# Praise for God's Umbrella

Mary Alice Murphy has done the very difficult. She has brought the "Greatest Generation" in southern New Mexico to life again by her skillful interviewing of World War ll Veterans. I have known the author for many years, and I believe this is her finest work. Don't miss this exciting piece of history!

> —Dianne Hamilton, retired New Mexico legislator, who represented District 38, where many of the interviewed veterans lived

These were quite the stories. I knew personally many of the veterans in this book, including several who were P.O.W.s of the Germans or Japanese. My hat's off to these men. They were already somewhat hardened just from living through the Depression. They were young and most of them more than willing to fight for our country. They endured all kinds of hardships but were up to the task.

Vietnam veterans do have an understanding of how these men lived, training with long walks and runs and living on little food in squalor. Those who became P.O.W.s in World War II, we'll never know the fear and deprivation of living day-to-day hoping to make it through a day or night. Except through our friends, who were captured by the North Vietnamese Army or Viet Cong.

> —Frank Donohue, Vietnam Veteran and past commandant of the Gaffney-Oglesby Marine Corps League Detachment 1328

Engaging and colorful histories. A must read for anyone interested in military history and those who served from southwest New Mexico.

—Diane C. LeBlanc, Captain, US Navy (Ret.)

While at basic and advanced training, and in Vietnam, 1971-72, I had the opportunity of meeting soldiers and conversing with them about their past and mine. I understand the mental and physical issues will not fade away.

The bond between each creates a family of its own for those of us who served our country with pride and honor. Our Buddies will not be forgotten, as they make each of us believe there is a God and prayer serves its purpose. Blessings to those that stayed home and to those who did not make it home. The memories of lost family members remain alive.

This book has been an inspiration. I strongly feel that reading it will help in making you, the reader, give from your heart the respect that each veteran has earned.

—Armando Young Amador, Vietnam veteran and secretary of Vietnam Veterans of America, Chapter 358

# GOD'S UMBRELLA

# GOD'S UMBRELLA

## SOUTHWEST NEW MEXICO

## WORLD WAR II SURVIVORS

### MARY ALICE MURPHY

God's Umbrella: Southwest New Mexico World War II Survivors

Copyright ©2018 Mary Alice Murphy


ISBN: 978-1-940769-97-4

Publisher: Mercury HeartLink

Silver City, New Mexico

Printed in the United States of America

contact the author at  mam@maryalicemurphy.com

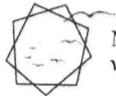


Mercury HeartLink
www.heartlink.com

# GOD'S UMBRELLA

## CHAPTER 1

### A YOUNG GIRL IN POLAND IS PULLED INTO THE WAR

## CHAPTER 2

### THOSE WHO JOINED BEFORE WORLD WAR II BEGAN

## CHAPTER 3

### VOLUNTEERING TO SERVE IN 1941

# CHAPTER 4
## THE DRAFT BROUGHT THESE MEN INTO THE SERVICE OF COUNTRY IN 1941

# CHAPTER 5
## VOLUNTEERING TO JOIN IN 1942

# CHAPTER 6
## DRAFTED IN 1942

# CHAPTER 7

## VOLUNTEERING IN 1943

# CHAPTER 8

## DRAFTED IN 1943

## CHAPTER 9
### VOLUNTEERED IN 1944

## CHAPTER 10
### DRAFTED IN 1944

## CHAPTER 11
### VOLUNTEERED IN 1945

# CHAPTER 12

## IN TRAINING
## DURING WORLD WAR II,
## BUT SERVED MOSTLY
## AFTER THE WAR

# CHAPTER 13

## TOO YOUNG TO SERVE,
## BUT FOUND A WAY TO SERVE
## IN A DIFFERENT CAPACITY

This book is dedicated to my father,

Joseph Francis Baingo,

who proudly served his country

as an enlisted man in World War I,

stayed in the U.S. Army Reserves

between the wars and served as a translator

in Allied Occupation Headquarters in World War II,

having achieved the rank of captain.

# ACKNOWLEDGEMENTS

Many thanks go to Christina Ely, the former publisher of the Silver City Daily Press, for giving me the opportunity to meet and tell the stories of these men and women who served in World War II all over the world and for giving me permission to put them into a book. Many Saturdays from 2008 to 2010, the Daily Press Weekend Edition featured these stories as told to this author/reporter in each veteran's own words. Most were living in Grant County, New Mexico, at the time of their interviews, but a few lived in other nearby counties and were interviewed over the years, with the latest in 2018. Current photos were taken at the time of interview.

Without the patience and support of my dear husband, Don, this book could never have been completed.

I also wish to thank Charlie McKee for her editing expertise, fact-checking and for "translating" what was published in the newspapers in Associated Press style to Chicago Manual of Style.

Thanks also go to Stewart Warren, who did the design work to make the book look its best for publishing.

Doug Oakes had input into the cover and chose the photo he felt would best represent the veterans, whose military and combat lives form the basis for this book.

And my thanks especially go to the veterans who were willing to share their stories with the reading public to help in the preservation of history.

# INTRODUCTION

Two brothers named Salas returned from their time as prisoners of war. The brother, Felix, who became a P.O.W. in the Bataan Death March, said to this author: "God had an umbrella over me." It became the inspiration for the title of this book.

Can you imagine being a mother during the war and having two of your sons be prisoners of war at the same time—one in the Pacific and the other in Europe?

Can you imagine being a young Hispanic teenager, who has never traveled far from home and now is serving in a far-off country, in a strange culture, and you find yourself a prisoner of war?

The two brothers, Felix and José Salas each knew the other was serving, but neither knew his brother was a prisoner of war.

The Grant County, New Mexico Salas family had to go through that emotional trial.

What about the soldiers who wanted to "see the world," but never got to travel away from their stateside post?

Why did so many young men from land-locked Grant County and the surrounding area join the Navy? Many had heard about, read about or seen pictures of the ocean, but had never had the chance to see it. This was their ticket out of town. Others thought the Navy would be easier than the

Army, because they would be in ships and not across from the enemy in trenches as soldiers were in Europe.

Some of them found out the hard way that the Navy was no safer, when their ship or smaller boat was shot out from under them or they became Japanese prisoners of war in the Philippines, during the Bataan Death March.

How would you feel if, after months of training, you suffered an accident of friendly fire and spent the rest of the war in hospitals?

Another story recounted by a sailor was about the letter he wrote for a young Marine, who wanted it addressed to President Franklin Delano Roosevelt, who, it turned out, was the Marine's father.

And then one young man from Grant County volunteered for three wars—World War II, the Korean War and the Vietnam War. Why? He'll tell you his story.

One fortunate young draftee served as a dog trainer throughout his service.

One woman was a child, six years of age, living in Poland when the Germans and Russians invaded—precipitating World War II. When she was seven years old, her parents were taken away, and she had to figure out how to provide for her sister, who was five and a half years old, and her brother, who was four years old.

Some of those who served wanted to volunteer but were drafted before they had the chance. Others trained for military service. Some served on ships, others in airplanes and many on land.

Several were in training during the war, but it ended before they had a chance to do their part, although some served immediately after the surrenders.

A few performed important jobs stateside, but most saw action in the Pacific or European theaters, with at least one serving in Africa. An unlucky few became prisoners of war but survived to give their accounts.

Conflicts leading up to World War II had begun as early as 1931, when Japan invaded Manchuria. Nazi Germany and Fascist Italy began militarized invasions in 1936, with other European countries being drawn into the global war from 1938 until the "official" beginning of World War II, usually listed as September 1, 1939, when Germany invaded Poland and two days later Britain and France declared war on Germany. The United States declared war on Japan on December 8, 1941, the day after Japan bombed Pearl Harbor. Then, from December 11 to 13, 1941, Nazi Germany and its Axis partners declared war on the United States, bringing the United States into a full-scale war on several fronts.

Most of the veterans who recount their experiences here became involved in the conflict as the war spread and the United States needed more soldiers, sailors, Army Air Forces members and Marines.

Where were some of these men and women when Pearl Harbor was bombed and war declared?

Marine Leonard Pritikin was on furlough and riding horses with a friend. Thomas Foy, who would later survive the Bataan Death March, was at Clark Field in the

Philippines. Jason Baker, who later spent his whole service in the Pacific Theater, was in Portland, Maine. Mason De Young was halfway to Iceland. Bill Harrison was on the USS Kakaskia. Frank Baca was at church with his parents in Hot Springs (now Truth or Consequences), New Mexico. Dick Johnson, a member of the reserves, was at his United States Forest Service office doing some work on that Sunday. Bob Johnson was studying at the University of Utah. Genevieve Johnston was training to be an Army nurse and was treating an older German lady at the time they heard the news.

God had an umbrella over each of these men and women, who lived and served during World War II—the natives of Grant County, New Mexico, and the surrounding area and those who later moved to the area.

# CHAPTER I

☙

# A Young Girl in Poland is Pulled into the War

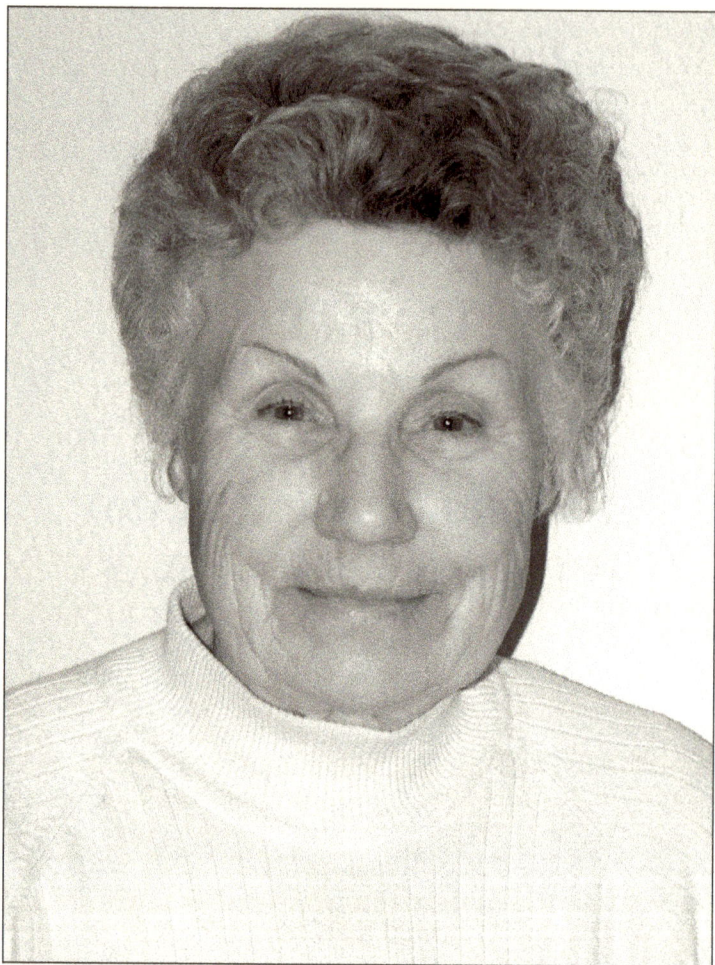

# Fila, Irene

## DOB about 1932

DOB (date of birth) about 1932, Irene Fila was impacted by two conflicts—the German and Russian invasion of Poland, which precipitated World War II, and World War II itself.

The first, the Russian invasion of the eastern part of Poland, where Irene lived with her family, occurred in 1939, soon after she had finished first grade.

"I was six (years old)," Fila said. "My parents were getting me ready for second grade."

As a result of Germany's entrance into the country, Polish teachers, doctors and lawyers were arrested and taken to Siberia.

"My father's family was taken to Siberia and they did not survive," Fila said.

To protect the remaining members of the family, somebody always kept watch at home.

"When he heard the rumblings of big trucks, my father hid us—my brother, sister and me—under the snow," Fila said. "We spent the night in the snow pile. We were so frightened, we didn't feel the cold."

The Russians brought in teachers to educate the children in the Russian language.

"The Polish people were Catholics," Fila said. "The teachers were brainwashing us that there was no God, but it was Stalin and Lenin that gave us everything."

She came home one day with homework. She said she was kissing the picture of Lenin in the book.

"In my child's thoughts I thought my parents were lying to me," Fila said. "I got such a spanking. My mother said, 'what we teach you at home is holy. Don't repeat it.'"

At school the next day, Fila said the teacher asked her if she believed in God. She replied that she did not and was allowed to go outside and play.

"I was living a lie," Fila said. "You start growing up overnight. I felt like two persons and had to remember what to say to whom."

In March or April 1940, the Russians came to the house "and took my mother away." Two months later, the family found out she was working as a laborer digging to build an airport.

"A few months later, they took my father and his horse and buggy," Fila said. "I was seven years old; my sister, five and a half; and my brother, four.

"I was crying because I did not know how we would survive," she said, "but when I heard my sister and brother crying, I told them we would go to the fields."

They found wild sorrel and boiled it to eat.

The Russians had taken the horses and pigs, and only three chickens and an old cow remained.

"The eggs had to be given to the co-op," Fila said, "so there was nothing to eat. I found a rotten potato and made a soup."

Because they had no bread, she gathered acorns, dried them, ground them and made "bread" using the flour and water.

"It was so hard, we were crunching it," Fila said.

She made a soup from carrots that she found growing. Edible roots and grasses from swamps kept the children fed. She also tried milking the cow. She managed to get half a glass of brown milk out of the udder.

"I gave it to my brother," Fila said. "He said he wanted white milk, so I told him it was chocolate. I started taking eggs and told the man who would collect them that the hens weren't laying."

One day about six months after their father had been taken away, "we could see a horse and buggy coming very slowly toward the house."

It was their father, who was paralyzed. Fila got an old sheet and tied it to her father to pull him out of the buggy.

"I know (my) father fell hard to the ground," she said. "The three of us dragged him into the house over the step. Father only had strength in his arms. We got him into the bed. I don't know how, but we did. He told me to find a certain woman in the village to help him. I told her that we had no money, no meat and no potatoes."

Fila said the woman put on her father's back tall glasses that had been heated on the stove. The glasses were filled with hot water and cooled a bit with cold water.

"The glasses were sticking to his back and the flesh was growing," Fila said. "The bubbles of flesh were black. The woman stuck a needle into the fire to sterilize it and punctured the bubbles. Black blood came out, but the woman said that after a few treatments my father would be able to walk."

Fila said the woman returned another day and did the same treatment to her father's legs, then returned to massage his back and legs.

"I remember one morning my father moved his legs," Fila said. "The woman lifted him and stood him between two tables, where he began taking a few steps."

Several months later, the children's mother returned. She had pneumonia but treated herself and recovered.

Russia occupied the area for eighteen months, during which time people started having meetings at the family's house to figure out how to survive. They would hide whenever trucks came to the house.

Then the first bombs from Germany began raining on Poland and the family wondered why the Jewish people were moving toward Russia.

"It was a very harsh winter and many German soldiers died," Fila said.

Before the Russian invasion, Fila's grandfather had lived and worked in the United States. When he returned, he purchased land and his family was doing well.

"I was always dreaming that I would be fancy in America," Fila said. "My grandfather taught us English. The bubble broke when the Germans came. They arrested my aunt, who was a fashion designer. They broke all her fingers because she wouldn't tell where firearms were hidden. She couldn't confess because she didn't know. She was taken away. For two or three years we didn't know where she was."

The son of the farmer where Fila's aunt labored was in the German army, and he wrote to the family to tell them she was alive and where she was.

"There were some good Germans," Fila said.

Two of her grandfather's sons were "chopped up and killed with axes." Two other sons hid in the forest. One died of pneumonia.

"When my grandfather became ill, we think with stomach cancer, of which he ultimately died, my grand-mother asked me to take care of him," Fila said.

"When I said the Gestapo was coming, my grandfather told me nothing would happen," Fila said. "He would get these attacks. When the Germans opened the door, my grandfather was oozing blood, so they put a quarantine sign on the house. He squeezed my hand and I gave him a few drops of water."

When Germans began rounding up Jews, they found places to hide.

"My mother was baking extra bread and I didn't know why," Fila said. "One night, I made myself stay awake. I heard a knock on the window and my mother gave a Jewish man a loaf of bread."

Her family would put out clothes, blankets and food, and they would disappear.

"Some of the Jewish people had dug a cave under an overturned tree," Fila said. "My father was also hiding Jewish people under the barn floor, but the Germans began coming to the house so often, they moved to another place."

The Russians had brought Ukrainians to Poland. They were burning houses and villages. Fila's family's house and the village were burned.

"It was like hell getting loose on earth," she said. "We hid and waited three or four days until it was quiet."

They took refuge in the parish church, but the church was destroyed.

The Germans sent a tank to help the villagers and proceeded to kill every Ukrainian they could find.

"The Germans said: 'We have helped you. Now you help us,'" Fila said.

The family was taken to a city, where the Germans gave them food and crowded people onto a train and took them to a three-story building.

"My mother said, 'We are not going inside. It smells like dead bodies,'" Fila said.

Later, they were loaded back onto trains, where Fila found a medal with St. Joseph on one side and Mary and Jesus on the other. Her mother told her to hold it and not to show it to anyone.

"It was like a treasure to me," Fila said. "It was my shield to keep the family safe."

She said what saved the family was that they were all blond and blue-eyed; Hitler always sought people with those traits.

Others were tortured and cremated.

"I will never forget the smell of burning bodies," Fila said.

Her family members were later taken to work on farms.

"It was 1943 and I was 11 years old," Fila said.

She and her mother were taken to a farm, where Fila remembered eating dirt to survive. Because lye had been poured on their heads to make their hair fall out, the farmer thought Fila was a boy and dressed her in Tyrolean pants and a cap. When a neighbor woman discovered she was a girl, she was given one of the farmer's shirts.

"I looked like Charlie Chaplin," Fila laughed.

They remained on the farm from 1943 to 1945.

"On May 9, 1945, we could hear rumbling," Fila said. "My mother was milking cows and I was peeking outside. Suddenly I saw American tanks. She threw the bucket of milk down and ran. My mother was kissing the feet of the Americans, and I was crying. We still stayed at the farm for three months until we were taken to a displaced-persons camp."

Because she still dreamed of living in America, Fila said, she studied lots of languages, as well as typing and shorthand.

"On October 24, 1950, we arrived in America," she said.

She soon found a job using her linguistic and clerical skills.

GOD'S UMBRELLA

# CHAPTER 2

ભ

# THOSE WHO JOINED BEFORE
# WORLD WAR II BEGAN

# Johnson, Richard C. "Dick"

## DOB 8/19/1915 DOD 7/18/2014

"My military career started when I went to New Mexico A & M [later New Mexico State University]," Richard C. "Dick" Johnson said. "I spent two years in Reserve Officers' Training Corps (ROTC) and two advanced years toward a second lieutenant in the reserves."

When he graduated, he could not get a commission because he would not be twenty-one years old until August. So, in 1936, he joined the United States Army Reserves as a second lieutenant and joined the United States Forest Service to work as a ranger in Arizona.

"I was at the office one Sunday morning, and my wife called me and told me that Pearl Harbor had been bombed," Johnson said. "I took a physical at Fort Bliss and found out in January that I had passed. I received orders to report for extended active duty to the Infantry Replacement Training Center at Camp Walters, Texas, on February 1, 1942."

By March 3, he was reassigned to the 82nd Division and arrived at Camp Claiborne, Louisiana. He was assigned to the 326th Regiment, M Company, a Heavy Weapons Company and to the 3rd Platoon, which was the .50-caliber machine gun platoon.

"I don't think I studied as hard on anything in college as I did on the various manuals my first six months in the Army," Johnson said. "I really studied the .50-caliber manual, so I knew all about the weapon."

In 1942, Army Ground Forces circulated a letter asking for volunteers with skiing, mountain living, ability with pack animals or forest ranger experience to join the 87th Mountain Infantry.

Johnson moved his wife Evelyn and their sons to Olympia, Washington, where he was assigned to H Company, 2nd Battalion. Their next stop was the newly constructed Camp Hale in Colorado, where Johnson learned to ski with a forty-pound rucksack on his back.

"I never learned to be very good, particularly in downhill skiing," Johnson said. "I had enough endurance that I could do quite well in cross-country skiing."

Around the middle of June word came that the 87th would be assigned to the Pacific theater, so the troops took amphibious training in San Diego under the Marines, which he described as operating strictly "by the numbers."

One part of the training consisted of climbing down rope nets from ship deck to landing craft beneath.

"We did not look as sharp as they thought we should, and on one occasion I saw the Marine major check his watch at the start and then again after we finished," Johnson said. "He looked at his watch two times at the end, shook his head and left without saying a word. We had bettered his time by quite a bit. I was proud of our men."

The unit was made part of Amphibian Task Force 9, heading toward Kiska, Alaska, the last of the Aleutian

Islands held by the Japanese. Almost everyone aboard the ship was seasick, except for Jerry Turner, Ev Bailey, Art Brodeur and Johnson. Brodeur and Bailey soon also become seasick, but Turner and Johnson never did.

The ship was unloaded at Adak, Alaska, where the men set up camp, checked weapons and did some training.

After two days of attacking and reaching objectives on Kiska, no Japanese had been sighted and no combat encountered.

"We learned later that the Japs had moved out right under the Navy's nose, in the cover of fog and night, just a few days before our attack," Johnson reported.

He, along with forty officers and 100 enlisted men, was called back to Camp Hale in Colorado.

His next stop was the Officers' Advanced Course No. 51 in Fort Benning, Georgia, starting February 9, 1944. He received his "diploma" May 9. Orders reassigned him to the 10th Light Division, 85th Regiment, 1st Battalion, B Company command at Camp Hale. Next, he headed to Camp Swift, near Austin, Texas, where the soldiers received combat training.

The following stop was Camp Patrick Henry, Virginia, where the troops spent Christmas and New Year's Day. On January 3, 1945, they boarded the USS West Point, which was a former luxury liner, and headed east in the Atlantic Ocean. They landed in Naples, Italy.

"As we walked down the gangway the next morning, we met a couple of British officers who welcomed us to

Italy and said, 'We're jolly glad to see you lads, and soon you will see why,'" Johnson said. "We also saw a number of young Italian boys holding out some empty tin cans begging for food handouts.

"I think that I realized then why we were in this war," he continued. "Sure, we were fighting for our country, but I thought, 'I am really fighting this war, so my two boys won't have to be begging for food like those kids were.'"

"Our division was ordered to take Mount Belvedere," Johnson said. "We remained under cover at the foot of the mountain, so the Germans would not be aware of the buildup below them."

The 1st Battalion, of which Johnson was a member, was given orders to mount an assault on Mount Gorgolesco to the east.

"I led D Company up the slope in almost total darkness," Johnson said. "Daylight hit B Company just a little short of the top, and they came under terrific fire from the enemy positions. Shortly afterward, C Company also came under fire. We took Mount Gorgolesco about 7 a.m. after calling on artillery for counter barrage."

Most of the men dug in and did not expose themselves. Their next objective was Mount Della Torraccia.

"Our air force dropped bombs on the enemy positions, and sometimes we were farther ahead than they thought, and their bombs came down real close to us," Johnson said. "The only wound I got during the whole campaign came from a piece of shrapnel from a 'friendly' bomb that made a cut on the back of my left thumb. There was enough snow in most places, so that bombs would penetrate fairly deeply into the snowdrift, which would muffle the explosion."

For his command during the Gorgolesco attack, Johnson received a Bronze Star.

General Mark Clark forwarded the following message to the 10th Division: "You men have done a damn fine job." To this remark General Willis Crittenberger added, "Four attempts have been made to take this high ground, but you are the only ones who have held it for long. I have had thirty divisions in the Corps and this is one of the best."

The second phase of the attack began March 3, with orders to take Mount Della Spe. B Company took the mountain.

Johnson was the only one of the three original heavy weapons company commanders in the 85th not killed in Italy. He was later named an executive officer for the 1st Battalion.

A large number of German divisions still guarded the Po Valley, and an allied assault began on April 14. Because he was at the battalion command post, Johnson said he had little contact with the details of the push, but kept the situation map. He reported that by 6 a.m. on April 20, A Company had taken the first road junction in the Po Valley.

"With our breakthrough into the Po, the backbone of the German resistance was broken," Johnson said. "The fighting now became fast pursuit with small local engagements. Local residents came out to cheer us on and many brought such things as fresh eggs, vegetables, flowers and even milk."

He said that, during one day's march, the men stopped to eat their lunch of C rations right next to a field of young, green garlic.

"We pulled some up, cleaned them fairly well and ate them like green onions," Johnson said. "They sure tasted good, but we probably smelled of garlic for at least a week."

He said the enemy forces were so disorganized by the speed of the division advance that many of their units, of any size, had been cut off or bypassed.

"In one instance, a clerk from one of the regimental headquarters, armed only with a fountain pen, received the surrender of a company-sized unit," Johnson said.

They took the town of Villafranca and its airport.

"During the evening, a [German] Focke-Wolf 190 landed at the airport, and although the pilot escaped, the plane was taken intact," Johnson said. "It was carrying a German payroll, and Sergeant Case, a battalion headquarters staff member, commandeered it."

The 85th and 86th regiments were sent to cut off the Germans last escape route by Lake Garda. On April 2, they received word that the Germans in Italy had unconditionally surrendered at Allied Headquarters in Caserta.

The 1st battalion sent a small detail to check a road pass east of Brenner Pass to ensure that no Germans or Austrians crossed in either direction.

When the troops returned to headquarters, they went through several tunnels, in which the Germans had set up manufacturing equipment to build or repair aircraft.

By May 8, the Germans throughout Europe had surrendered. May 9 was designated VE Day for victory in Europe.

On May 19, 1945, Johnson was promoted to major.

Toward the end of June, the 10th Mountain Division prepared to go to the Japanese front, but on August 14, the Japanese surrendered and World War II ended.

After he returned to Camp Patrick Henry, it took Johnson two and a half days to get to Fort Bliss in El Paso, Texas, for discharge. The train arrived on August 28, 1945.

When Johnson traveled from El Paso to Albuquerque, he stopped at the Regional Office of the Forest Service, where he asked to return to the United States Forest Service. Following his termination leave from the Army, he was assigned to the Infantry Reserves and went to work at the Lakeside District of the Sitgreaves National Forest.

He stayed in the Army Reserves and was promoted to lieutenant colonel on April 24, 1956. He was transferred to Retired Army Reserves on February 18, 1963.

Johnson retired from the United States Forest Service as the Gila National Forest supervisor on December 3, 1973.

GOD'S UMBRELLA

# PRITIKIN, LEONARD

## DOB 5/17/1920 DOD 07/19/2018

Many Marines took part in World War II and Leonard Pritikin was one of them. He volunteered almost two years before war was declared in the U.S., which followed the bombing of Pearl Harbor, Hawaii.

"I'm a Marine all the way," Pritikin of Silver City said. "There's no such thing as an ex-Marine, just civilian Marines."

He volunteered for the service in February 1940.

"I was home on furlough when Pearl Harbor was bombed on a Sunday of December '41," Pritikin said. "War was declared on Monday and my furlough was canceled on Tuesday. I was riding horses with a friend and came home to find out."

"They didn't have to cancel my furlough," Pritikin grumbled.

He did his training at the Marine Corps Recruit Depot in San Diego, California after he volunteered.

When war was declared, he was sent to Great Lakes Naval Training Station where he remained until May. Marines served gate and brig duty.

When Pritikin joined the 9th Reserve Battalion in 1940, he planned to be a thirty-year Marine. The Reserves were called up in October 1940, when the National Guard was made federal.

"The Marine Reserves were already federal. They just had to activate," he said.

He was sent again to boot camp in San Diego.

"I had already had all this training and at the end of boot camp, they apologized for making me go through it again," Pritikin said. "It was all right. It didn't hurt me."

Leonard Pritikin was then sent to New River, North Carolina, and joined Company D of the 3rd Marine Division.

He was there from the end of May 1942 until the end of August when the company was transferred to the West Coast. The Marines embarked on the SS Lurline, a Matson Line ship. After fourteen days, they arrived in Tutuila Island, Pago Pago, American Samoa.

"We were there for nine months, doing maneuvers," Pritikin said. "Then in 1943, we went to New Zealand for more training."

From New Zealand the unit was sent to Guadalcanal.

"We landed August 7, exactly one year since the 1st Marine Division had landed on the island," Pritikin said. "We were sure the Japanese would try to bomb us out since it was the anniversary, but they didn't."

The troops did have to dig holes to get underground before they unloaded the ship.

"And then maneuver, maneuver, maneuver, training all the time," Pritikin said. "Before we shoved off for

Bougainville up the slot [of the Solomon Islands] from Guadalcanal, we had to test-fire all weaponry."

That's when a cloverleaf, with six .81 mm mortar shells fell 1,000 yards short and "wiped out me and my machine-gun nest."

He said the men were used to hearing shells flying over their heads, but "you don't hear the one that hits you."

Six of his comrades were killed and ten ended up in the hospital.

"I was hurt the most and spent sixteen and a half months in the hospital until I was discharged in January 1945," Pritikin said. "And that was the extent of my time in the service."

His legs were shattered in the friendly-fire accident. At first, he was in the hospital on Guadalcanal—Mobile Hospital 8—where he was in and out of a coma for nine days.

"And then they put me on a hospital ship—the USS Tryon—and sent me to Espiritu Santo Island in the New Hebrides for a month," Pritikin said. "I never set foot on the island. They carried me everywhere."

He traveled back to the States on another Matson Line ship, the SS Matsonia, where he was treated at Mare Island Naval Hospital near Vallejo, California, until he was discharged.

"I told them I was in the Marines for thirty years and they couldn't kick me out," Pritikin said. "They said, 'Yes, we can.'"

He said September 20, 1943, was his "day of infamy."

"Every September 20, I have a drink to my six comrades who died—Fortin, Franklin, Viens, DiBilaggio, Croswell and Peters. I can't forget their names," Pritikin said.

A few years ago, he called two guys from the outfit—one in Ohio and one in Florida—and they said, "Cheers," and drank to the memory of the six men who died that day.

"Ralph Croswell was the bugler of the company," Pritikin said. "I was the section leader and he kept pestering me to let him fire the machine gun. That day I let him, and he died. It's a shame I killed the guy who just wanted to fire the machine gun, but he did get to fire [it] before he died."

He said the machine gun was ruined by the shells. Although it was repaired, it would never fire again.

"The mortar guys were sick about killing their friends and comrades," Pritikin said. "Friendly-fire accidents are part of war."

Pritikin said he is named after his great-grandfather, a Russian soldier who was a veteran of the Charge of the Light Brigade of the Crimea.

# Denham, Monroe

## DOB 1/5/1920 DOD 12/16/2011

Monroe Denham went into the service in July 1940, when he volunteered.

"I was in the Navy when the war started," Denham said. "I was living in Tularosa, New Mexico, although I was born in Oglesby, Texas, on January 5, 1920. I haven't been back there since I was a baby."

He was living with his sister and brother-in-law when he decided to join the Navy.

"I had a brother, Dan, who was eleven years older, in the Navy, so I joined in El Paso," Denham said. "They shipped me to the San Diego Training Center. I served at North Island Air Station, at San Diego, from 1941 to 1944."

He began his service as a seaman, but after training became an aviation machinist mate.

"I worked on airplanes," Denham said.

When an aircraft carrier arrived that had airplanes, usually SBDs—scout bombers built by Douglas Aircraft Company—the planes would be overhauled and sent back to service.

"I worked in the shop on eight-hour shifts," Denham said. "We had to know what we were doing. We worked on the single engines and then sent 'em back out."

The only two-engine planes he saw were P-38s.

"One time when I was at North Island, there was an airplane dogfight over the bay," Denham said. "They crashed into each other. One chute opened immediately. The other one had to get out of the way of a piece of airplane above him before he could deploy the parachute. He was all right, but when they picked up the one whose chute had opened immediately, he was cut in half. When he was hit, it busted his chute pack open."

In another instance, Marines were flying in a transport aircraft, training to be paratroopers.

"One of them jumped out of the plane. His chute caught on the tail wing," Denham said. "He was hanging head down. There was no way to pull him back in, so the plane flew over the bay into calmer air.

"Another pilot went up with a guy in the cockpit," Denham reported. "The pilot flew his plane underneath the Marine hanging by his chute. They grabbed him and cut off the shroud."

Denham said he ran to sickbay to see the guy.

"He was all bloody, but he lived," Denham said. "They said he went back to paratrooper training. It was a freak accident."

One time when he was working at the airplane shop, he and several other fellows were outside smoking, because they were not allowed to smoke inside.

"The hangar I was working in was right on the bay," Denham said. "There were some benches where we could sit, and a big sandbox was at the corner of the building.

"I was sitting on the back of the bench, with my feet on the bench" he said. "A P-38 was coming in. All of a sudden, we heard .50-caliber guns going off. One shell hit the sandbox, and another hit the building right over my head. I froze.

"The pilot forgot to safety his guns," Denham said. "When he turned, it tripped them. Nobody got hit, but the pilot sure heard about it."

The P-38s had only one pilot, and the SBDs had a pilot and a gunner/radioman in the rear seat.

In February 1944, Denham was sent to New Caledonia, an island in the western Pacific Ocean.

"I was in VS-57, a submarine patrol squadron," Denham said. "We patrolled to sink subs. The squadron sank one [Japanese] sub before I got there. By the time I got there, the war had moved north of there, but we still had sub patrol."

When he flew, he manned the .30-caliber machine guns in the back of the SBD.

Squadron members were sent out daily on patrol. On April 1, 1944, Denham made aviation chief machinist mate.

"I didn't go on patrol every time," Denham said. "Then when I was made chief, I didn't have to go out on patrol anymore. I was a line chief and assigned to see that the group of men under me kept the planes up and did what they were supposed to do. Each one was assigned to take care of a plane."

He said his brother Dan saw more action, because he was aboard a ship.

"Dan had been in the Navy before, and he went back in in 1939," Denham said. "I didn't see him again until 1945."

In June 1945, Denham was transferred to the Pacific Fleet and in July to Honolulu, Hawaii.

"I was in a Carrier Aircraft Service Unit in Hawaii when the bombs were dropped on Hiroshima and then Nagasaki," Denham said. "I was there when the war ended."

In December 1945, he was shipped back to the States and had a 30-day leave.

His mother and stepfather were living in Central (now Santa Clara), so he went to visit them.

"I got there on Christmas Eve," Denham said. "It was the first time I had seen my mother in three or four years. It was quite a coincidence that my brother got there two days after Christmas. It was the first time my mom and I had seen him since 1939. It was quite a homecoming."

His sister, Anne, was also there, so "we were all there with my mother that December."

GOD'S UMBRELLA

He was discharged July 18, 1946, out of San Pedro, California.

"I was in the Navy for six years during the war and never saw action," Denham said. "I didn't mind at all."

After the war, he went to El Paso and worked for El Paso Natural Gas for years. One of the places to which he was transferred was Douglas, Arizona. There he met his wife, Mary, a nurse.

"We had fifty-two and a half years together," he said.

They lived all over the West before moving to Silver City after twelve years in Lordsburg.

"I had a service station (in Silver City)," Denham said. "Then I was a Borden distributor; bought the Broasty, where we cooked chicken, kind of like KFC. It was in a building, a different one, where Grandma's Café is. I sold it and went to work for Phelps Dodge and retired in 1982."

GOD'S UMBRELLA

# VANOVER, ANDERSON "ANDY"

## DOB 10/20/1922 DOD 02/09/2009

In 1939, Anderson "Andy" VanOver, who later came to live in Silver City, volunteered, but was turned down and told to come back when he turned eighteen years old.

He joined the Army Infantry—"cannon fodder," as he called it—on his birthday, October 20, 1940.

Of the seventeen people who were in his company at Fort Thomas in Covington, Kentucky, he said most had had a choice of going to jail or joining the Army and chose the latter.

"They trained us and then we trained the draftees we got," VanOver said. "I didn't come back home until 1945."

His company was moved in late 1940 or early 1941 to Michigan, where they "tramped all the snow down to ice."

"We did Tennessee maneuvers," according to VanOver, where they marched with Springfield rifles and eighty-pound packs from Michigan to Tennessee, with a major standing on a hill, saying, "Only thirty more miles, men."

"We marched twenty-five to thirty miles a day from daylight to dark," VanOver said. "Jeeps would come in hauling machine guns and mortars. I was a corporal and I said, 'Guns are in, men, pick 'em up.' I got into a fight and was back to private."

Then the soldiers turned around and marched back to Michigan, arriving in June. VanOver was sent to Fort Bragg, North Carolina, for jump school. In mid-August 1941, the unit readied for overseas assignment and was sent to Iceland. Under British control, they were to clean out German radio relays, he said.

When they hit a storm in the North Atlantic, some nurses and officers were in a gun pit aboard the ship and got washed out onto the deck by a large wave.

"We had to drag them back in before another wave hit us," VanOver said.

He remained in Iceland until the first part of 1943.

"People think Iceland's cold," he said. "It was miserable, but not cold."

His unit was assigned to the British military until December 7, 1941.

"They called [the ships] frigates, but they smelled like fish, so I called it a fish ship," VanOver said. "We would go for inland runs to bomb installations."

He trained for a short time in England and during that time received one pass for a short leave.

"I came back, and the company was gone," VanOver said. "The cooks fed me and said, 'go out on the road and flag down a truck and it will take you where you want to go.'"

He next spent six to eight months in Ireland for intensive training, which consisted of thirty minutes of exercises, cleaning up bunks and rolling up gear before a light breakfast, after which they took mess gear and washed it. Then, they put on full gear, got a peanut butter and jelly sandwich for lunch, and ran nine miles behind a Jeep onto the parade ground, which he said was a cow pasture. Following this were two hours of intensive exercise.

"I didn't think anything would make me sore, but it did," VanOver said.

After live ammunition practices, they returned to base at 5 p.m., had a light meal and for twenty-five miles, they ran half and walked half.

"We would fall by the side of the road and sleep until trucks picked us up and hauled you back to start over again in the morning," VanOver said. "We could run across France."

From August 4 to September 15, 1944, VanOver served with Gen. George Patton's 5th Infantry of the 3rd Army. VanOver was originally in the 1st Army, but was among those pulled out to form the 3rd Army.

He jumped to Saint Lo, France, and the first drive was to Angers. The Germans had mined a bridge with boxcars full of mines.

"We got to the bridge and cut the wires to the explosives," VanOver said.

Germans were trying to blow up the bridge with explosives strapped to their bodies, but the American riflemen killed a lot of them. The Germans blew up when they were shot.

"We got into Normandy," he said. "The units were there, but they couldn't go ahead because the Germans were pushing back. We were a bunch of hillbillies from the mountains of Tennessee, Kentucky and West Virginia. We relieved the unit and just pushed right on through."

VanOver was a mortarman and ended up as section leader.

"We would eyeball the distance to protect the riflemen," he said. "We got so good, we could drop a mortar round into a foxhole."

After the Germans took one of the company's medics and bayoneted him "to pieces, we didn't take prisoners."

During the battle for Hill 183, VanOver said trucks had to haul away the dead.

"The poor Germans were stacked like cordwood," he said.

After Angers, the units were relieved and sent to the Argonne Forest, where VanOver said the trees were still just stubs left over from a battle there in World War I.

Because the men had no goggles, their eyes got sunburned. VanOver said he took out the folded shelter he carried tucked in to his belt at his back, and, because he couldn't see well, spread it out to sleep on what he thought was a pile of rocks. The next morning, he discovered it was a heap of old mortar shells, some of which, he found out later, were still live.

Next he went to Metz, France, which had never fallen to an armed force "until we took it."

Just before Metz, the American soldiers were attacked.

He went down to a gully to check on the men.

"The air burst over me and knocked me down," VanOver said. "I took off my helmet and there was a cow turd in it."

Shrapnel went into his shoe and burned "all the meat off." He also had shrapnel slices on each shoulder. Some of the shrapnel came out two years later, he said.

"I went to the medic, but I saw people worse off than me," VanOver said. "I went back, washed my foot and sock and rolled off."

He was still limping weeks later toward the end of December, after a trip to Luxembourg and France. His captain asked him why and sent VanOver to a hospital. After he put sulfa powder on it and cut the toe of his sock, his foot healed.

"It was the dirty sock," VanOver said. "We didn't get socks every day."

The hospital was at the edge of a river in Luxembourg. The soldiers shot steel cables across, and hooked boats onto the cables to cross the river.

They then went through the Ardennes toward Bastogne, Belgium.

"We got two-thirds of the way, the sun came out and everything happened," VanOver said. "The bombers and fighters could go in and drop ammunition."

One of the German jets came down the river trying to defend the Rhine. VanOver grabbed a john boat and, halfway across the river, the jet came back and dropped a bomb.

"It rocked the boat, but we didn't turn over," VanOver said.

He said Patton got stuck in the middle of the Rhine on a personnel carrier.

"He asked me how I was doing and I said fine. Patton said he was fine, too," VanOver said. "We told each other to be careful."

VanOver's commanding officer was supposed to take the railway station and decided to cross through buildings nearby to get to the station.

"We could hear a shell coming, so we ran into the police station," VanOver said. "The lady there showed us there were no Germans, but lots of weapons."

He said if his commanding officer got a bottle of whiskey, he would save VanOver a drink and vice versa.

"We found a cellar full of pink champagne, so I brought him some," VanOver said.

His next stop was the Ruhr Pocket, where the Americans "roared up the Autobahn in tanks and trucks and got it cleared off."

"The last day of the war, we were supposed to clear out a forest," VanOver said. "It was May 8 or 9 when they radioed up and told us to pull up and wait, because the 'war's over.'"

Everyone was seasick on the trip across the ocean, he said, except for him, so he got the job of "captain of the head."

There was a disposal unit trough along the side of the ship. One day when the guys were being sick into it, VanOver took a wad of toilet paper, lit it and sent it down the trough. "I lost my stripes again," he said.

After he returned to the United States in late June 1945, VanOver became one of the original NASCAR stock drivers.

GOD'S UMBRELLA

# FOY, THOMAS P.

## DOB 10/19/1914 DOD 10/8/2011

Thomas P. Foy joined in 1940 and fought in World War II. He recounted his experiences up to the Bataan Death March, which he survived.

Troop F of the cavalry, the original National Guard unit in Silver City, was sent to Fort Bliss in El Paso, Texas, to train for the war.

According to Foy, Troop F "went down to fight in Cuba," during the Spanish American War and "a number of the boys from Silver City were with Colonel Theodore Roosevelt when he stormed San Juan Hill."

"Troop F was one of the highest-rated units in the Army," Foy said. "It was converted in October into an artillery unit—Battery G of the 200th Coast Artillery."

Although he was not an original member of the 200th, he joined it later.

"I had just returned from school [Notre Dame Law School, from which he graduated in 1939] and had a job working as a clerk with Woodbury, Wilson and Woodbury," Foy said. "As fate would have it, mine was one of the first names drawn out of the hat for the draft. I wasn't going to let them draft me. I wanted to join the National Guard. Mr. Woodbury said, 'You won't get out until the war is fought,' but he promised me a job when I got back."

Foy listed some of the names of those in Troop F. They included Johnny Turner; Clyde Ely, whose father had been the commander of Troop F; Raymond Twaits, an officer; and Alvin Bayne, who was called "Sweets."

"I went to school with all of those guys," Foy said. "I joined up January 4, along with Calvin Graef."

He said he had no time to go to officers' candidate school, so "I shipped out as a private."

"The irony was that the day after I signed up, the National Guard was federalized," Foy said.

He was appointed as assistant battery clerk, because "I could type, and the battery clerk couldn't."

Captain Hazelwood of Albuquerque took over Battery G and soon said, "Foy, I don't think we're going to get along."

He told me he was looking for officer material for Battery H in Taos, "so I went to Battery H."

"At this point I had been fifteen days in the service," Foy said. "Captain George gave me a fast introduction to the Army and he guided me, and we became good friends."

He soon met a Captain Hutchinson, "who asked me if I knew anything about communications, and I said, 'Sure. I can answer the phone.' He gave me a book to study—a communications manual. I studied it for two weeks and then went home for the weekend. I got back Sunday night. He said, 'Congratulations. You're the sergeant of communications.' I built the communications unit up from the worst to Number 1. I had some Indian boys doing communications between the batteries. I built up the first Code Talkers, although they weren't as good as the later ones that got us out of Clark Field [in the Philippines] to Bataan."

He said most of the Indians had not volunteered but were drafted.

When they were assigned to units, the officers picked out Indian men who could speak different dialects.

"The one used by the Code Talkers was seldom used by other tribes," Foy said. "When the Japanese captured us, the first question they asked was 'What code did you use?' We just gave them our name, address and serial number."

The Japanese never broke the Navajo Code Talkers code.

"We got everyone out of Luzon down into Bataan with no casualties," Foy said. "We were assigned to protect the Clumpit Bridge into Bataan. From Christmas Day until New Year's Day, we were protecting the tank battalion infantry soldiers and the anti-aircraft group."

He said they cut the 200th Coast Artillery almost in half to make the 515th Coast Artillery the night after Clark Field was bombed.

"It left us about 800 men. There were not quite as many in the 515th," Foy said. "They had to get all their equipment in Manila. I stayed in the 200th. This was December 1941."

The 200th stayed at Clark Field protecting the planes that had been destroyed.

"Right after Pearl Harbor, the Japanese knocked everything out," Foy said. "There were seventeen B-17s on the field that had just returned from missions. From a total of thirty-four B-17s at Clark, seventeen were sent down to Mindanao and on to Australia. Out of our P-40s and P-41s, I think seven were left intact."

Bataan was about 100 miles from Clark Field.

"There were three little airstrips on Bataan to protect," Foy said. "All our batteries from the 515th and 200th ended up there. Some were converted to heavy gun units to repel the Japanese. They did a good job. I was still in communications at that point."

In January, sixteen or seventeen men were commissioned as officers and Foy became a second lieutenant and was transferred from Battery H to Battery F—the group from Carlsbad.

"In Bataan, we ran out of ammunition. We had no medicine at all. We didn't have food. We ran out of gas," Foy said. "The Japanese sent in a new army that had been slated to take Australia. They thought they would knock us off in a minute."

He said the only supplies the Americans had were individual medical supplies that had been issued.

"They went to the doctors, which were scattered out with the different units," Foy said. "We established a hospital on Bataan and put the medicines in one place."

Capcaben was where the soldiers made their last stand.

"It was a nightmare and a mess to go from Bataan air strip to Capcaben—about 50 miles," Foy said. "Our Battery F, the 1st platoon, didn't get the message to stop at Capcaben and went on down to Mariveles. Our orders were to blow all the ammo dumps between Capcaben and Mariveles. We were caught before we could get to Mariveles." The Japanese were behind, to the side and in front of them.

"They surrounded Manila Bay and Corregidor was below us," Foy said. "One of my platoons made it to Corregidor."

He said General King "could see the writing on the wall. He had orders not to surrender, but he said rather than leading men to slaughter, he would take responsibility for a surrender. He did not surrender Corregidor and some of the troops were left to defend themselves."

Foy said the island of Corregidor was bombed by the Japanese for thirty days.

"They pulverized it," he said.

The troops consisted of about 1,800 members of the 515th and 200th, along with a tank battalion from Minnesota and "others from up and down the Mississippi. We also had 50,000 to 60,000 Filipinos in the Army."

"All of these groups, about 70,000 men, were in the Death March," Foy said. "They were Americans and Filipinos and other nationalities who were commissioned into the Army."

The men were marched in small groups of about 100 from Mariveles and other towns at the tip of the Bataan Peninsula to San Fernando. It took each group about five days to cover the 65 miles. The march began after the surrender of the Bataan Peninsula on April 9, 1942 by Major General Edward King Jr.

The Bataan Death March resulted in the deaths of thousands from starvation, mistreatment by their Japanese captors and disease. Those who survived the march ended up in prisoner-of-war camps, where thousands more died from the same maladies and mistreatment.

According to the history of the Bataan Death March at the New Mexico National Guard Museum, at least 10,000 men—1,000 Americans and 9,000 Filipino—died in the march and more died in confinement camps, as well as in the "death ships" transporting them to the Japanese main island.

# CHAPTER 3

☙

## VOLUNTEERING TO SERVE IN 1941

GOD'S  UMBRELLA

# CARTER, JACK W.
## DOB 03/16/1923 DOD 05/08/2015

Jack W. Carter of Silver City, volunteered for the Army on May 6, 1941 when he was nineteen years old and ended up with the United States Army Air Forces. He joined in Owensboro, Kentucky, where he was born and raised and did his basic training at Fort Knox, Kentucky.

"Yes, the gold was there," Carter said.

He became a top turret gunner on the B-17 "Flying Fortress."

In early 1942, he was sent to Lakenheath, England, home to the Royal Air Force. Carter left there to take part in the invasion of North Africa.

"I flew fifty-eight combat missions in the B-17," Carter said.

When his plane was targeting the Shell oil refinery near Berlin, it was shot down. The date was March 16, 1943.

"The pilot told us to bail out," Carter said. "I bailed from 30,000 feet. My parachute opened, and as I drifted downward I could see thousands of peasants with rifles running toward me. My .45 wasn't going to do me any good."

While he was still heading toward earth, a German plane, a Messerschmitt 109, made a pass at him.

"He wounded me in the arm and the bullet came out my elbow," Carter said.

By the time he got out of his chute on the ground, it was late afternoon and getting dark.

"An SS trooper was coming up the dirt road on a motorcycle," Carter reported. "I greeted him face-to-face as a man. When I noticed him moving to the rear of his cycle, probably going for a gun, I picked up a stake on the ground beside me. I hit him in the face with the stake. It dropped him. I took his pulse, which I couldn't find. He wasn't breathing, so I tossed him into a ravine.

"Before I tossed him, I took his three hand grenades," Carter said. "They came in handy. It was nighttime by now. I met an ammo truck and blew it up with a grenade. It was probably heading to the Russian front. Then I met a fuel tanker, sneaked up, surveyed it good, opened up the tanks and threw the grenade in. It blew sky high."

Soon after that, Carter was captured. It was March 16, 1943.

"They took my shoes and socks and everything," he said. "I had to walk twenty miles barefooted in freezing weather and snow. I ended up with frozen feet."

He was taken to Buchenwald, a concentration camp, which also housed prisoners of war.

One evening in 1945, he was taken to Luckenwalde, another prisoner-of-war camp, where he was interrogated.

"That's where Axis Sally came into the picture," Carter said. "She was an American woman who spoke German and English. She was caught in Germany when the war broke out. Hitler kept her as a translator.

"I was being interrogated by Hitler and his guards face-to-face," Carter said, with his eyes blackened by having been busted by rifle butts from his guards. "I told Hitler if that was the best he could dish out, I can stand anything. I spit in his face, and he left.

"I stayed at the POW camp until we were liberated by the Russians in May 1945," Carter said. "I'm lucky to be alive. I thought the Germans would shoot me."

He said the 1st Ukraine Army under Marshal Zhukov liberated the prisoners.

"We could hear gunfire in the distance when the Russians were moving up," Carter said. "Everybody was hollering, especially the Russians in the camp. Russian women who had been stealing and hiding guns shot off the padlock.

"It was the first time I had been in daylight," he said. "We were kept in darkness. The light hurt my eyes and I said, 'Let me back inside.' It was May 5, 1945."

The next day the United States Army 83rd Infantry Division arrived to liberate the Americans who were held at Buchenwald.

"They were still fighting the Germans, and P-51s were working the front lines," Carter said. "I was sent to a field hospital, where they cleaned me up as best they could. I was air-evacuated to Paris to the 98th General Hospital."

He spent six or seven days at the hospital, where doctors operated on his left shoulder.

"The doctor told me he took out 100 to 150 pieces of shrapnel that ranged from one to ten millimeters in size," Carter said. "I was then ferried by air back to the United States, where I ended up at Bowman Field in Kentucky."

After his return from World War II, Carter was assigned to flight engineering school and became a flight engineer.

He stayed in the service and served in the 2nd Bomb Group, 33rd Bomb Squadron in Korea, where he flew twenty-eight combat missions on B-29 aircraft. By then, he was in the 22nd Bomb Group. He has attended 2nd Bomb Group reunions.

While Carter was still in the service, he married Helen Irene Michaels. They had been married twenty-eight years when she died.

"If the squadron needed entertainment, she went and got it," he said. "She was a dance professional and appeared in a movie."

Carter spent seventeen years, three months and six days in the service.

GOD'S  UMBRELLA

# POOLE, WILLIAM "BILL" H.

## DOB ABOUT 1925

DOB about 1925 William "Bill" H. Poole, who lives near Silver City, always said that he would become a pilot in the service, but his friends told him he would need a college education.

"I became a pilot by a devious route," Poole said. "On July 1, 1941, I joined the Army Air Corps with a high school friend, R. L. Cheek. I was only sixteen years old."

Cheek, according to Poole, "spent the whole war as a prisoner of war (POW)."

Poole said becoming a pilot occurred by "pure happenstance." A glider program came about because of the invasion of Crete.

"I couldn't apply to become a glider pilot, because I didn't have my birth certificate," Poole said. "I had just turned seventeen. It was 1942. A kid who slept about three bunks away had his birth certificate and he applied and was headed out the next day. He said, 'Come on and go with us.'"

Poole still didn't have a birth certificate, but he went with his friend who said the sergeant needed people and would probably put him on the orders.

"That's exactly what happened," Poole said. "I got put on the orders and he told me to be there at nine the next morning. I escaped the education and the age requirements. I was flying Army aircraft at age seventeen."

He was shipped to Randolph Field near San Antonio, Texas, where he stayed for about three weeks. Then they headed to Spencer, Iowa.

"I soloed and was flying alone by July 1, 1942," Poole said. "By mid-September, I had logged about 200 flying hours and was doing 'dead-stick landings' with the engine off and propeller stopped day and night."

In the fall of 1942, by way of Albuquerque, he was sent to Fort Sumner, New Mexico, where a new aerodrome was being constructed. The men moved into tents and started flying gliders.

By February 1943, it was decided that there were too many glider pilots, but that, for men who had not "washed out" of Army Air Forces Pilot School and if they could pass the written exam, the education requirement was forgiven.

"This was what I always wanted," Poole said. "I went to Air Corps Pilot School in the class of 1943 and graduated Dec. 4, 1943."

The class was the first to receive instrument training. Primary flying school was in Blythe, California; basic flying school in Bakersfield, California; and twin-engine advanced flying school back in Fort Sumner. Upon his graduation and receiving his wings and commission, about eight of the group were sent to B-25 transition school first at Mather Field near Sacramento, California, and next to Deming,

New Mexico, where they learned to fly combat aircraft. He said he liked the B-25s, because "we kids considered them hot rods."

"Those of us who attended transition went to overseas training as a first pilot and picked up a co-pilot, a bombardier, a navigator and three gunners," Poole said. "I checked out in the B-25 at Las Cruces Auxiliary, which is now the city airport. In January 1944, there were new runways with runway lights and nothing else. No buildings."

Transition was completed toward the end of February and the B-25s were flown back to Sacramento. The men boarded a train and traveled through Cheyenne, Wyoming; Omaha, Nebraska; Chicago, Illinois; Cincinnati, Ohio; and south to Greenville, South Carolina.

"I had reached my nineteenth birthday, January 1, 1944," Poole said. "My new co-pilot, Wilton 'Pete' Soerens, had just graduated from pilot school. He was twenty-five years old. The bombardier and the navigator were twenty-three years old. One of the gunners was forty-two."

In mid-July, the crews were flown to Savannah, Georgia, where each of the twelve first pilots signed for one new B-25 aircraft. The next day they took a five-to-eight-hour test flight over water to check for fuel consumption.

Next stop was Palm Beach, Florida, where they were briefed on over-water flights to Borinquen, Puerto Rico.

"We knew we would be flying overseas to combat, but we did not know whether we would be sent to the South Pacific, Europe or China-Burma," Poole said. "A flight to Puerto Rico indicated Europe or China-Burma. Once the first leg of the flight was in progress, we could open sealed orders to determine whether we were flying to Tunis, Tunisia, or Karachi, Pakistan. This prevented personnel telephoning their route to family or friends.

"Our route was Puerto Rico; British Guiana; Belem, Brazil; and Natal, Brazil," Poole said. "We overnighted at each destination. We then flew about 1,500 miles east to Ascension Island."

Those destined for the Mediterranean and Tunis flew north to Liberia; then to Dakar, Senegal; Marrakech, Morocco; and finally, Tunis. He said his "closest fuel problem" was between Dakar and Marrakech, because they had to fly 300 miles east of the coast, because the Germans were in Spanish Morocco. No guns were on board, except for the officers having .45 caliber pistols.

"We got down to seventy-two gallons of fuel left (out of 982 gallons), which was only thirty minutes of flying," Poole said. "I was always a serious pilot and never had any accidents.

"From Florida to Tunis was ten days of very laborious, slow, hard flight due to the minimum power setting to economize on fuel," Poole said. "We flew six to eight hours per day at about 150 miles per hour. The aircraft struggled at this speed, when normally the aircraft flew at 200 or more miles per hour."

Most of the 12 crews he had trained with were assigned to the 12th Air Force, 57th Bomb Wing, 310th Bomb Group. Poole was assigned to the 379th Squadron of the four squadrons in the 310th Bomb Group. Each squadron could muster eighteen B-25 aircraft and several "spares," which filled in if an aircraft dropped out of formation due to mechanical problems.

Poole's post was Ghisonaccia Gare, Corsica. He and his wife, Patsy, returned to Corsica about twenty years ago.

"I saw my washwoman, Marie Thou, who was about forty or forty-five during the war," Poole said. "I found a fellow who was an eight-year-old during the war. He said he was at the airfields all the time and got run off a half-dozen times a day. He showed me a pile of tail-fin crates that were still there. We made what we called 'bomb stools,' out of the steel crates. He had one that you could still read the stenciling on.

"I don't smoke, so during the war, I traded smokes for candy—Mars, Snickers and Hershey bars," Poole said. "I would take and pick up my laundry twice a week. Marie reminded me when the kids saw, they would come, yelling, 'Hey, Joe. Bonbons.'"

First pilots who arrived fresh from training had to fly co-pilot with a seasoned combat pilot to test their reactions.

"My first and second combat missions on August 4 and 5, 1944, were to bomb the Avignon, France, rail bridge over the Rhone River," Poole said. "I still own a piece of the shrapnel that came through the right side of the pilots' compartment on my first mission. It went about a foot aft of my head and ricocheted around the compartment without hitting the pilot or me."

He flew thirteen missions in southern France, including as first pilot during the invasion of southern France [Operation Dragoon] on August 15, 1944.

"When we invaded southern France, the Germans started fleeing, because they knew [General] Patton was on his way," Poole said.

He flew the rest of sixty-seven missions out of Ghisonaccia primarily into northern Italy—from the Apennines to the Po River Valley and Brenner Pass areas—into southern Austria, eastern Italy and Yugoslavia.

"One time, we were going someplace, nice sunny day, when all of a sudden, we were hit with flak," Poole said. "The airplanes scattered, but soon came back into formation."

They moved to Fano, Italy, after dropping bombs on Rovereto, Italy. On April 9, 1945, the "big push" to get the Germans out of Italy began.

"We were a great distance from the front, but we could feel the concussions from the big guns at night," Poole said.

"On the ninth, every aircraft we had was in the air. I was Number 2 on my sixty-ninth mission. We went up to bomb the Germans where they were dug in. About 325 B-25s dropped fragmentation bombs. Every six airplanes had 792 of them. The British Army walked through the hole we made. They said the Germans were crazy from the four days of constant shelling and then, "here we came with the bombs."

A "box" of six Allied airplanes overtook the lead group during this mission and started dropping bombs through the lead airplanes. Eight bombs hit Poole's plane. Six went right through and two stayed in the airplane. One tumbled around in the engine compartment and broke off the fuse. "A miracle," he called it. One exploded inside.

"I always wore a winter or summer flying helmet, to protect my ears," Poole said. "I didn't hear the bomb hit. George Jolly was perforated. Everyone on the crew went back to help him and came back and told me he was dead. After we flew the badly damaged aircraft over the Adriatic Sea, where I dumped the bombs, we crash landed at Fano, destroying the airplane. I walked away from it."

He credited his glider training for landing and keeping the uninjured crew safe.

"Within an hour, I heard George wasn't dead, but they flew him out in the middle of the night and I figured he was buried. I thought he was dead all those years, but he was still alive," Poole said. "I found him in the 1980s. He was living in Cape May, New Jersey. I met George again in Denver. We spent the whole day together."

On August 19, 1945, Poole was sent out on the seventieth mission, slated to be his final one. It was to Rovereto, where almost always a plane was shot down.

"I said, 'Why don't you increase the odds?'" Poole said. "About eighteen B-25s were ahead of us and they were getting the hell shot out of them. We got over the area and there were no shots. It was in the waning days of the war, and the Germans were no doubt having trouble getting ammunition, and they had evidently used everything on the preceding planes. Another miracle."

He was awaiting transport to the United States in Naples on May 8, 1945, when peace was declared. He was sent to Atlanta, Georgia, where he was discharged effective July 12, 1945.

During his four years of service, he was awarded a Distinguished Flying Cross, eleven Air Medals, and five Battle Stars.

Then he had to finish high school. Next, he obtained a bachelor's degree in general business from the University of Southern California in June 1949.

# Harrison, James William "Bill"

## DOB 06/22/1922

In late June 1941, when James William "Bill" Harrison was attending business college in Oklahoma City, Oklahoma, and working on his grandparents' farm, Navy recruiters came to town.

"On July 7, I was inducted into the V-6 Navy Reserves," Harrison said. "On July 21, I was on active duty."

He went in as a yeoman third class.

"My first job was as secretary taking a court martial," Harrison said.

By October, he was on the oil tanker, USS Kakaskia.

"I had been in the service for a year and was on the Kakaskia when war broke out," Harrison said. "We were at Mare Island, California, and workers were in the process of welding guns to the decks."

In just a few days, the ship headed to San Pedro, California, to take on fuel.

"We got to Pearl Harbor in January 1943," Harrison said. "It was still a mess."

He served in the South Pacific taking fuel from San Pedro to Tonga Island.

"We met the fleet coming from the Atlantic Ocean, just before the Battle of the Coral Sea," Harrison said.

The oil tanker was pumping aviation fuel to the USS Yorktown during the zig-zagging that the fleet was doing to try to avoid submarine attacks.

"The whole fleet did the same turns," Harrison said. "Everyone else zigged and we zagged."

The boom was crushed, and the rubberized steel hose uncoiled and got stuck in the Kakasia's screws.

"We were trailing oil in the Coral Sea and were dead in the water," Harrison said. "We had to cut the steel out of the screws."

The ship was required to return to Hawaii for repairs. The oil tanker that took the Kakasia's place was sunk during the battle.

The Battle of the Coral Sea was the first that the United States forces won, thanks to the air support, he said.

The Japanese ships were on their way to New Guinea and on to Australia, but the fleet was so badly damaged that they never went onward.

Harrison served as a petty officer second class on Admiral Chester Nimitz's staff, in what would nowadays be called public relations.

"We wrote all the press releases," Harrison said.

During the Battle of Midway, he injured his hand and was sent back to the United States for medical discharge.

"But I didn't take it, because by the time I got back, my hand was working pretty well," Harrison said. "I was transferred to the VF-36 Squadron in Seattle."

After that he was sent to Whidbey Island, Washington, then to Ream Field in San Isidro, California.

"The commanding officer, the personnel officer and I would take a group and turn them into a squadron," Harrison said.

He said that at that time, "enlisted men were less than nothing and officers were gods."

The V-12 program gave the opportunity to enlisted men to attend universities in the United States for officers' training.

"In 1943, I was transferred to Southwestern University in Georgetown, Texas," Harrison said. "I had the choice between Southwestern and Yale, but I chose the smaller school because I was a small-town boy and I wanted the individual attention."

He enrolled in courses in naval engineering and pre-law. After Southwestern, he, as a reserve midshipman, attended the University of Texas in Austin.

"I was there when the war ended," Harrison said. "I spent four years, three months and twenty-seven days in the Navy without any combat. My service was without any distinction whatsoever."

While serving under Nimitz, Admiral Richard Byrd came into the office as the Allied Naval Base Inspector. He needed a yeoman and interviewed and selected Harrison.

"I had a leave coming and he told me to take it," Harrison said. "I did and when I got back, Byrd had had to leave early, so I missed him and didn't go."

Also, while in Nimitz's office, Harrison was asked to take and write a letter for a Marine.

"It started out 'Dear Dad,'" Harrison said. "He talked about things he shouldn't have been talking about in a letter. After he left, I said that the letter needed to go through the censor and I needed to know where to send it, too. The young Marine was Elliot Roosevelt and the 'Dad' was President Franklin Roosevelt. I got ribbed a lot about that."

Another experience Harrison recounted took place on Tonga Island.

"I went ashore and saw a fellow trying to get a car started," Harrison said. "I had worked with my dad in his filling station, so I got the car running by drying off the spark plugs. The fellow asked me if I would like to meet Her Majesty the Queen."

The queen had moved out of her palace preparing it for officers' quarters, so she was holding court in the Free Methodist Church.

"There was a large chair and a few smaller ones," Harrison said. "Probably the largest black woman I've ever seen came out. Her name was Salote Tabu. She could trace her ancestry back more than 600 years. We visited. She was a very intelligent and nice lady. And what I especially remember was what she said: 'We want your American Christianity, but not your American Christians, because they don't do what they say.'"

He reported that she later moved all the women off the island, so the bloodlines would not be mixed with other ethnicities.

"I felt most fortunate to be in the Navy and not the Marines," Harrison said. "We were all kids when we went in, and I was one of the grunts who got it done. I have the utmost respect for the gold-plated heroes in the Army."

Harrison served as Silver City town manager after moving to town in 1969. He counts among his ancestors his great-great-great-great-great-great-great-grandfather, President William Henry Harrison.

"He was the perfect president," Harrison said. "He didn't do anything and died a month after taking office."

GOD'S UMBRELLA

# HILL, JACK

## DOB ABOUT 1921 DOD 04/20/2016

Jack Hill of Silver City said he went through civilian pilot training at New Mexico State Teachers College, where a Navy recruiter signed him up for the service in 1941.

After he passed his physical in August, he received primary flight training in Long Beach, California, and then spent two months in Dallas, Texas, for ground school and physical training. He was sent to Corpus Christi, Texas, and to a new airfield in Kingsville, Texas, for the final two months of fighter training.

"I graduated in September 1942," Hill said. "My first orders were to North Island, near San Diego [California]. There weren't enough ships to send us overseas, so we did odds and ends. I flew ferry trips to Dallas and to Sand Point, near Seattle, Washington."

Hill went into the service with two friends from Silver City—George Harsch, who did not make it through training at Long Beach, California, and Bud Collins—"my very best friends."

Collins served as a pilot on the aircraft carrier USS Enterprise. On one mission, one of his wing mates ran out of gas. He went back to mark the spot until a destroyer could pick up the wing mate. When Collins returned to the carrier, someone on board thought he was the enemy and fired at him.

"Others died, too, and we lost him," Hill said.

In November 1942, Hill was transferred from dive bombers to torpedo planes, where he flew the Avenger.

January 1943 found Hill in Chicago to qualify for and make carrier landings on the USS Wolverine in Lake Michigan.

After six weeks, he was back in San Diego, with orders to go on the USS Enterprise.

"But before I caught it, it got damaged," Hill said.

He was assigned to the USS Sangamon, a converted oiler, which became an auxiliary aircraft carrier.

"Three of us acted like one big carrier," Hill said. "One ship carried fourteen torpedo planes, fourteen diver bombers and thirty fighters. A big carrier would have three times that."

He flew missions in the Solomon Islands and Guadalcanal, Mondo Bay, the Russell Islands and, for his last trip, Bougainville.

A lot of the time, Hill was based on Guadalcanal. On his second trip to the island, he lived in a Quonset hut, with no screens. He could hear rats scratching at a can of hard candy.

"The ships would come in and dump supplies on the beach," Hill said. "We would get three-gallon cans of peaches and only pry the lid up partway. We hung a can by wire from the eaves, and the next morning it had rat doo in it."

During landings on the ship, Hill said, "we just had to trust the signal officer. We knew what the plane would do. It wasn't that hard."

"Landings were better than takeoffs, when we were flying with a full load of armament," he said. "Sometimes we flew off the end of the ship, not going too fast. I liked the catapult better."

His planes were shot up several times.

"I had several holes and I lost a wingtip on one mission," Hill said. "I flew a lot of night missions."

He described his service as "pretty good and I made a lot of good friends. I saw a lot of good country and a lot of bad country."

Guadalcanal received more than 300 inches of rain a year and he said the coral island was hot and humid.

"It was better living on the carrier," Hill said.

The carrier returned to the United States in the fall of 1943.

"Being a replacement pilot, I got to come back, because I had flown enough missions," Hill said. "I was required to fly thirty to return. I had flown thirty-seven."

He was ordered to Jacksonville, Florida, for several months, and helped open a new training field near Miami, Florida, for new pilots from Corpus Christi, Texas, or Pensacola, Florida.

"We had whole crews teaching subjects such as navigation, night flying and carrier landings," Hill said. "For most of the rest of my career, I was in Norfolk, Virginia, and Gros Isle near Detroit, Michigan."

He said he accrued plenty of required points to be discharged after "a little over four years. I got out in October 1945."

Hill said he tried to start a Civilian Air Patrol unit in Grant County, but "we never could get an airplane. We had a trainer upstairs at City Hall, but we never got civilian pilot training off the ground, although we had about twelve ex-Army, Navy and Marine pilots. Cap Besse, a retired Navy officer, taught two-way navigation at the college."

Hill is a native of Grant County, having been born in "the big hospital that used to be on the hill" in Tyrone, New Mexico.

When he was about one year old, his family moved to Hurley, New Mexico, where he grew up. After his freshman year in high school, the family moved to Silver City.

"It's been home ever since," Hill said.

After the war, he returned to Silver City and said he flew some with Thurmond Yates and with Dr. Jack Cobb.

He taught mathematics for ten years at Cobre High School, and then spent the rest of his teaching career at Silver High School, where for four years he served as principal.

GOD'S UMBRELLA

# BAKER, JASON

## DOB 09/25/1918 DOD 5/8/2010

Jason Baker of Lake Roberts was originally from Massachusetts. He was living in Portland, Maine, when he heard about the attack on Pearl Harbor that started the Pacific Theater of World War II for American troops.

"The next day I got a telegram to report to the Philadelphia Navy Yard," Baker said.

He received basic training for officers at the rifle range "to sharpen our skills."

"From there we got word that we were going to take a ride," Baker said. "There was a mixture of troops on a train to the West Coast."

Within twenty-four hours of arriving in California, he was aboard ship heading to New Zealand for more training.

"The people of New Zealand are the most wonderful and accommodating people," Baker said.

His next stop was Guadalcanal where he arrived in 1942.

"It was a beautiful island, but we had nothing to eat for the first week, except coconuts," Baker said. "I sent fellows up the trees to retrieve the fruit. Our food was still aboard the ship."

He was assigned to the 1st Marine Corps Division, 3rd Battalion, 5th Regiment, Company I on Guadalcanal.

Major General Alexander A. Vandegrift commanded the 1st Marine Division, the assault landing force.

"I was with the first troops to land on Guadalcanal and as a first lieutenant was sent to help clean it up and secure Henderson Field," Baker said. "We stayed there until we secured the island, and we wanted to make sure all the coconuts were eaten up."

On the morning of August 7, 1942, the 1st Marine Division landed across the north beaches east of the Tenaru River.

"We spent a lot of time at the mouth of the Tenaru River," Baker said. "It was a great place to cover the beach."

A major ridgeline stood a way back from the coast.

"I thought it would be a great place to set up camp," stated Baker. "I was told a general was coming up to see me. It was Vandergrift and he told me it looked a good spot because it was high ground."

Malaria sickened many of the troops and Baker was no exception.

"I had trouble with it for a month or so," Baker said.

While on the island, he said he played poker on a stump with General Merritt A. "Red Mike" Edson, renowned for the Edson's Raiders, a special operations-type force within the Marine Corps.

"Guadalcanal was a heck of a battle," Baker said. "I was told that it took years to get rid of the unexploded ordnance left on the island."

Thirteen days after "we wound up Guadalcanal," Baker's unit headed to Australia. They ended up in Melbourne.

"I was in the hospital for a while, but I can't remember why," he said. "When I was well enough to leave, they sent me for a rest in Tasmania."

While on the island, with what he described as "a perfect harbor," Baker said he met some people who owned and lived on a lot of property.

"They had a beautiful yacht," Baker said. "After the war, I found out the yacht was owned by a movie star."

He also served for a short time off the coast of New Guinea and briefly in New Britain.

"A lot of us were in Australia for almost a year," Baker said.

# Anderson, Roy

## DOB 06/09/1921 DOD late 2015 or early 2016

Roy Anderson, of Silver City, signed up to be in the Army Air Forces following the attack on Pearl Harbor in 1941.

Having also served in the Civilian Conservation Corps in the 1930s, Anderson couldn't find a job upon his release from the CCC, so he traveled from his birthplace in Cloquet, Minnesota, to live with his uncle in Rockford, Illinois, where he volunteered.

"I was supposed to go to Air Corps training, but I was sent to Chanute Field, Illinois, and then to Tulahoma, Tennessee, where I was assigned to the 33rd Infantry Division," Anderson said. "It was not what I wanted, but I went through basic and got expert and sharpshooter certification."

Because a radio operator course was also available, Anderson took it.

"The whole outfit was to be shipped to Tacoma, Washington," he said. "I had a weekend pass, so I went to Nashville and talked to a colonel about my wanting to serve in the Air Corps. He said he would check into it."

The troops, including Anderson, were sent to Tacoma, so he went to Bremerton, where he "ran into" a brigadier general.

"I 'cried,' not real tears, on his shoulder," Anderson said. "Within a few days, a lieutenant came to me and said, 'You're wanted at headquarters.' That's where I found out I was being transferred to the military police. I went through the training, but this was far from what I wanted.

"One day, I heard, 'Anderson, get your gear. You're being shipped to San Antonio, Texas.' Nine of us went."

The nine were given tests. One of the questions was to list their education degrees.

"I didn't even have a high school degree, but I took the tests and passed them," Anderson said. "As a kid, I always had my head in a book."

He was shipped to Chickasha, Oklahoma. The first thing he did in his new Air Forces cadet uniform was spend half a day with his flight instructor in a BT-19—a two-seat, open-cockpit plane. Then he went through ground school.

"Virgil Petty was my instructor," Anderson said. "He was a barnstormer, a crop duster and did acrobatic flying. He took a liking to me and told me he was going 'to teach me things.' If I went to a single-engine fighter, I could go quickly right or left or upside down. He said, 'You're a natural' behind the stick."

His next stop was Coffeyville, Kansas, where he almost lost his instructor.

"We were in a BT-19, which had a canopy," Anderson said. "It was open maybe two feet. I'm sitting there in my cold-weather clothes with my helmet on, my seat belt buckled and with my parachute. He's the instructor. He rapped the stick back and forth and said, 'Take 'er up.' I got her off, but he's cussing me before we got off the ground. We got about 5,500 feet. The canopy still wasn't shut. He told me to do this and that and then said, "Is that all you learned in basic?" I did a half roll, and all of a sudden, kerplunk. He wasn't strapped in, no parachute and didn't close the canopy. We flew back. He was white as a sheet and the other guys asked me what happened."

The next thing Anderson heard was, "Anderson, report to the commandant on the double." The sergeant asked, "What's going on?"

"I went in to see the colonel, who was commandant of the cadets," Anderson said. "I held my salute. He bawled me out and said, 'You had a damned good record in basic. You must tell the instructor what you're going to do.'"

Anderson was next trained on two-engine planes in Frederick, Oklahoma. A Major Reeder taught a couple of the cadets how to "fly under the hood," using instruments.

"We graduated and got our wings," Anderson said.

He was sent to Sedalia, Missouri, to train on larger, multiple-engine planes, such as the C-47 and C-46 cargo planes, as well as CG4A gliders, with no engines.

He learned how to tow gliders, using a hook on the rear of a plane, which hooked onto a cable on the glider to take it airborne.

After this training, he had two sets of wings [badges representing his pilot status]—one for airplanes and one with a G on it for gliders. His next stop was La Guardia

Air Field in New York, where he was assigned to a C-47. He and his crew were sent to the Bahamas.

"I'd never flown over an ocean before," Anderson said. "Before flying the ocean, I did a violation. I wanted to see the Statue of Liberty, so Ervin Bohlmfalk and I buzzed her and blew a kiss to her as we banked by."

After the Bahamas, the crew flew to the Azores.

"We were seeing an awful lot of water," Anderson said. "We stayed down where we wouldn't have to use oxygen. Three-quarters of the way there, the crew chief asked when we were going to get there and if we were lost. We had no idea where we were, but then we saw something dark on the horizon and landed on a postage stamp in the Azores."

Next were stops in Casablanca, Morocco; Algiers, Algeria; and Cairo, Egypt. Their next orders were to Karachi, Pakistan, and on to India, where their orders sent them to the Assam Valley.

"Our assignments were to take food and supplies and drop them to Merrill's Marauders, who were building a road from Lido, India, to Mandalay, Burma," Anderson said. "At a Las Cruces reunion of the China-Burma-India campaign veterans, Lloyd Hackenberry told me: 'You're the one who killed my ass.' There was one clearing for our drop. His mule, Dynamite, took off to eat grass and my 2,000-pound load hit his mule. I told him I was sorry."

Anderson also flew "The Hump," [the eastern end of the Himalayas over which Allied pilots flew military transport from India to China to resupply the Chinese war effort and for the United States Army Air Forces based in China.].

"I flew a C-46, called a 'Dumbo,' over "The Hump," he said. "It held 4,000 pounds and was sluggish and slow. I told them to get me a C-47 and I'll fly 'The Hump.'"

He made "quite a few trips" to Kunming, China, with the 10th Air Force.

"It was one of the most dangerous and treacherous places to fly," Anderson said. "Seven hundred forty-six C-46 and C-47 planes went down in 'The Hump.' It was called the Aluminum Trail, because of all the crashed planes."

He recounted a story of one trip.

"I had an assignment to take supplies to Kunming," Anderson said. "We carried our own gas, and everything inside the plane was tied down. The flight was dangerous because the air currents were pushing us around and up and down. We were hit with hail the size of golf balls hitting the fuselage, then we had rain, snow and ice. On this trip, we had a sudden jolt and a rough ride. I had to keep resetting the instruments. All of a sudden, we hit an air pocket and everything went upside down.

"We were at 25,000 to 26,000 feet altitude and all of us were belted in," Anderson reported. "Then I saw two peaks. By instinct from my training with Virgil Petty, I kicked the rudder as hard as I could and went between the peaks sideways and then straightened out. The altimeter showed we were 300 to 400 feet off the ground."

A later assignment was to move troops from eastern China on the coast to the western boundary of the country, because the Japanese wanted to take over China.

On one such ferry of troops, it got really hot and one of the Chinese opened a door in the plane.

"All of a sudden, the plane is going down," Anderson said. "I said, 'Erv, go back and see what's going on.' He reported that the troops were making a lot of noise and having fun playing a game. 'They threw a soldier out the door without a parachute,' Erv said. We did a count and were missing seven Chinese troops. The loser of the game got sent out. I later found another pilot, Milton Bulls, who had also had a similar experience."

On another flight, the load wasn't tied down properly, and the plane stopped to get gasoline and food.

"When we went to take off, the load shifted and we were tail-heavy," Anderson said. "We hit the ground and sheared the landing gear off because there was no place to land. I struggled to get out of the canopy and hit my head, shoulder and leg. I had a big gash in my leg. No one was around, so I had a kit in my pocket with a needle and thread, and I sewed the gash up and blotted it with my underwear. We walked far enough to get a ride, with my crew partially carrying me.

"I was airlifted to a hospital," Anderson continued. "The doctor looked at me and cussed me out for a sloppy job of sewing. I didn't tell anyone else about my leg, because I didn't want to go back home."

He did get sent home at the end of the war. He traveled on the USNS Marine Phoenix, and spent most of his time on deck with the captain, who explained about currents and whales and porpoises. They landed at Fort Lawton, Washington.

Anderson was a flight officer from June 27, 1944, to May 9, 1946. He received the World War II Victory Medal, the Asiatic-Pacific Theater Medal and the American Theater Service Medal. His sister, Lillian, and his brother, Robert, also served in World War II.

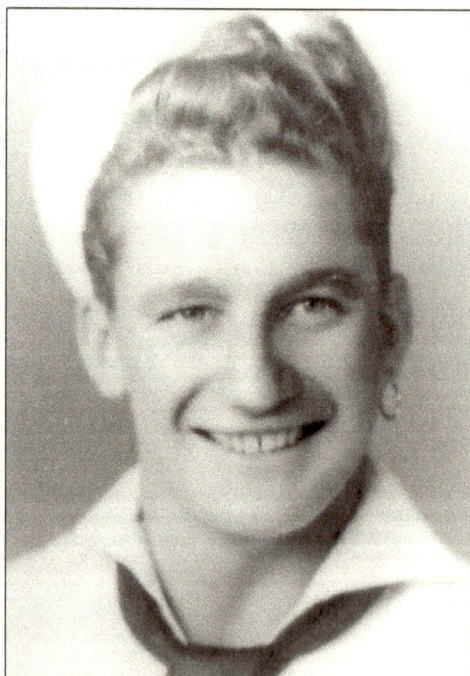

# De Young, Mason A.

## DOB 9/12/1924 DOD 2/8/2011

Mason A. De Young enlisted in the United States Navy in August 1941, when he was sixteen years old.

"My dad signed for me," De Young said. "We were living in Minneapolis, Minnesota, at the time. I told him I wanted to go into the Navy and he said, 'Damn good place for you.'"

He began his service September 15, 1941, when the war was still only in Europe. But in the last years of his service, he served in the Pacific.

"I was assigned to the USS Tuscaloosa, a heavy cruiser, but I never got aboard it," De Young said. "I stayed on the USS Hilary P. Jones, a Destroyer 427."

Three times, the ship escorted British convoys to Iceland.

"The third time, we were halfway to Iceland, when the Japanese bombed Pearl Harbor," De Young said. "Although I wasn't seasick, others were chronically seasick."

Each trip took about a month and because the galley was on the main deck and the waves were high, the cook couldn't get to the galley, so the crew ate the life raft rations.

"Once, the ship rolled seventy-eight degrees without capsizing," De Young said. "German planes came out of

Norway to attack us above the Arctic Circle. Very seldom was it calm. We didn't have much anti-aircraft on the destroyer. We had five-inch guns and depth charges, which we used when we had contact with submarines."

In 1942, after required repairs to the ship, "we changed scenery," De Young said. "We went to the Caribbean to look for German supply ships and subs. It was much better weather.

"I was on a boarding party, with a few other guys and an officer," he said. "We would go aboard and inspect the ships. They let us aboard. If they didn't stop, they would get sunk. I was just a seaman, but I had a .50-caliber machine gun."

Next, his ship headed to Norfolk, Virginia. The commissary steward there received money to buy food for the ship's crewmembers, but he pocketed it and got twenty years in prison.

"After Norfolk, we went to North Africa," De Young said. "We were covering landing ships at Casablanca and patrolled between there and Gibraltar. The French were tied in with the Germans, so we had to contend with them a little bit."

He said he got to go ashore in Casablanca, but it was "dirty as hell."

Back in Norfolk, in 1942, he went to torpedo school and came out as a torpedoman third class. He was transferred to the USS Renshaw DD 499, another destroyer.

"In New York City at Pier 92, I was assigned to guard duty, guarding prisoners who were going to Leavenworth," De Young said. "I was walking my beat, and a guy said, 'Hey, Mac, do you know how to handle that .45 on your hip? You gotta shove that clip in first.' I was so embarrassed."

In January 1943, the ship traveled through the Panama Canal headed toward the South Pacific, "where we spent an eternity. We crossed the equator on February 18, 1943."

The next stop was the island of Espiritu Santo, where he received training as a gunner.

"We spent a month or so trying to fool the Japs," De Young said. "We were going day and night. We would go to an island to get ammunition, then speed to different islands bombarding Japanese bases. We bombarded all of them—Borneo, Truk, Guadalcanal, Iwo Jima, Bougainville, Tarawa and the Marshall Islands. We were fighting off Japanese Zeros and torpedo bombers."

A lot of the Japanese planes were suicide bombers.

The Renshaw and the USS Pringle headed to the Kuta Gulf, where, although they were outgunned by the Japanese, who were shooting eight-inch guns to the destroyers' five-inch guns and 40 mm and 20 mm guns, they knocked out an airbase, an oil dump, a submarine and several landing crafts.

The next week, in the same area, the group was hit hard by the Japanese fleet and lost a cruiser and a couple of "tin cans," as destroyers were nicknamed.

During this time, De Young said he and the other crewmembers spent twenty-four months at sea without setting foot on land.

"We all got a little 'funny,'" he said. "We had a song-and-dance guy called Queenie who used to sing 'I Went to School with Maggie Murphy.'"

In 1944, the destroyers continued their bombing missions.

"When I got a .50-caliber machine gun, the skipper called me 'Trigger-Happy Torpedoman,'" De Young said. "I was a spotter. A shipmate named Taylor said, 'I saw De Young throw a crescent wrench at a Japanese Zero that came between the stacks.' I missed."

One time when the destroyer was escorting a couple of mine sweepers along the west side of Bougainville, the ship picked up a radar contact that the Japanese fleet was headed toward the ship.

"I thought, 'This is our end,' but our big task forces cut them off," De Young said.

After another Christmas at sea, De Young said, the crew spent four days in Sydney, Australia.

"Wow, we sure had a great time," he said. "They make good beer. When we left port, there were twenty or so girls trailing us in small boats through the channel. Some were hanging on our screw guards and shouting, 'Don't leave.' They loved the Americans, because we saved them from the Japs."

The ship was headed for Espiritu Santo when a lone Japanese Zero dropped a bomb, just missing the fantail, but putting a dent in the destroyer.

"The sad part was that we had smuggled booze aboard and hid it in the aft steering room," De Young said. "It all got broken."

After repairs in San Francisco, California, the destroyer headed back to the South China Sea, where they covered the landing at Lingayen Gulf in the Philippines and were there when General Douglas MacArthur made his famous "I Have Returned" speech.

The Japanese hit the destroyer with a torpedo at midships portside and made a twenty-foot hole.

"It killed eighteen buddies and wounded several more," De Young said. "We worked like hell to keep her afloat. I went around putting the depth charges on safety, so if we went down, she wouldn't explode. Queenie was blown out and scalded. He was red like a lobster. I was sure he had died, until I saw him years later at a reunion."

At the time of the interview, De Young said his son-in-law fought in the Gulf War and was returning on a destroyer.

"I flew to Hawaii to see him and rode back staying in officers' quarters," De Young said. "It was better chow than we had and it was the same for the enlisted men and the officers."

The food was not the same for all the troops when De Young was serving, he said.

"One time, we were going to have beans and the officers were having roast chicken," he said. "I'm a little guy and I stepped into the galley and snatched a chicken that was being handed out on a silver platter. We ate the whole thing and threw all the evidence overboard. The incident was investigated, but nobody confessed."

De Young was in combat the whole time he was in the Navy—more than four years. He also spent all four Christmases at sea.

He was discharged at Great Lakes Naval Station on October 15, 1945. In the Pacific he earned nine Battle Stars and earned another for his work in North Africa and the Atlantic Ocean.

# CHAPTER 4

☙

## THE DRAFT BROUGHT THESE MEN INTO THE SERVICE OF COUNTRY IN 1941

GOD'S UMBRELLA

# SALAS, FELIX

## DOB 2/14/1923 DOD 7/12/2009

"God had an umbrella over me," Felix Salas said of his years as a Japanese prisoner of war following the Bataan Death March.

He remembers clearly the events leading up to his induction into the United States Army on March 18, 1941, when he was seventeen years old.

Because the Depression was "rough, I quit school in fifth grade and started looking for a job," Salas said.

He was young, and his family did not have a car, so he hitchhiked or took advantage of a twenty-cent bus ride to and from work.

By the time he was seventeen years old, Salas said, he had been working a lot, and "I knew how to work."

When he was drafted into the Army, he had added four years to his age in order to get work. He was working at the copper mines in Grant County, New Mexico, near where he lived, and a list of draftees was compiled. He was in the third group to be drafted.

"But the lady at the post office couldn't find my notice," Salas said. "It took three days to find it and by that time I had received a mean letter telling me I was going to be court-martialed if I didn't report."

Julio Tafoya gave Salas and three friends from Santa Rita, New Mexico—Manuel Muñoz, Vicente Ojinaga and Pablo Gutierrez—a ride to the bus to go to Santa Fe, New Mexico. Another man from Mimbres, New Mexico—Reynaldo Salaiz—was on the same bus to Santa Fe. Salas and Salaiz roomed together. The third day, they were put on a bus northward to Albuquerque, New Mexico, and then back south on a train to Fort Bliss, Texas.

"I had long hair," Salas said. "Some guys cried when they shaved our heads."

Salas was assigned to the 200th Coast Artillery, H Battalion, with Indians from Taos, New Mexico.

"We were shown the showers and washbowls and were told to shave," Salas said. "I hardly had a beard, so it didn't take me long. We had 5 a.m. reveille and had to hurry to fix our beds and clothes, then we ran to line up."

Salas was assigned to a 37 mm Gun M3 (cannon) as part of a seven-man crew. He said Corporal Norvell Tao was "tough, but kind. He liked the way we worked."

For seven months, he and the rest of the battalion were trained as infantry, coast artillery and anti-aircraft soldiers. The crews were drilled in shooting at a light that simulated an airplane.

'We hit it more times than anyone else," Salas said. "We won, so they gave us three choices—to go to Alaska, Louisiana or the Philippines. We chose the Philippines."

The men were put on a ship after reaching San Francisco, California.

"The ship started rocking," Salas said. "Everyone got sick. I got sick, too. The more the ship moved, the more the poor guys got sick. I was lying in my bunk close to the windows. I saw the ocean going up and down and really got sick, but not again after that."

After a stop in Hawaii, the men were on their way again.

"When we arrived at our debarkation point, we could see shacks of bamboo with grass roofs," Salas said. "We wondered how we could sleep or take baths, but we were taken to our barracks, where we had canvas cots. The walls were bamboo strips."

Around the first of December 1941, the troops arrived in Luzon, Philippines, at Fort Stotsenberg, which included Clark Field.

By early 1942, American troops had retreated to Bataan.

Salas said his group took up position on a hill. With their 37 mm Gun M3, they had 1,000 rounds.

"We started shooting and sometimes could see planes smoking down to the beach, so we could see good results," Salas said. "Within a couple of weeks, they cut us down to fifty rounds, then twenty, ten, and then, nothing except what was in the clips.

"The Japanese hit the airstrip at Bataan, and we were told to burn our trucks and after crossing a bridge to burn it," he continued. "I cried. What are we going to do without our cannon? They gave us infantry-style, .30

caliber machine guns and told us to shoot and we did. Then the order came to throw away our ammo, including the cartridges on our belts. We found some old white sheets and tore them up and put the pieces on the ends of our rifles. The Japanese grabbed our rifles and put us like cattle into a corral. It was April 10, 1942."

He said they found a water trough and washed their faces and filled their canteens.

"They hit us in the head or anywhere," Salas said. "Good thing I was short, because they missed me."

It was a three-day walk to San Fernando with no food or water for his group.

"They called for 150 men to go on detail," Salas said. "I jumped at it. I knew how to work."

He soon came down with malaria.

"I got to the doctor, but he didn't have anything and just told me to drink lots of water," Salas said.

He said he became delirious. Then he sprained his ankle and had to limp with a bamboo pole. Each morning when he awoke, corpses were on either side of him.

"'Help me, Lord, help me,' I begged," Salas said. "I used to dream of home and crying for Mama."

The prisoners were fed rice and watery soup.

"I still have my original cup from when I entered the Army," Salas said.

Dysentery was a common problem for the prisoners as the water they drank was usually contaminated. Diphtheria also struck the men.

"I almost died [of diphtheria]," Salas said. "I was lucky because they had some medicine."

He lost so much weight from having malaria and diphtheria that, when he encountered Vicente Ojinaga, his "compa" (friend) did not recognize him.

"He was working in the kitchen and would bring out burned bits of rice," Salas said. "We divided it with [Luis] Mendoza and [Pablo] Gutierrez. Vicente said to me, 'Come on, Felix. Eat some more.' He begged me not to die."

Within a couple of weeks, Salas was stronger and could work on details. He was shipped to Japan on one of the prisoner transport ships.

On January 30, 1944, he and other prisoners arrived in Japan, where he was put to work as a blacksmith in a factory making bolts.

"When I was accused of collaborating [by other prisoners], I said, 'I'm not collaborating. I'm [working hard and] trying to save Felix to get home to see Mama,'" Salas said.

One day, he and the other prisoners saw a "big cauliflower smoke," Salas said. "An Australian doctor, a major, told us it was an atomic bomb. We said, 'What's that?' He told us and said the Americans did it."

By this time, a Japanese officer whom "we used to cuss in every language we knew" told them that he didn't have food for the prisoners and "didn't even have food for his family."

"We found two horses that were thinner than us," Salas said, "and told him to take the horses to feed his people. We found a Holstein and I shot it between the eyes. By that evening, we were eating steaks."

When they heard American planes overhead, they wrote in lime [on the ground], "805 [the number of men]— we need 6 [cigarettes] and 6 [sweets]."

A plane dropped "goodies," including Hershey bars.

"I got four and ate them," Salas said. "Japanese ladies and children were picking up things, too. I ate another one and couldn't breathe. The doctor said my body wasn't used to it. I couldn't throw up, I couldn't go to the toilet. Finally, it melted away."

Soon they were on an American ship, where they had mattresses, sheets, blankets and pillows, and hot showers, soap and towels. Salas said when they yelled, "Chow," he soon overdid it again. The next morning for breakfast, he asked for hotcakes, two fried eggs, two sausages and coffee.

He next saw Ojinaga in Manila, where "we hugged and cried and kissed each other. 'Compañero,' he said, 'I thought you had died. You were on the list.'"

After a long trip back to the United States and to Fort Bliss, Texas, for separation from the Army, Salas arrived home in Santa Rita on October 30, 1945.

GOD'S UMBRELLA

# RENTERIA, MANUEL

## DOB 3/31/1920 DOD 7/15/2017

Manuel Rentería was born in Valedón, Hidalgo County, New Mexico, on March 31, 1920. He was a lifelong resident of Hidalgo County.

Rentería received his draft notice in March 1941. On October 15, 1941, he was called to get ready to go to Santa Fe for his physical. "We waited for the bus and it drove us to Santa Fe. We had supper, got to our room and were told to be ready for our physical the next morning. On October 16, we got up, ate breakfast and marched to the National Guard, where I passed the physical."

"They put us on a train on October 17, for Fort Bliss, Texas, where I was sworn into the Army," Rentería continued.

He said a few days later after arriving in Fort Bliss, they were shipped to Fort Sill in Oklahoma to be part of the newly created Army 27th Division. He received a few weeks of training there.

"We were at Fort Sill, when the Japanese bombed Pearl Harbor," Rentería said. "We were then sent to Fort Ord, California, about two months after Pearl Harbor to embark for the Pacific-Asia operation.

"Our company commander called us to the ship's deck to see the Golden Gate Bridge," he said. "He knew many of us would not see it again. I said to myself, 'I will return. God is great. He will bring me back.'

"In March 1942, we got on a boat for three or four days [out of California]," he recounted. "Then we went back to the base. We were told it was so the Japanese would think we were moving out. On the fourth day, we went on the water again. They told us, 'We're moving for good this time. We're not coming back.' We were part of about 100 boats. We didn't know where we were going, but we went for many days and nights.

"I served with the United States Army 27th Division Field Artillery on a machine gun," Rentería said. "We were told we were going to the Philippines, but when the Philippines fell to the Japanese, we turned back to Hawaii.

"We landed in the Hawaiian Islands, and the first thing I saw was Pearl Harbor all torn up," he said. "Little girls and boys lined the area holding flags.

"We were trucked to a field and built our Army camp," Rentería said. "I don't know how long we were there. We got in boats again and this time, we were told to look for enemies, that we were getting close to the Japanese enemies. We were told that we were there for two reasons—to get killed or kill.

"We invaded Okinawa," he said. "Almost four years I was there. We were always fighting. It was bad.

"We always knew when it was mail day, but we didn't get mail often," Rentería said, "maybe every two months. We ate a lot of C-rations in the field, where I was a lot.

"In Okinawa, I saw a lot of blood, a lot of dead people," he said. "I used to say to my friend, 'We're not going home,' but the next day I would say, 'Yes, we're going home.'

"When I did get back home, I stayed at home with Mom and didn't go out for weeks," Rentería said.

One morning when the troops were out in the field scouting, still in Okinawa, they saw a chicken, and all of them said, "Chicken for dinner." They caught it, killed it and had chicken for dinner. A few weeks later, they saw another chicken and thought, "Chicken for dinner," but, when they saw the chicken was eating worms from a dead soldier's body, the thought of a chicken dinner was totally out.

"I was discharged on October 17, 1945, four years to the day after I went in," he continued. "They asked me if I wanted to volunteer and that I would get more money and more stripes. I was a corporal. I said, 'I want to go home and see my folks.'"

Rentería had three brothers in the service. Daniel was in the Navy and also fought in Okinawa. Two served in Germany—Ramon and Ernesto.

"Ramon was the oldest, and we all made it back home," Rentería said.

Once the battle in Okinawa was over, he said they had to stay two more months waiting for transportation back to the States.

"While we were waiting, an offer came over for volunteers," Rentería said. "I asked what we were volunteering for and they say they needed help to move our troops who had been Japanese prisoners of war to hospitals.

"I volunteered because I had friends from Lordsburg who were prisoners; my neighbor was one of them," Rentería said. "For three days, I was seeing the same prisoners. They were so thin, their clothes wouldn't stay on them. I said, 'One in the bunch I think I know.' His name was Marcus Cardenas. When they were together, I called out his name and he jumped. When I asked him, he said, yes, he was from Lordsburg. I told him, 'I know you. You used to have a lot of horses.' He said, 'I don't remember you.'

"I said, 'I'm from a big bunch of brothers,'" Rentería recounted. "He looked at me and began to cry. The more he cried, he made me cry. When I told him I was Manuel, he was kneeling and crying. I told him, 'As long as you've been a prisoner, I've been here. We're doing this for you. I'll be here a few weeks more.'

"One day, they told us we're going home," he said. "Marcus said to me, 'Please go to my folks and tell them I'll be home soon.'"

The troops went first to Washington State where they took training lessons to adjust back to civilian life.

"When I got home, the neighbors came to see me and my mom," Rentería said. "I told Marcus's mom my story, and she started crying. I told her she would see her son as soon as he was not sick. They couldn't believe me.

"Within two years, I was in town, and thought I better go home," he said. "Who was standing there, but a man who looked lost? It was Marcus. I put him in the car and took him home. I went into his house and told his mom that Marcus was soon going to be there. I asked for coffee and went back to the car and brought him to his house."

Rentería said Marcus later moved to Silver City and then to Las Cruces to be close to Fort Bliss.

Rentería's daughter, Dora Martinez, said that her father told his dad, her grandfather, not to let the Cardenas family know how he saw Marcus, as just skin and bones, having to hold onto his clothes to keep them on.

Rentería stayed in Lordsburg and was active with the Veterans of Foreign Wars Post #3099 and with the Lordsburg Elks Club #1813. A lifelong member of Saint Joseph's Catholic Church, he was instrumental in raising money to build a new church and rectory in the early 1960s and helped with upgrades to the buildings over the years.

GOD'S  UMBRELLA

# MADERO, ROBERT

## DOB 10/3/1923, DOD 5/25/2009

Robert Madero of Silver City was drafted into World War II when he was eighteen years old.

"I went to the European Theater," Madero said. "Our company got the Legion of Merit for European Service."

He received medals for the occupation of Germany, the Good Conduct Medal, and five overseas stripes.

"I was a technician fifth grade," Madero said. "At first, I went to radio school in St. Louis, Missouri, and I was stationed at Scott Field in Illinois. They pulled us out of school because they needed 10,000 soldiers."

He was shipped to England and spent eighteen months near Manchester at Warrington where General George S. Patton had his headquarters.

During his time in England, he said, they had air raids and blackouts almost every night.

"One time, I was going on the bus to town," Madero said. "We went under an underpass and a big blast blew up a hotel as we passed it.

"I was at Warrington before, during and after the Normandy invasion," Madero said. "Two to three weeks after the war ended, I went to France and was in Rheims for the official surrender."

He said he went early in the morning, so he could get a good viewpoint.

"I went into a little restaurant," Madero said. "A GI was married to the French owner. He told me to go down the street to a certain hotel and get a room and I could watch the ceremony."

He got a room during a sprinkling rain. As it rained harder, the participants in the ceremony went into a building and "I didn't get to see the ceremony, but I did see General Eisenhower."

Madero started his service with the 8$^{th}$ Air Force, but was transferred to Patton's 3$^{rd}$ Army.

"I used to see him at Warrington when he went back and forth," Madero said. "We had reveille every morning. That's when I'd see him."

Madero was with automotive maintenance.

"I used to go pick up [Patton's] staff car to have it serviced," he said. "The car had painted windows. When I went through the checkpoint, the guards had to salute, because they couldn't see in."

Because of his job, Madero had access to vehicles.

"I drove all over the country," he said. "I went by myself, because the older soldiers were homesick and didn't have any interest in learning about the country where they were. The same thing in Germany when I got there. I went all over every chance I got. I also went to Paris whenever I could. I got to the top of the Eiffel Tower and to where they signed the World War I Versailles Treaty."

He also went to the cemetery near Château-Thierry, "because my folks sent me the Daily Press and I wanted to see where Grant County GIs who had died were buried."

He said he wanted to see the records, but the Germans had "blasted" the chapel. Madero went to Aachen, Belgium, which had been flattened, with nothing but a church left standing.

"The Germans didn't bother the Catholic churches," he said. "I went to Midnight Mass in Aachen."

The Third Army liberated Dachau, one of the camps where Jews were taken and where many were killed during the war.

"I saw it soon after liberation," Madero said. "They would dig a ditch with a Caterpillar tractor and throw the dead bodies in and cover them up. I saw the 'showers' where people would be taken, but they didn't send out water, they sent out gas to kill them. They would grind up the bones for fertilizer and make lamp shades out of skin."

The German prisoners of war "worked for us. They didn't want to go home because there were no jobs. They didn't try to escape because they got three meals a day."

He surmised that if the Germans had had more technology, they might have won the war, because they almost had the atomic bomb.

"After the war, the Germans were friendly," Madero said.

He spent twenty-eight months overseas.

"Personally, I wanted to go," Madero said. "I got to see half of the world."

Other places he visited while in Europe included the Brandenburg Gate in Berlin. Madero said he applied to go to college in Switzerland, but another fellow copied his application and was accepted.

"There was still a little discrimination then," Madero said.

Before the war, he worked as a painter's apprentice. When he returned he was given a job as a laborer.

"They told me as soon as there was an opening, I would get my old job back, but two other guys got in ahead of me, so I went to the New Mexico veterans' representative, Arthur Deck," Madero said. "He told me to go back to work and not say anything. I was unloading railroad parts the next day and Jimmy Sage, the foreman, told me to come with him. I stayed as a painter for three years before they laid off 900 employees, but I remained for thirteen years, before I went to work for the post office."

He stayed with the Postal Service until he retired.

Madero attended school with Betty Head Ely, the owner of the Silver City Daily Press until her death in 2006.

"It was hard to get a Daily Press delivery job, but I delivered the Albuquerque Journal in Santa Rita on my bicycle," he said.

After his retirement, Madero spent many hours volunteering at St. Vincent de Paul Catholic Church in Silver City.

GOD'S UMBRELLA

# CHAPTER 5

❧

## VOLUNTEERING TO JOIN IN 1942

# Baca, Frank

## DOB 3/6/1924 DOD 1/20/2011

Frank Baca of Bayard [New Mexico] joined the United States Army Air Forces in 1942.

"In 1941, I was in church with my parents in Hot Springs, New Mexico, now Truth or Consequences," Frank Baca said. "The priest announced that Pearl Harbor had been bombed."

He was a junior in high school and "I wanted to go into the service so bad," but his parents said, "No, we have plans for you to go to school."

He graduated from high school on May 27, 1942 and told his parents that he had made arrangements with the recruiter.

"I told them if they didn't sign for me, I would run away from home," Baca said.

On June 1, the recruiter took four young men to Santa Fe to be sworn in, then on a train to Fort Bliss, Texas, where they underwent aptitude tests and physicals.

"Two of us made the Air Force and were sent to Shepherd Field, Texas, where we took basic training," he said.

Next, Baca went to Lowry Field, Colorado, to armament school.

"I hadn't even shot BBs," Baca laughed. "Within a few weeks, I could shoot a .50-millimeter machine gun."

His next training was as a ball turret gunner in the bottom of a B-17. A train westward took him to Walla Walla, Washington, where he was assigned as an armament specialist with the 95th Bomb Group of the 8th Air Force.

In May 1943, he and about 25,000 other GIs traveled for six days on the Queen Elizabeth ocean liner, which had been retrofitted as a troop carrier. He was stationed at Framlingham Royal Air Base in Britain.

"The Jerries [a term for the Germans] tried to bomb us that night," Baca said. "They didn't hit anyone."

He said that Lord HeeHaw, a German man who broadcast on the BBC, announced, "We know you ninety-fifthers got to England and we're ready for you."

A good friend of Baca's at headquarters told him that orders had come in that anyone with his experience could be a ball-turret gunner.

"It was a two-week training," Baca said. "I was very good, because I had good eyesight, was eighteen and eager to go fly."

He was put in the 336th Bomb Squadron and assigned to a lead group.

"I was assigned to the Holy Terror. That was the name of the airplane," Baca said. "Captain Thompson was the pilot. Our first mission was to France targeting airfields. The crew already had eight missions, but I replaced the gunner who froze his feet."

He didn't see any fighters but was told he would see some.

"Two or three missions went by and we went to Germany," Baca said. "I got to see a lot of fighters. It was January 7, 1944, and the crew had completed fifteen missions when we got shot up bad."

The captain was hit, and the plane became the "Holey Terror," with 200 holes, so Baca was assigned to another group.

During a mission over the port of Wilhelmshaven, Germany, the plane he was in was hit and "we had to pull out of formation, because two engines were in trouble."

Germans liked stragglers and the pilot told the crew they would be attacked.

"'Here come eight fighters, you guys. Fire every gun at 'em,' the captain said," Baca reported. "We started home over the English Channel and the captain told us to throw out everything. One guy who liked to gamble had to throw $4,000 overboard. We could see the white cliffs of Dover and we were losing altitude. As we approached Horman, where they had moved us, we were at about 300 feet and there was a big tree in front of us. The right wing caught the tree and the plane fell to the ground. The plane landed in front of a house where three women were sitting drinking tea."

Everyone survived the crash. A truck picked them up from the base, which was about three miles away.

"They called me 'Bunky,'" Baca said. "One of the mechanics, who liked me, said: 'The only time Bunky looked like a white man is right now.'

"They gave us another airplane," he said. "It was my third plane. It was getting expensive. It was a new plane with two more guns. I was on my twenty-third mission. I had to fly twenty-five to finish my tour."

The commander told him that more than likely he would finish his tour and asked him what he wanted to do.

"I told him I want to go home," Baca said. "I wanted to be a pilot, so they assigned me to Biggs Field at Fort Bliss, so I could train gunners, after my furlough. Man, I thought I was all right."

On his twenty-fifth mission, a daylight raid to Berlin with more than 1,000 bombers in formation one mile deep, Baca was shot down by a Fokker 190 on his way back home.

"The fighter was at one o'clock and low to attack from below," Baca said. "When he was framed in my range, I could see the bullets bouncing off. He had a 20 mm machine gun and he hit our gas tank. A stream of fuel was pouring out and we were on fire. We were told to abandon ship.

"I didn't have a parachute on because gunners didn't wear them," he continued. "I got my parachute snapped on, put my hand on the pull cord. I don't know how high I counted, but I jerked so hard, my shoulder was sore, like I had been hit by flak."

He landed and could see Germans in blue uniforms from where he was hiding in the grass in a ditch.

"They couldn't find me," Baca said. "I took my compass and headed toward France. I still had my wristwatch and it was noon when I started out. At six, I saw a civilian on a bicycle; he said, 'Raus mit,' and I got up."

The German took Baca to his house where a woman and a girl also were.

"It was February and I was cold and scared," Baca said. "We couldn't understand each other, but I understood when he told me to sit at the table."

The man turned him over to German soldiers and he was taken to a building outside Bremen, where a captain told him, in English, "The war is over for you."

"I think I knew that," Baca said. "They took me in a car to an interrogation center in Frankfurt, and threw me into a little cell, with no bunk, only a little bench, for the night. The next morning, I had cabbage soup and was taken to the interrogation room. Another captain said, 'I speak English just like you. I went to school in Cleveland, Ohio.'"

When he was asked why soldiers were going to England, Baca said he didn't know anything. After the ninth or tenth day, Baca said the captain pulled out a manila folder and showed him the list of the whole airplane crew, which he said scared him.

"He wasn't too bad, but he would get red in the face when I wouldn't answer his questions," Baca said.

He and other prisoners of war were taken to Stalag Luft 7 in Lithuania, then later to Poland, always traveling in boxcars.

"The camp conditions were lousy," Baca said, "and we wouldn't always get our Red Cross parcels, which had one week's rations for one man. They would put two to six men on a parcel and also give us black bread, which was eighty percent sawdust and weighed about nine pounds."

They were given cooked barley in the morning and usually had to depend on the parcels for lunch. The Russian prisoners were in charge of the kitchen and were treated worse than the Americans, according to Baca. He said the latrine situation was bad and the prisoners were given only three or four seconds to stand under cold water for showers.

"On February 5, 1945, they told us we were going to move out in the morning," Baca said. "They kept marching us back and forth. We walked 640 miles in three months, sleeping outside in cold weather, and at farmhouses when we could."

While still in Poland, the prisoners cooked what they could find.

"We had water boiling and a little brown hen kept getting in my way," Baca said. "I was so hungry, I got a stick and whammed her and killed her. I went upstairs in the barn, and pulled the guts out and put her in the water."

The guards could smell the chicken aroma and said if the man cooking it did not give himself up, they would kill eight Americans.

"No one squealed and I took the chicken and stuck it in the hay, and threw out the water and all the evidence," Baca said. "It was half cooked, but it was good. I hid it in my beat-up topcoat and ate it when I could."

"On May 27, 1945, an English tank came toward us," Baca said. "The officer flipped up the top and said, 'You are free men now.'"

They walked eighteen miles in three days to the American lines.

"There they were with white bread," Baca said. "To me, it looked like angel food cake."

They were flown to Belgium, where they were "really liberated, deloused, and given clean clothes and haircuts." At Camp Lucky Strike in France, they were fed fried chicken, he said.

"I got home on June 18, 1945," Baca said, "but I didn't know my parents had moved to Bayard. I got off in T or C and started walking home from the bus station. I saw a cousin who told me [my parents] didn't live there anymore. He took me to my uncle, who took me to Deming. Because gas was rationed, another uncle took me to Bayard.

"My cousins said there's a pretty girl named Lily we want you to meet," Baca said. "We've been married for sixty-two years and raised five children—Elmo, Jerry, Greg, Pamela and Michelle."

Two of his younger daughter's sons are Marines and have been to Iraq and back. One has also been to Afghanistan and back, and the other one is now stationed in Japan.

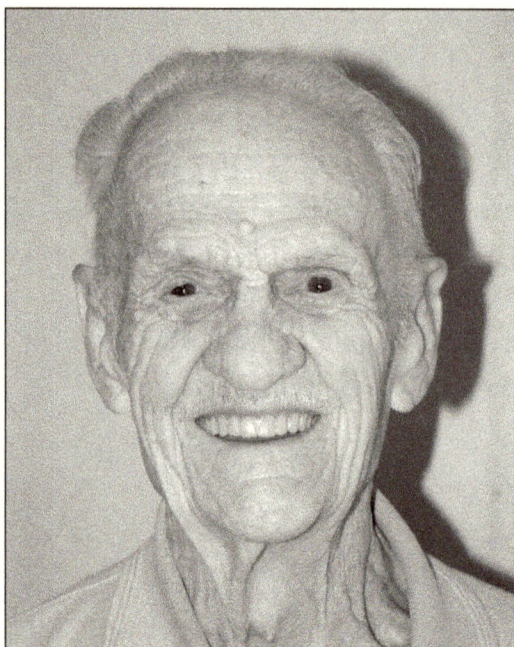

# VEEDER, ARTHUR K.

## DOB 11/29/1916 DOD 06/12/2018

Arthur K. Veeder served in World War II after being commissioned by taking ROTC at Colorado School of Mines in Golden, Colorado.

"I graduated May 1, 1942, and on May 2, I was inducted as a second lieutenant," Veeder said.

He was sent to Fort Leonard Wood, Missouri.

"I had a platoon of sixty-four I had to teach," Veeder said. "We were in the Engineer Corps. I taught them how to shoot, build pontoon bridges and fixed bridges, and how to install barbed wire and landmines."

He spent nine months at Fort Leonard Wood.

One time during his teaching stint, he was trying to teach the recruits about being on a Cossack post, [which according to the dictionary is a onetime outpost consisting of four men forming one of a single line of posts].

"I had a one-act play worked out," Veeder said. "I wanted them to know that there was nobody they could trust. One guy asked me for the password. I mumbled it. He got closer to me, and I still muttered it. He finally got close enough that I grabbed his gun. He hung on and danced around with me hanging onto the weapon. He was a little guy, and I lifted him up off the floor, but he hung on. He—Maleshevshi was his name—was a good man. I think he probably made a good one at the Cossack post if he ever got on one."

After they built the fixed bridges, "we had to have dynamite training, so we would blow them up," Veeder said. "I was fascinated with the pontoon bridges. We put one across the Big Piney River in Missouri."

He described it as a river with a slow current.

"If it had been faster, the pontoons might not have been as effective," Veeder said. "It was fifty or sixty feet wide, slow-moving and deep. It lent itself well to that training."

His next post was Fort Ord, California, with the 110th Engineer Battalion, where "we were training for combat."

"I got sick before the gang went to the Aleutian Islands," Veeder said. "They sent me back to Missouri for treatment."

He wasn't the only Veeder boy in World War II.

"There were four of us brothers in the war," he said. "Lloyd was in the Air Force and was awarded four citations. Ross was in the Maritime Service. He lived in Silver City for a long time. Harold was a clerk."

Veeder was medically discharged in December 1943

# WILSON, BYRL

## DOB ABOUT 1923 OR 1924

Byrl Wilson of Silver City, and his twin brother, Dick, joined the Army Air Corps together on June 8, 1942. They were nineteen years old and lived in Winslow, Arizona.

"We decided to go to Phoenix [Arizona], and take the test for the Army Air Corps," Wilson said. "We went in to be pilots."

They were inducted and sent to Abilene, Texas, for training and detachment. During this training each brother accrued ten hours of flight time in the pilot's seat.

Next they went to Santa Ana, California, for testing to be a pilot.

"My brother made it, but I washed out because of my depth perception," Wilson said. "I would bounce the planes when we landed. I thought the world would come to an end because I didn't get to be a pilot, but, of course, it didn't."

On April 5, 1943, Wilson's brother was sent with the 15th Air Force to Italy as a pilot of B-24s. Wilson went to McGill Air Field in Florida, where he was trained as a gunner, an assistant engineer and an armorer.

After Florida, Wilson was assigned to the 8th[h] Air Force, 747th Bomber Group, 711th Squadron stationed near Stowmarket, England.

A production of the play, Blythe Spirit, by Noel Coward was being put on in the town. The crew was asked if their plane could be christened with the name of the play.

"We made an agreement with them, with the approval of the general, that when we finished our missions, we would fly back to the states and go on bond rallies," Wilson said, "but we didn't have the chance."

At first, the planes and crews were required to fly fifteen missions, but that number was soon raised to twenty-five and then thirty-five.

"Our crew was lucky because it got a top position in the bombing group," Wilson said. "That put us over the top of most German fighters, but, unfortunately, we still took heavy flak.

"The flak was horrible," he continued. "Every trip it seemed impassable. We flew right through the black clouds formed by it."

On one bombing raid, he remembered seeing a Messerschmitt Me 262, one of Germany's first turbojet fighters.

"I held my machine gun right on the pilot and put a good volley of rounds into it," Wilson said. "Abruptly, its nose turned straight down. I don't know if I hit it or not, but it sure went out of there fast."

Wilson's twin was shot down on his third mission while flying over Yugoslavia. The crew parachuted out, but his brother's chute got hung up in a pine tree. The underground found him, hid him and got him out of the country and back to friendly lines within three months. The rest of the crew was captured and spent time as prisoners of war.

"Our hardest mission was over Merseberg, Germany," Wilson said. "Our vertical stabilizer was shot off; the right wing tip was shot off; the bomb-bay doors wouldn't open all the way; the left engine was hit and oil was streaming out of it; and we had more than 200 holes in us, but not a soul was hit."

Because he was the armorer and was tasked with pulling the bomb pins to make sure they were ready to drop, he had to release the 500-pound bombs by hand and roll them out, one at a time—12 of them.

"We couldn't wear a helmet, flak vest or parachute in the bomb bay," Wilson said. "I just had on a jacket and it was cold in there."

The crew members were all about the same age, with Wilson being the youngest by two months and the oldest not more than two years older.

"We flew at 22,000 feet altitude and had to have oxygen for emergency use," Wilson said. "We had those little walk-around bottles."

He said the radioman always got airsick. One time when the plane was returning from a mission, the radioman thought he saw three fighters and he called over the intercom that there were three fighters incoming at three o'clock.

"I reprimanded him with my boot," Wilson said. "The planes were P-47s, an escort for us."

Another time, the tail gunner was in his position on what was like a bicycle seat. A piece of flak came through the bottom of the plane and cut the twin gun grips right out of his hand.

"We had a good crew and we were close," Wilson said. "Somebody was sitting on our shoulders. We were lucky."

These were men who benefitted from God's Umbrella.

After the crew finished its thirty-five flights, a new group of men took over the plane. On the crew's first flight, no one came back. They were shot down and all were killed.

"We didn't have a chance to use the plane for bond rallies because of it being destroyed," Wilson said. "We were sent back to the United States, and because we had enough points, we were discharged in 1945."

Wilson was discharged as a staff sergeant and has lived in Silver City since 1947.

# DOWNS, HELEN

## DOB 08/21/1917, DOD 04/23/2016

Helen S. Downs of Silver City went into nurse's training in 1940 at Cooper Hospital School of Nursing in Camden, New Jersey, after she got out of high school.

"In December 1941, the war began, and I joined the Army in June 1942," Downs said.

She was Helen Shipman at that time.

She trained at Camp Lee, Virginia, for a month until she was transferred to Walter Reed Hospital in Washington, D.C. She also served at the 67th Station Hospital in Fort Riley, Kansas, before boarding the USS Mauritania in Newport News, Virginia. The ship traveled for three weeks, with one stop in Rio de Janeiro, Brazil.

"I'll remember it as long as I live," Downs said. "We were always in blackout on the ship and I woke up one morning and we were in Rio. We were not allowed to fly the flag while en route. That morning, the Mauritania was flying the biggest American flag I've ever seen. There was not a dry eye on the ship."

She spent time in Durban, South Africa, living in a hotel on the beach, and then traveled to Leopoldville, with a refueling stop for the airplane in Elizabethville—the location of an American station hospital with runways built by Pan American Airways.

Downs's unit was made up of five nurses from New York and New Jersey, and five from Minnesota and Wisconsin. They left Leopoldville for their first station in Accra, Ghana, arriving in November 1942.

"Pan American had set it up and turned it over to the Army," Downs said. "We were in a stone building which was screened. It was supposed to be for Pan American Airways guests."

Madame Chiang Kai-shek of Taiwan and entertainer Martha Raye had stayed there.

"We were there six months," Downs said. "We took care of GIs who were malaria patients. I was the head ward nurse. We also had native medical trainees who had been well trained by the British."

On duty, the nurses were never allowed to wear slacks.

"We had slacks for off duty time," Downs said. "We did get to get rid of stockings in Africa, because it was the tropics."

Her next post, from March to August 1943, was the 93rd Station Hospital in Dakkar, Senegal. Dakkar was the supply base for Allied Forces pushing back the Germans in North Africa.

"I was one of the first nurses to get to go on rest leave," Downs said. "I went to Marrakesh, Morocco, and spent the night in the hotel where [Winston] Churchill used to write."

During her ten-day leave, Downs took a truck ride to Mogador, where artisans created wood works. She also went to a place where silver was made into jewelry and other artwork.

"As a child I had always wanted to go to Africa," Downs said.

She said South Africa was very much like England, Australia or New Zealand.

Flying on a DC-3 airplane back to her station, she and the other passengers sat in bucket seats.

"A colonel gave me his sleeping bag and I curled up on the seats," Downs said. "I felt like I had been beaten afterward."

When she returned to the hospital, an X-ray of her chest showed a lesion, so she was sent back to the United States.

"I flew to Brazil again on the way back, and stayed for two or three days," Downs said, "then to Trinidad for a refueling stop. Out of Puerto Rico, we had engine trouble. I took everything out of my B-4 bag and stuffed it in my pockets. I would have gone straight down if the plane had crashed into the water."

Ten days later, in Miami, Florida, she came down with malaria.

"I had a reaction to the drugs and was in Miami more than a month," Downs said. "Then I was sent to Fitzsimmons Army Hospital in Denver, Colorado. After six months, I was still recuperating."

She had a month's leave and then was sent to Fort Carson, Colorado, where she served until the end of the war.

"On D-Day, I was on night duty as supervisor," Downs said. "I went to supper at midnight. We always listened to a band on the radio. That night, the band wasn't on, but D-Day had started. We sat there all night and listened. The next morning, the hospital was like a beehive. Everyone was so excited. I was at the hospital for D-Day—the end of the European War—and the end of the Japanese War."

She was promoted to lieutenant at Fort Carson. Downs was still in the service when she married Eric Downs in March 1945. She had met him in Africa, where he was flying B-26s. He became a prisoner of war after landing at what he thought was Roberts Field in Liberia. He was surrounded by French troops, who took him prisoner for nine months.

"I met him as a malaria patient in Dakkar in December 1942," Downs said.

He was there only a month, but they kept in touch.

"[My service] was a wonderful experience," Downs said. "The GIs were so sick with malaria, but such good patients. We worked hard and we played hard. I can never tell you how much we loved those GIs. They fought so hard.

"I've always enjoyed my life," Downs said with a big smile.

# GROVER, KEN

## DOB 1923

Ken Grover volunteered for the Navy in 1942 from Port Orchard, Washington.

"I graduated from high school, went and took a vacation at a horse ranch in Montana first, and then joined the Navy," Grover said. "In high school, I was taking a radio class."

If he received his Federal Communications Commission (FCC) license, he could get a special deal called the V3 Program in the armed services.

"That was interesting to me, so I joined up," Grover said.

He went to boot camp in San Diego at the Naval Training Center in July 1942. Then he went to the University of Colorado in Boulder for three or four months of radio training, learning Morse code and how to type on a Navy typewriter with a "mill" keyboard. It had special characters for radiomen to facilitate communications during the war. It had a key for the numeral 1 and a zero with a line through it to differentiate from the letter O. These were necessary because most communications were enciphered, with letters and numerals mixed together.

"We had routine classes every day," Grover said. "We were out at five in the morning for exercises, back at work until four in the afternoon. We lived in the university's men's dorm, and lights out was at nine-thirty at night."

After graduation, he received his radioman third class insignia. The men were told they were going to be shipped to San Francisco for Christmas leave.

"That was a joke," Grover said. "They put me aboard a transport, and we spent a month zigzagging across the Pacific to New Caledonia."

On the way across the ocean, the troops were fed only two meals a day.

"It was a hot, messy place to eat," Grover said. "We were packed in like cordwood. There were too many people, and the facilities were too small."

He said they were told the ship was a converted French cattle-hauling vessel. "I don't think they did much converting," Grover laughed.

Just out of San Francisco, the transport ship encountered large swells.

"Most everyone got sick, and the place was a mess," Grover said, "but I didn't get sick, so I ate all I wanted."

He reported that the ship hit a place in the Pacific near the equator where the "water was like glass. Other times it was not so peaceful."

The ship arrived at New Caledonia the end of January 1943. Most of the fighting had moved north of the island by then. The island is about 1,000 miles from Australia and about an equal distance from the island of Fiji. Reefs surround the island, and they served as a barrier to keep the Japanese Navy away.

"The cruiser USS Chicago escorted us over there," Grover said. "When it left, it got sunk [by Japanese aerial torpedoes in the Battle of Rennell Island, in the Solomon Islands, on January 30, 1943]."

Grover was stationed on Île Nou, which is about two miles long and half a mile wide. The island lies about a mile across the water from the harbor at Nouméa.

"I was a dry-land sailor and didn't see combat," Grover said. "At the receiving station, I was out with a group picking up canned food and putting it in big trucks for transport," he reported. "I opened a gallon can of fruit cocktail and ate at least half. I still can't eat fruit cocktail. I didn't feel too good afterward."

He served as a Navy Weather Central radio operator until the latter part of May 1944.

"As an operator, I gathered information for the South and Central Pacific from various islands," Grover said. "They came in encoded groups of five characters, all numbers, then the weather people decoded it, and we sent it out along with their observations at seven sharp each morning."

The only time they didn't send it out was January 16 and 17, 1944, when the area was hit by a typhoon that knocked down all the transmitters and receiving equipment. The wooden structures withstood the strong winds, but the metal Quonset huts lost their roofs.

"I remember watching the roof fly over the bay," Grover said. "At that age, you don't have much fear of what can happen. It's the only hurricane or big wind like that I've ever been in."

None of the weather people forecast the storm. It took two days to rebuild the transmitters.

At first, the information was sent using a hand key, but later Grover got a speed certificate to send it with a "bug, a semiautomatic way to transmit." Grover made the dashes and the machine made the dots. As he was training new operators, they got a new punched paper-tape method for transmission.

"It almost led to a calamity," Grover said. "They sent it out to the code-practice oscillator, which gives off a tone like it's sending, but it didn't go out. They got me out of bed and down there, and I got it out in a hurry."

They later learned that the Japanese could decode the weather within a day.

During his stay at Île Nou, American troops in Nouméa were unloading ammunition when it exploded.

"We ran out of the radio shack," Grover said. "Then the shells started landing, and we ran back inside. Some magnesium caught fire and burned for a couple of days."

He made a deal with the Navy that if he stayed extra time to train Navy radio operators, he could have two weeks of vacation.

"I got it extended to four weeks until they started looking for me," he said. "I hadn't gotten on the list to go back to Nouméa on provided transport. That cost me a little bit."

His vacation was in Sydney, Australia, and he finally got a ride on the USS Saratoga, the only Navy fighting ship he was aboard.

"I still love Australia and love the people," Grover said. "Betty [his wife] and I went back to visit."

While he was playing baseball on the beach on Île Nou, Grover stepped on a piece of brain coral and fell over.

"They gave me an Ace bandage and said it was a sprained ankle," Grover said. "I continued to have trouble with it. A number of years after I got back to the States, a fellow student at the University of Washington told me to go see an orthopedist."

Grover went to the Veterans Administration hospital, where his ankle was fused, which "got rid of most of the pain."

In May 1944, Grover returned to the United States "in luxury class on a Liberty ship with hot and cold running water. No more salt-water baths, and only a two-week crossing."

He landed back in San Francisco and was given a month's leave in transit to school in Chicago for a review of math and to enter a technicians' program. The entire curriculum took a year. When he finished the pre-program, he was sent to primary training for three months in Clarksville, Arkansas.

"They closed us down and sent us to Dearborn, Michigan, to the Ford plant," Grover said. "Next was to the Chicago Navy Pier, where we went into a number of things, such as receivers, transmitters, and sonar. We got as far as sonar when the bombs dropped [on Japan], but did not complete secondary training."

Because troops had to be 100 percent ready for action, they had to do calisthenics.

"I couldn't do them because they tore up my ankle," Grover said. "My points came up and I got out on Christmas Eve, 1945."

# Hawkins, Rob

## DOB 01/27/1915 DOD 7/12/2015

"I had a choice: get drafted and go into the Army, or volunteer and go into the Navy," Buckhorn, New Mexico, resident Rob Hawkins said.

He went into the Navy on November 18, 1942 and was discharged October 28, 1945.

Hawkins was the only one who left Silver City at that time, he said, but five or six Grant County men went into the Naval Construction Battalion (Seabees). They included George Bearup, George Turner, Joe Cobb, Dick Hayes and a man from Santa Rita, whose name he didn't remember.

"I wish we still had some of those men we had in World War II," Hawkins said. "I thought General MacArthur was one of the smartest men we had."

Hawkins took basic training at Camp Perry, Virginia, for six weeks. He was then sent to Camp Endicott, Rhode Island, under the Marines.

"The instructors were nice," Hawkins said.

From the East Coast, he was sent to the West Coast, then to Alaska, which was a territory, to Adak in the Aleutian Islands.

"It's halfway between Seattle [Washington] and Tokyo [Japan]," Hawkins said. "I spent eighteen months there, mostly building a naval base. It wasn't so terrible cold, just miserable, because it was always drizzling or snowing. In the summertime, it rained all the time."

In 1944, Hawkins was sent back to the United States, where he joined a group heading to Okinawa, Japan.

"I was driving a truck or oiling shovel," Hawkins said. "Each truck had a driver and an oiler. I was usually the oiler, greasing the gears of the shovel. We were building runways. There wasn't a whole lot of fire on us, but the Japanese had their snipers, who were holed up in caves."

The main Japanese fight force had been "whipped out," he said, so only snipers remained.

While he was in Okinawa, he left the company he was in to unload supplies from a ship and was left to guard the hold.

"It was a load of [canned] pineapple," Hawkins said. "I put a couple or three cans in my duffel bag. The ship was riding low, but after we unloaded it, it rose about twenty feet.

"We had to drop our duffels overboard, and I could just see the cans busting open, so I waited until others had been dropped," Hawkins said. "Mine bounced a time or two, but the cans didn't break."

He talked about the food served to the troops.

"We had carrots and peas on the table twice a day," Hawkins said. "We called it rabbit food or buckshot. I don't eat them much anymore, only once in a while."

The troops had K-rations and C-rations to eat most of the time.

"One old boy said he would rather have K-rations," Hawkins laughed. "One time he would eat the insides and throw the box away. The next time he ate the box and threw the insides away."

The troops worked seven days a week and twenty-four hours a day. Hawkins said a person always worked from six o'clock to six o'clock, whether it was night or day.

"It didn't hurt any of us," Hawkins said.

"I was in Okinawa when the war ended," he said. "I had enough points to get out of the service."

A cousin who served in the Coast Guard during World War II told Hawkins that the Army "does the work," the Marines "get the glory," and the Navy "gets the pay."

"I chose Navy, but I didn't get much pay," Hawkins said.

He said he found it kind of embarrassing how "light" he had it during the war, because so many people had it so much worse.

Hawkins lived in Grant County from the time he was twenty-two years old. After the war, he went to work for

Kennecott Copper Corporation and subsequently retired after thirty-one years.

"At that point, I had spent half my life with Kennecott," Hawkins said. "I played cowboy for a few years after that, as long as I could get on my horse."

GOD'S UMBRELLA

# Rodriguez, Edwardo S. "Lalo"

## DOB 01/08/1921 DOD 04/03/2016

Edwardo S. "Lalo" Rodriguez of Bayard was born in Gila, New Mexico.

In July 1942, he "left a good paying job with Kennecott" and volunteered for the Navy.

"I wanted to see the world," Rodriguez laughed, "but I didn't know I was going to see nothing but water, water, water for more than three years."

He went ashore only when the ship he was assigned to—a cruiser, the USS Indianapolis—was in harbor for repairs.

His basic training was in San Diego, California, and Bremerton, Washington. From Bremerton, he was sent to protect Alaska from attacks.

From Kodiak, Alaska, he was put aboard a transport ship to go to the Indianapolis.

"We patrolled the Bering Sea to protect the Aleutian Islands from attacks and to make sure no further supplies would get to the Japanese through the winter to the summer of 1943," Rodriguez said.

At one point, the ship was sent to San Francisco, California, for several months of repairs. He said the yard workers worked day and night and never stopped.

"San Francisco was home to me, because I had two aunts, cousins and several friends from this area living there," Rodriguez said. "I enjoyed times with them partying, dancing, skating. To me, it was a vacation every time we came back."

When his money would get short, he would take on shifts in the shipyard.

"They always needed workers," Rodriguez said.

The Indianapolis had been in the South Pacific before he boarded it.

"It survived the battles of the Coral Sea and Santa Cruz," Rodriguez said, "but the Japanese had more experience, so they beat us, and we had heavy losses."

After the Aleutian Islands campaign, the ship went to the United Statesfor supplies before heading to Tarawa in the Gilbert Islands. Rodriguez was aboard.

"We first secured the islands the best we could, and the planes came to protect the Marines when they landed. There were heavy losses. It was a bloody place," Rodriguez reported.

The ship continued to the Marshall Islands.

"It took us seven months to reclaim the islands from the Japanese," Rodriguez said. "The weather was bad. It was so hot. I weighed 149 pounds when I enlisted, and got down to 119. I had blisters where I sweated the most. Heavy guys had them all over their bodies."

When it was too hot to sleep below deck, Rodriguez said, he would sleep under one of the guns, because "it was cool. Below deck was unbearable."

Between the weather and the enemy, "we hardly had time to sleep and eat," he said. "We were in contact with the enemy all the time."

He was also on the ship during the bombardment of Palau in the western Pacific.

"We had carriers, battleships and destroyers," Rodriguez said. "The Japanese knew they had no chance to engage us, so we had only small losses."

The ship headed to Honolulu, Hawaii, for minor repairs before preparing for Tinian, Saipan and Guam in the Marianas Islands in 1944.

"There were heavy casualties in the Marines," Rodriguez recalled. "Japan decided it would come back in full force, but we secured the islands and managed to offset their plan. We knocked down around 300 or 400 Japanese planes. Our planes and guns fouled up their attempt to retain the islands.

"The next day we picked up some of our pilots who couldn't make the return trip," he continued. "Some had returned in the dark, but it's risky to turn on the lights on the carriers. "

The ship stayed in the area through August, and in September 1944, returned to the Mare Island Naval Shipyard in California for a break and for the ship to be overhauled.

"They gave us leave for twenty days, but it took longer to repair," Rodriguez said, "so I went to Los Angeles and worked for Aluminum Company of America."

For his military pay, after money was taken out to support his family, of which he was the oldest, and to pay for clothes and food, he had about fifteen dollars left, so he had to go to work.

He was in Gila and Silver City for Christmas—"mostly Silver, because there wasn't much activity in Gila."

On December 29, 1944, he was back in San Francisco and then on to San Diego.

"We went to Tijuana," Rodriguez said. "On January 1st or 2nd we left for the Central Pacific. We were headed to Iwo Jima with carrier forces. We went in before the battle. We would bombard it at close range with tons of lead, but [the Japanese] were underground."

The Indianapolis also supported carriers to bombard Tokyo and the Japanese mainland, he said.

He recalled a humorous story. A fellow the other sailors called Submarine was on board their ship.

"One day the officer on duty came by when we were all on our forty-millimeter gun duty," Rodriguez said. "Someone said something to Submarine, and the officer looked around and said, 'Where, where's the submarine?'"

"We were running back and forth," Rodriguez said. "We were always on the move except to get fuel and ammunition. After Iwo Jima was secure, we headed to Okinawa for occupation."

He said during the Marianas occupation, and during the attacks on Iwo Jima and Okinawa, Admiral Arch Spruance was in charge of the whole fleet.

"He was given credit for losing fewer ships than other admirals," Rodriguez said.

"We had heavy attacks from suicide planes where we were bombarding the capital," Rodriguez said. "A suicide plane slipped through the defenses and crashed on our ship. It crippled half the ship."

"The suicide plane killed several sailors and flooded eight compartments," Rodriguez said. "The plane was headed toward the bridge, but one of our gunners clipped his wing, and he landed aft. I was just getting out of bed, and felt the impact. I went on with my duties, because I didn't know what had happened until the injured started showing up.

"We were diverted to a harbor occupied by the enemy," he continued. "We had to patch up enough to head out for repairs. During our stay, the Japanese would swim out with ammunition to attack the ships. Our guard caught one, but he fell overboard, and we didn't know whether the attacker was on board. We didn't find him, so he must not have gotten aboard."

After ten days in the emergency harbor, the Indianapolis set sail for the United States, escorted by destroyers, because it was traveling slowly due to damage. A trip that should have taken seven days took sixteen before arriving in San Francisco. Of the four propellers on the ship, two were damaged.

During the ship's stay in San Francisco, Rodriguez was transferred to gyrocompass school and assigned to a new ship—a destroyer, the USS Harwood. He said he was transferred because the Navy needed trained people for the new ships that would be sent to the Pacific.

"I was put on a training ship and never boarded the Harwood," Rodriguez said. "During that time I heard the news about the sinking of the Indianapolis in the Philippine Sea by a Japanese submarine. Then I was told that, just a few days after the bomb had been detonated at White Sands, my ship had delivered the parts and the uranium for the bomb that was dropped on Hiroshima.

"I would have gone down with the ship, because the submarine struck near where my sleeping quarters had been," he said. "It had only been fourteen days that the Indianapolis had been without me.

"When I heard the news, I was paralyzed, because it was quite a shock losing all my friends," Rodriguez said. "I felt like a deserter, like I should have been with them.

"God had other plans for me," Rodriguez said. "I thank him daily."

Before he was discharged, he was assigned temporary duty on shore patrol at Oakland, California, for four hours every other day.

"We got sixty-nine cents for meals," Rodriguez said. "We would take off our border patrol insignia and put our pants over our leggings and go to shows, while we were on duty."

On October 8, 1945, he was discharged at 10:40.

"My ears were busted; my eyes were bad," Rodriguez said. "I had to have someone drive for me. I made a claim, but it wasn't accepted."

He went back to his old job with seniority at Kennecott but could do only jobs inside because he couldn't stand the glare of the sun. He spent forty-two years at the Hurley, New Mexico, concentrator, until his job was eliminated with the closing of the facility. Then he worked for a time at American National Bank. In the summertime, he would work the camps for the Forest Service when fires were being fought.

"I worked until I was seventy-two years old, when I quit to stay with my wife," Rodriguez said.

# SENSANBAUGHER, RAY

## DOB 1/8/1923, DOD 1/19/2013

Ray Sensanbaugher, born in Silver City, said, "I was one of the first babies born in Grant County that year."

As a youth, he was one of the original paperboys at the Silver City Daily Press, when it was still in the Bell Block of buildings on Broadway, after the purchase of the Silver City Independent by Clyde Earl Ely, Sr.

Don Lusk was the editor of the Independent and stayed on as the editor of the Daily Press, Sensanbaugher said.

In the fall of 1942, he and three friends at New Mexico State Teachers College "were upset with what had happened to the 200th," he said, "so with each of us boosting the other, we volunteered for the United States Army."

Max Reynolds of Luna, Frank Goble of Cliff, Jess Lee—described by Sensanbaugher as "quite a singer who sang as a teenager at churches in town"—and Sensanbaugher joined up together.

"There was a bus line here, Parrish State Lines," Sensanbaugher said. "Fred Parrish had lines to Lordsburg, Deming, Las Cruces and El Paso. He took high school teams to sports events, and his buses took draftees and volunteers to Fort Bliss, Texas. We volunteers and a bunch of draftees left from behind the courthouse. There was no jail there then. It was on the third floor of the courthouse."

He said the buses ran three or four times a week with young men traveling to Fort Bliss to join the war effort.

"They tested us, figured out whether we were in good enough health to go," Sensanbaugher said. "We were all separated. I was at Fort Bliss about a month and was accepted into what sounded like a good deal, until it fell apart—the Army Specialized Training Program."

One of the famous members of the ASTP was Henry Kissinger, according to Sensanbaugher.

"The program fell apart on D-Day," he said. "They needed us."

The men were to have about eight or nine months of rigorous infantry training.

"When I volunteered, the last thing I wanted was infantry," Sensanbaugher said, "but we were to become officers and be sent to college."

The program was planned to allow the recruits, who had received high test scores, to get a four-year degree in one year's time, going to school seven days a week at a university that offered degrees in the subjects of the program. They included engineering, linguistics, science and mathematics.

"After a month at Fort Bliss, I was sent to Camp Maxey, Texas, just off the Red River where Texas, Oklahoma and Arkansas come together," Sensanbaugher said. "Camp Maxey was constructed in a hurry. It had barracks, running water and a sewer system. However, I was put in what was called the 'Jap Trap.'"

Originally designed to house captured Japanese soldiers, it wasn't well finished. Plywood created the bottom half of the walls, and the rest was screened, with roll-down curtains in case of rain.

"But we didn't capture enough Japanese prisoners," Sensanbaugher said. "They preferred to commit hari kari."

The Jap Trap had no plumbing, and the troops had to dig trenches to use as latrines. It was also surrounded by guard towers.

"It's amazing we didn't get sick," Sensanbaugher said. "They had planned for plumbing. We complained that we needed showers, because 'we stink,' but were told that if we got overseas we wouldn't have a choice."

He said the time spent at Camp Maxey was one of the "most difficult parts of soldiering. Sometimes we thought we were the prisoners. It was a rigorous eight or nine months."

The building was cold, because only the curtains covered the windows. They were issued leftover World War I gear, including leggings with hooks, as well as bayonets.

"I saw a guy get killed on the obstacle course," Sensanbaugher said. "He fell and the bayonet stuck him.

"They were going to make us good second lieutenants," he said. "Then the summer came, and I found out what humidity was. We also had plenty of bugs. During maneuvers we got chiggers. I had never heard of them before."

Finally, Sensanbaugher was sent to Sam Houston State University in Huntsville, Texas.

"When I said I was in Huntsville, I had to explain that I was at the university, not the state penitentiary," Sensanbaugher said. "It was study, study, study. I didn't want to flunk. I was studying civil engineering. As a joke, we called it SI, and said they didn't teach us spelling, just math."

Then came D-Day, June 6, 1944, in Normandy, France.

"We lost a lot of men on D-Day," Sensanbaugher said. "Those of us at Sam Houston were halfway through our degree, but the Army needed a bunch of people quick."

He said a general in Washington, D.C., must have said, "For heaven's sake. We have several thousand people in the ASTP program. That's where we can pick up some soldiers."

"Just like that, we got orders to throw everything we owned into duffel bags," Sensanbaugher said. "We at Sam Houston got sent to Camp Maxey, but not the Jap Trap this time."

Sensanbaugher contracted double pneumonia and was out for almost three weeks.

"I thought I was a goner," he said. "I thought I was the only one who didn't make it to Europe, but I found out at a reunion of the 99th that quite a few of us didn't make it overseas because of pneumonia. A bug must have gone through."

The 99th Infantry Division played a pivotal role in the Battle of the Bulge, with its somewhat inexperienced troops holding back the Germans on the northern front.

"They left from Virginia, and I was hoping I would get well enough to go," Sensanbaugher said. "Talk about a guilty feeling when I didn't go. I'm proud to say the 99th really showed its colors and ashamed to say I wasn't part of it."

His last stint in the Army was at Camp Hood, Texas. He was discharged from McCloskey General Hospital in Waco, Texas, in early 1945.

"I had a lot of GI Bill, so I went to New Mexico State University in 'SI,'" he laughed. "I'm glad they're extending the GI Bill to veterans of more recent wars, because they deserve it."

GOD'S UMBRELLA

# JOHNSON, ROBERT L.

## DOB 1922

Robert L. "Bob" Johnson was born in Silver City. When he was nineteen years old and studying at the University of Utah, Pearl Harbor was bombed on December 7, 1941.

"Most of my friends enlisted, but I had a knee injury, and had to wait until it was healed about February or March of 1942 before I could join up," Johnson said.

His date of enlistment in the Army Air Forces was May 1942, but he was not called to active duty until November 11.

"I always thought that was appropriate to be called on what was then Armistice Day," Johnson said.

The girl who would later become his wife, Patricia, "saw me off at the train."

Johnson went into training as an air cadet and completed primary training.

"Then I had a health problem, and I hate the term 'washed out,' but that's what happened," Johnson said.

He was sent to Chanute Field, Illinois, and then to Detroit, Michigan, for further training.

In January 1944, Johnson was sent overseas on a Victory ship.

"It took us thirty days to get to Italy in an enormous convoy," he said. "When I came home, it only took five days on the Queen Mary, where the covered swimming pool was the mess hall."

When the convoy entered the Mediterranean Sea and passed by Gibraltar, he reported that, because everyone was still seasick from the rough trip across the Atlantic, the captain asked for volunteers.

"I kept volunteering throughout my service," Johnson said. "I should have learned."

He was asked to man one of the anti-aircraft guns.

"We were off Tunisia when we were attacked by submarines and aircraft," Johnson reported. "We were protected by destroyers whipping in and out of the convoy."

He was glad to be on deck behind the guns, because the men below deck who dispatched the anti-submarine shells heard the loud reverberations of the shell, and felt like they were being attacked.

Two anti-aircraft balloons floated about 200 to 300 feet above the boat.

"One morning, we found them shot to pieces by our own guns," Johnson said. He saw at least two ships go down during the bombardment.

The convoy landed at Naples, Italy, and Johnson was sent to Foggia in the middle of the plains area of the country, where many aircraft landing areas were located.

"I had been trained as a mobile oxygen operator," Johnson said. "B-24s were assembled there for bombing missions to Romania and Germany. Anywhere from fifty to 300 would take off. They made a thunderous sound in the valley. That's where I spent the war, as an oxygen manufacturer."

Air, through compression, was cooled to liquefy it. Then the oxygen was "boiled off, grabbed and stored in inflatables similar to balloons." Next, the oxygen was pumped into cylinders and shipped to the aircraft.

When the weather was good, Johnson said, the Italian "bambinos" would gather around "waiting for us to give them some food. It was a happy time to watch them."

After the war in the European Theater ended with Germany's surrender, the troops were slated to be shipped to the Pacific.

"Again I volunteered," Johnson said. "They told us never to volunteer, but I did. Well, Japan surrendered, and the war was over, but I was sent to go with Occupation Headquarters to Landsburg, Germany. We traveled over Brenner Pass.

"I got an easy job. They put me in charge of coffee and doughnuts. I worked until nine a.m., and then again in the afternoon."

He said he would save the coffee grounds, and trade them with the Germans for haircuts, clothing, and other items he needed.

"It was a terrible thing to see the Germans so desper-ate," Johnson said.

Fraternization between Germans and Americans was prohibited.

"It was against the rules for me," Johnson said, "but I was single. One day, I was walking through the park and saw a fraulein who motioned to me to sit by her on a bench. She couldn't speak English and I couldn't speak German, but we communicated a little.

"While we were sitting there, two discharged German soldiers went by with their German shepherd dog," he continued. "One of them said 'sitten' to the dog. I stood up and the dog growled at me. I was pinned there. When the two men got about a quarter of a mile away, one of them whistled and the dog left. The fraulein went one way and I went the other."

If a girl was caught fraternizing, her head was shaved, so everyone knew what she had done.

"It was a terrible time for everyone," Johnson said.

During his stay in the country, he went skiing at the Zugspitze mountain.

By 1945, he had accumulated enough points to get out of the service, but it was too late to see his mother, who had died that year. Neither he nor his brother, David, who was also serving in Europe during the war, made it to their mother's funeral.

I got home on December 24," Johnson said. "Foolishly I hadn't let them know I was coming. I went walking up to the front door, looked through the window, and could see a fire in the fireplace and my father in his chair, talking to my aunt, who was visiting.

"I sent Patty roses on Christmas Day," he said. "We got married September 9, 1946."

He sent the photo of himself, taken in Rome during his stint in Italy, to Patricia.

"It was what kept me going," she laughed, "but I didn't know he was holding a cigar behind his back."

GOD'S UMBRELLA

# SIMON, GENE

## DOB 3/15/1916, DOD 5/8/2012

Gene Simon joined the Navy in late 1942.

"I didn't want to get drafted, so I joined up and applied to be an officer to become a ninety-day wonder," Simon said.

He spent three and one-half years on the USS Belleau Wood, a combat aircraft carrier built on a Cleveland class cruiser hull. It went everywhere from the Tarawa Atoll to the surrender in Tokyo Bay, Simon said.

"For seventy-nine days, we were cruising around Okinawa," he said.

During this time of doing the same thing day after day, the ship received a message from the commander of the screen of destroyers that circled the aircraft carrier and a couple of battleships. It read: "Refer to Bible, Hebrews 13, Verse 8. No irreverence meant."

The Bible text is: "Jesus Christ, the same yesterday, today and forever."

Simon served as a recognition officer. He was taught the Renshaw Training System for Aircraft and Ship Recognition by the Ohio State University professor for which the system was named.

The system was devised to prevent airplanes and ships from being shot at with "friendly fire" from their own gunners. Simon said the system saved many lives.

Simon said digits were flashed for maybe one second, and then pictures of Japanese planes, until the officers recognized them. The second sequence of photos helped in differentiating between parts of American planes and those of Japanese planes

"The concept was not to read from left to right or top to bottom," Simon said, "but we looked at it and grabbed it visually."

The system allowed recognition officers to recognize an enemy or friendly ship or airplane within one-twentieth of a second.

"Your job was to get on a ship and see planes coming out of the sun and you had to determine whether they were friend or foe," Simon said.

The commander of the ship was Captain Pride, the only "mustang" admiral in the Navy, Simon said. A mustang refers to an officer who started as an enlisted service member, and came up through the ranks to become an officer.

"He was one of the best the Navy had," according to Simon.

One "beautiful Sunday morning," the USS Belleau Wood was hit by a Japanese kamikaze pilot.

Simon's station was on the starboard side and the executive officer, Commander Ballinger, was pacing the deck, because five-inch shells were "swishing over the fantail."

Because the Japanese planes were coming, the ship's planes had "their props going, were fully armed and ready to go," Simon said. "After we were kamikazed, guns started going off and bullets were spraying everywhere."

A splinter shield to protect the eleven people on the bridge was perforated with holes.

"One other guy and I didn't have a scratch," Simon said. "I get goose bumps now when I think about it."

While the ship was in Okinawa, a typhoon hit and another ship, the USS Pittsburgh, lost its bow.

"The skipper said if we roll more than thirty-seven degrees, we're going over," Simon said. "It rolled thirty-four and thirty-five degrees, but we didn't go over."

Everything was lashed down, but some of the sailors were seasick.

"One guy we called 'Salty Sweat' looked green," Simon said. "He said, 'everything's coming up, but the food tastes better coming up than going down.'"

After the Japanese airplane hit the ship, the USS Belleau Wood was repaired at Hunter's Point, California. Simon received an eight-day leave, the only leave he had during his stint in the Navy.

"When we got on land, we could hardly walk, because the land didn't move," Simon said.

San Francisco was fogged in, but Simon finally got to Los Angeles.

They were rescheduled for a flight at 2:00 a.m., but another fellow and Simon made their own arrangements and got on a Western Airlines flight, with both of them sitting in the same seat.

"The plane we were supposed to leave on crashed in the San Fernando Valley and killed twenty-seven people," Simon said. "I didn't have time to wire my change of schedule. Everyone back home thought I was on it. When it came across the ticker tape, I was told my father-in-law went white and went into his office and closed the door, but I wasn't on that plane."

After Okinawa, the ship sailed to Espiritu Santo in the New Hebrides Islands.

Simon recounted a story that happened at Espiritu Santo when he was officer of the deck and a bunch of officers and sailors came back from shore liberty. He said he always had deck duty "at the wrong time."

"They were tanked," he laughed. "I told a couple of our heftiest Marines to pull a launch up to the dock and stack them in whenever it was level with the dock, but don't overdo it because they might suffocate. They were two and three deep."

It was Simon's job to get them aboard, but the drunken officers and sailors couldn't get up the Jacob's ladder.

An airplane crane with a cargo net on it was lowered to the launch and "the Marines put them in and we hoisted them aboard."

After a cold shower in their clothes, they were thrown in their bunks and "we didn't lose a guy."

He also told a story about the communications officer, Sam Gallu, who was Fred Waring's choral director in Pennsylvania.

"Humor kept us going," Simon said. However, the executive officer, Ballinger, "smiled briefly only once every three months," according to Simon.

Once when Gallu was drunk, he staggered up to Ballinger, who should have been addressed as Commander. Gallu said: "Mr. Ballinger, the only reason we're whipping the Japs is because they got two naval academies and we only got one."

"Veins stood out on Ballinger's neck and I got as far away as I could," Simon laughed.

Simon received two Silver Stars and three Bronze Stars—the equivalent of thirteen combat stars, because each Silver Star equals five Bronze Stars. He also was the recipient of the Presidential Unit Citation and the Philippines Liberation Medal.

He said he also "has a ninety to ninety-five percent hearing loss, courtesy of the United States Navy and the four .40-millimeter quads around the splinter shield on the bridge."

Simon talked about those he served with during his Navy career. "What was sad was there were five kids in my division," "All of them were younger than I am. I used to get Christmas cards from all of them. Then one year, I got four, then three, two, one. Now none of them is left."

"While I wouldn't want to repeat my experience, I wouldn't exchange it for anything," Simon said. "Sixty-three years ago, I got out of the Navy, but I remember everything like yesterday."

GOD'S  UMBRELLA

# CHAPTER 6

억

## DRAFTED IN 1942

GOD'S UMBRELLA

# Vasquez, Rafael

## DOB about 1920-23

Rafael Vasquez said he was going to join the Air Force, but "before I could, I got my [draft] notice in Silver City."

Although he was born in El Paso, Texas, he considers himself a Silver City native, because his family moved to town when he was a small child.

Vasquez joined the Army on July 1, 1942, as a United States Army Band member, because he was a proficient trumpet player from having an orchestra with two of his brothers.

Vasquez traveled to Fort Carson, Colorado, for basic training. He was assigned as an instructor to train a drum and bugle corps.

Because he used to go hunting, he was an expert rifleman, so he and three other members of the band requested a transfer into the infantry because they wanted to see action overseas.

Vasquez was transferred to the 8th Infantry Division, scheduled to be shipped overseas.

"While at Fort Carson, I got to see President [Franklin D.] Roosevelt wish the troops good luck and godspeed," he said. "In 1943, in Virginia, I boarded a ship headed for France. It took us two months to make the trip, because there were many delays due to enemy submarines. We landed in Le Havre, France."

As part of General George Patton's force, his division advanced across France into Germany. From 1943 to 1945, he said the troops were always on the move.

"We always had plenty of food—K-rations," Vasquez said. "The cans of chicken were my favorite."

"I was in the crossings of the Moselle River and the Rhine River," he said. "It was during these crossings that the worst part of my experience in the war took place. I thought that would be it for me, but I never got touched."

During the Rhine River crossing in landing boats, he said, the Germans lit up the skies with flares so bright it made it look like daylight.

"Many boats and lives were lost in the crossing," Vasquez said. "The boat that I was on made it to shore, but, during the landing, many men in front of me and around me were falling. There were so many that I had to run over the fallen soldiers. It took more than a day to overtake the Germans."

He described the crossing events as the Germans' "last big stand" in 1945. More American reinforcements were brought in and from there "we had the Germans on the run. En route to Berlin, the Germans surrendered."

The troops were in Germany in a small town, near farms, when Germans overran them.

"I hid in a barn in the hay by myself and they didn't find me," Vasquez said. "The Germans were hurrying to move because the Americans were advancing. When the Americans came, I came out of the barn.

"We celebrated with the Russians," Vasquez said. "They could really dance and they were challenging each other."

The Russians put on a show of dancing and rifle maneuvers, and the Americans also displayed their rifle moves.

He said the drinks were cider and vodka, and they also had French bread.

"We had a good time," Vasquez said. "But it was about the time Roosevelt died and the Germans said, 'Your president is kaput.' We said, 'So is Hitler. He was kaput first.'"

Vasquez was given a furlough and sent back on a ship he boarded in the English Channel. He was slated to be sent to the Pacific Theater.

"I was ready and willing to go," Vasquez said, "but I was here [in Silver City] when we dropped the bombs on Nagasaki and Hiroshima, so I went back to Fort Carson and got discharged."

For his service, Vasquez received the Bronze Star, which he said he received for "bravery, for not being afraid. I thought, 'If others go, I go, too. You get used to it.'"

"I liked [being in the Army and] serving in the war," he said. "I would do it all again."

Although he wanted to join the Army again, he said, "My mom wouldn't let me. She told me to go to school, so I went to New Mexico State Teachers' College [now

Western New Mexico University] here in Silver City. I was going to be a music and arts teacher, but decided I'd rather be a carpenter and construction worker."

About twenty-five men from Silver City joined at the same time, including his brother-in-law, Edmundo Madrid, who was married to Vazquez's oldest sister.

"He was taken prisoner in North Africa," Vasquez said. "We didn't see each other again until after the war."

Vasquez's brother, Rudy, served in the Marine Corps in the Pacific Theater during World War II. His brother, Mike Vasquez, served stateside because two brothers were overseas.

When the brothers returned from their service overseas, they were surprised to see a small child at home. They asked their mother who it was, and she said it was their little brother, born while they were gone.

Rafael and two brothers, Rudy and Mike, had an orchestra. After the war ended, they formed a big band, the Old Veterans Orchestra, with former GIs. The band played for dances and weddings all over New Mexico, Rafael Vasquez said.

GOD'S UMBRELLA

# MILLER, JACOB RANDOLPH

## DOB 10/09/1921

Jacob Randolph Miller was drafted in August 1942.

"I waited and took my turn. I was working at a metal-lurgic lab as a machinist for Mack Trucks," Miller said. "My boss wanted to get a deferment for me, but I told him I wanted to join the Army. I was living in New Jersey then."

Miller was inducted at Fort Dix, New Jersey. "They gave us our shots and issued our clothes. We went from there to Fort Knox, Kentucky, for basic training. I was there about six months. I went to radio school there. When I graduated, I got my first stripe. I was then sent to Camp Campbell, Kentucky."

He served with the armored force at Fort Knox and Camp Campbell. "I went into field artillery and was a radio operator in a Sherman tank, which I didn't much care for, so I complained. The first lieutenant took pity on me and designated me as a wire NCO [non-commissioned officer] for the 12th Armored Division. They issued me spikes to climb poles. As the wire corporal, I had to splice wire and climb poles. And for a while, I served on the midnight shift as a switchboard operator."

After about six months, a notice went up on the bulletin board that the Air Force wanted pilots and bombardiers. "I went to Louisville, Kentucky, took the test and passed it. I was accepted into aviation cadet training. I was shifted here and there, waiting for pilot openings in a college. After about three months, I went to the University of Pittsburgh for aviation cadet training. I was three weeks from pre-flight training in a Piper Cub, when the Air Force decided it didn't need any more pilots."

On the Sunday before Easter Sunday, 1943, "the Army took about 200 of us and sent us to Camp Ellis, Illinois. We went from college training to pushing wheelbarrows through mud in a new camp. We were a sad bunch."

The Army took him into the Medical Corps and he was trained as a medical technician. "In my spare time, I asked if I could be a truck driver. I got a government license. I drove Jeeps, three-quarter-ton and two-ton trucks. I also took basic training again."

He went from Camp Ellis to Fort Meade, Maryland. "I spent time working in the hospital for training and to get my equipment together. Then they sent me to Boston [Massachusetts] in November 1944, where I got on a big Dutch liner, the *Nieuw Amsterdam*, with about 7,000 other people on Armistice Day, 1944. It took off the next day. It was manned by an English crew. It took us seven days to get across the Atlantic, and we had mutton stew to eat every day. The last few miles to Scotland to land, we zig-zagged. We had accompanying ships to keep the German submarines away. We landed in a harbor outside of Glasgow."

The troops were put up in Quonset huts in a little town just outside Glasgow. "We were there for Christmas. In January, I started driving trucks, hauling our equipment to Liverpool [England]. We went down the low road and came back by the high road. Yes, they had a low road and a high road in Scotland. I made three trips with our equipment."

The Germans were flying and dropping buzz bombs over Liverpool. France had already been liberated. "You hoped you were somewhere else when the buzz shut off, because, when it quit, that's when it exploded."

"We loaded our equipment into a ship. We were in blackout, so we took off in the dark headed across the English Channel," Miller said. "We were going along, when all of a sudden the ship was kind of jumping up and down, and I thought, 'Oh, my, we hit a mine or something.' The captain came on the radio and said, 'Don't be alarmed. We thought we saw something in the channel, and we put it in full reverse.' We got to France, landed in the dark and unloaded the equipment the next day."

"We were put into camps named after cigarettes—the Lucky Strike, Chesterfield, 20 Grand and others," Miller said. "I went into Camp 20 Grand. They were staging areas for troops to go into action in Germany. We left Camp 20 Grand and went into action a while after the Battle of the Bulge. We went through Holland and Belgium, both where the Germans had already been ousted. It was still winter. We followed the 2nd Army and General Patton. We got within 1,500 yards of the frontlines. That was close enough. We were the 63rd Field Hospital. If you've ever watched *MASH*, it was just about like the MASH units. We had our good times and our bad times. We had some casualties. We were under Lieutenant Colonel Briguglio, like Colonel Potter [in *MASH*]."

Miller's hospital unit would set up in tents or in towns in empty big buildings. "We followed Patton through Germany," Miller said. "There were three platoons of us. We were broken into three different units. The other two units followed someone else, as we went through the war zone. Each platoon had its own surgeons and nurses and equipment. I was a medical technician. I would give shots and would assist the surgeons and nurses if they wanted this or that. I also could bandage wounds."

After the war was declared over in Europe in May 1945, Miller was a truck driver. "We set up in different places. One time we were set up by an airfield and were evacuating refugees, like the Polish and some Jewish, I guess. We were still in Germany when the war ended in Europe."

One of the bad happenings he remembers was at an airfield. An English pilot in a Spitfire did an inversion over the field and fell out. "He hit the ground and splattered himself all over the field. It was like he committed suicide."

"After the war, we ran a venereal disease clinic and gave shots to GIs, who were doing things they weren't supposed to be doing," Miller said. "I was a shot giver there. We gave them a shot of penicillin every three hours. Rank had no privileges. Those who came in were from all ranks. It was not too nice a job."

He said the only time he carried a gun was on guard duty. "I was fortunate that I never had to shoot anyone. I would have if it had been my duty and I had to. I was on the life-saving end."

"We were set up in tents at Atzenhain, Germany," Miller said, "when the war with Japan was over in August 1945. All three of our platoons were together. We spent our last get-together there."

When they were in Atzenhain, Miller had his driver's license and wasn't too far from Frankfurt, where he said everything had been flattened, except for the church. "We could buy cigarettes for one dollar and we sold them in Frankfurt for ten dollars. So, we did something illegal and not honest, but it wasn't really stealing. We furnished the residents the cigarettes and made a profit."

He said Essen was flattened, too.

"Then we went to Bad Nauheim, a beautiful town that was never touched by the war," Miller said. "It was a good-sized hospital, where we filled different duties. It was called Bad Nauheim, because it was a city with hot mineral baths.We got to go soak in the hot baths, which was really nice. That's where we were picked to go to Bremerhaven to get on a ship to come home."

When he was in Bad Nauheim, the government started giving the GIs trips. "I took a ten-day trip to Switzerland. That was really nice. I went skiing on Mont Blanc at 13,000 feet in December 1945, dressed in a T-shirt. Several of us went up in the tramway. Halfway up was a stop. You could feel the cable stretching. I thought, 'Is it going to break?'"

Miller also remembered going to Heidelberg. "It's a beautiful city with a castle on a cliff overlooking the

[Neckar] River. At the castle is a huge barrel that holds 40,000 gallons of wine. It had a dance floor on top. Every year in the good times, they would fill the barrel with wine. Apparently, there were a lot of vineyards there."

General Patton was hurt in a car accident. "I was in the same hospital with an enlarged spleen when he passed away at Bad Nauheim. "

Miller was officially discharged in January 1946 to Bremerhaven, where he got on a victory ship in the North Sea at the northern-most part of Germany. "It took seven days to go over and took us seventeen days to come back because of January weather. It was terrible. We had to go down to the Azores and back up to New York City because the ocean was so rough. I wondered a lot of times if that little victory ship would go all the way over when a wave hit. But it always came back up. And we would see a wave and think we were going through it, but we rode up to the top. It was terrifying. Ninety percent of those on board got sick, but I never did. We would go down in the hull to eat. They put the tables crossways, so they wouldn't move. One day I was sitting there eating, when somebody else's mess kit came sliding by full of what someone else had already eaten." He laughed, but said it wasn't funny at the time. "Nothing ever upset my stomach. I could eat anything; nothing has ever bothered me, never has."

On February 17, 1946, Miller was back in Fort Dix and was discharged where "I went in."

GOD'S UMBRELLA

# Chavez, Nicholas

## DOB 4/5/1921, DOD 6/24/2012

Nicholas Chavez of Mimbres was drafted into the United States Army and entered the service October 28, 1942.

Born in Santa Rita, New Mexico, Chavez said he was inducted into the Army in El Paso, Texas, and spent two weeks in basic training at Fort Bliss.

"I was sent to Camp Roberts, California," he said. "From there to Camp Hulen in Palacios, Texas."

He was there about two months and then was allowed to go home for a few days. After his leave, he traveled to New York and then to Bristol, England, from where he was sent to Liverpool and spent time there.

"We spent all our time in England until the Normandy invasion of France," Chavez said. "We went in on Omaha Beach in one of the later waves on June 7. There were too many [dead] soldiers all over the place."

His group—part of the 29th Infantry Division—fought toward the east in France, and then on to Belgium, Holland and Germany. He stayed with the same division throughout the war.

"I saw a lot of combat," Chavez said. "Many I was with were from Texas."

Chavez's son, Dennis, picked up the narrative from things he remembers his father telling him.

"He said that bodies and equipment were strewn all over Omaha Beach," Dennis Chavez reported.

According to his discharge papers, Nicholas Chavez served in Normandy, northern France, the Rhineland and Central Europe. He received the Victory Medal, the American Campaign Medal, the European-African-Middle-Eastern Campaign Medal and the Good Conduct Medal.

"He was a heavy-truck driver and carried troops and supplies," Dennis Chavez said. "He was in a lot of convoys that did nighttime driving with only one truck with lights. The others had virtually no lighting."

Dennis Chavez said one thing his father remembers clearly is coming under heavy fire in Germany and being forced out of his foxhole.

"'Everyone was running for their lives,' he told me," Dennis said. "He ran into the limb of a pear tree, and it knocked him out. When he regained consciousness, he told me, he was lucky it wasn't what he thought it had been."

Nicholas Chavez served with a comrade out of Texas named Macias, who was known as Mashus.

"He was a real clown, this guy," Dennis Chavez said. "He was always getting in trouble. He loved to go to town. They had a saying, 'Wind blew, s--- flew, we won't see Mashus for a day or two.'"

At one point in combat, the tanks and trucks came to a crossroads and couldn't get across without getting blown to bits. Mashus had pulled a prank not long before and had been assigned to a truck in front.

"He came back white as a ghost," Dennis Chavez said his father told him.

The Germans had dug a hole and set in it a Royal Tiger tank with nothing but the turret sticking out. Mashus's truck was badly damaged, and troops were killed and wounded.

"He wasn't, because he ran back," Dennis Chavez said.

The United States Army Air Forces were called in and they "blasted the tank."

"They went to the Rhine River and met the Russians on the Elbe River at the end of the war," Dennis Chavez said. "He remembers the Russians had a lot of women with them."

"It was their wives," Nicholas Chavez said. "They wouldn't talk to the American soldiers. We spent three years in Europe."

The weather could include two to three feet of snow.

"We had heavy shoes, but no snowshoes," he said.

Nicholas Chavez spent thirty days in a hospital in Germany at the end of the war, because he was in bad physical condition from a stomach ulcer.

After the stay in the hospital, because his division had already returned to the United States, Nicholas Chavez left

Germany with another division—the 453rd Bomb Group Division.

Dennis Chavez said the generals, colonels and majors had told the men that they were there to die, so he didn't expect to come home.

Nicholas Chavez arrived home on December 24, 1945.

"They told us not to leave the base [in El Paso]," Nicholas Chavez said, "but I called a taxi and went home. When I got back to base, I told the man who was mad that all I needed was a discharge out of the Army. I got it on December 31, 1945."

# CHAPTER 7

☙

## Volunteering in 1943

GOD'S UMBRELLA

# GOSE, RANDALL

## DOB 10/15/23, DOD 2/14/17

"I was in my second year of college at the New Mexico Military Institute," Randall "Randy" Gose said. "I said after a football game that if I got my second draft notice, I was going to leave and join the Navy and that's what I did."

He joined on January 23, 1943, and was sent to San Diego, California, for boot camp and sonar training.

Gose was nineteen when he enlisted and couldn't get a drink because he wasn't twenty-one years old.

"I was almost through sonar school, so one time, I changed my ID card and didn't do a very good job," Gose said. "The petty officer took one look at it and saw it wasn't right. I spent the night in the city jail. The commander asked me, 'Why did you do that?' I told him that, at home, if I wanted something to drink, I'd just go to the refrigerator and get one. He restricted me to base for the rest of school."

The commander told Gose he was sending him as far away from home as he could go.

"That was when he sent me to New Orleans, [Louisiana]," Gose said. "And then he put me in charge of two other people to go there, but I was the only one with a restricted tag."

In New Orleans, the men picked up the 173-foot-long USS PC (patrol craft) 1243, which had just come down the Mississippi River from Memphis, Tenn., where it was built.

The room he slept in had three bunks on one side, six bunks in the middle and three more on the other side. The men had to tie themselves into the bunk to keep them from falling out as the boat rocked back and forth.

"We headed across the Gulf [of Mexico] to Miami, Florida, for shakedowns," Gose said, "and there was where I found out about seasickness. We started out and went through a cyclone and for four days and four nights, I never did see the galley. It was just heave, heave, heave, and those dry heaves hurt."

He said the captain of the ship was the first one to get sick. A lot of the men were sick because they had never been to sea before.

After Miami, the ship was sent to Key West, Florida, and then started escorting convoys up the East Coast in the Atlantic.

"I had another four days and four nights of heaving," Gose said, "because the seas were very rough."

He said a boatswain on the ship had been on the USS Enterprise when it was sunk. He got off the PC-1243 because he said he'd rather be back on the Enterprise and being shot at than go around Cape Hatteras one more time. It was always rough around the cape.

"We'd go over one wave and then would be the next one," Gose said.

They kept the sonar pinging because "we hoped we'd catch us a submarine."

The patrol craft escorted a convoy up to New York and "then we had a couple of weeks of leave, where we got to go ashore. We got to know New York pretty well."

Every time they arrived in New York City, they were allowed to go ashore.

"On 32nd and 33rd streets, there was a bar and a dance floor, right next to restaurants," Gose said. "That underground railway was great. For a nickel, you could go all over New York."

The ship continued to escort convoys back to Miami and Key West and as far as Panama.

"The seas hadn't been as rough going to Panama, so I hadn't gotten sick," Gose said. "Coming out of Panama, we ran into a storm that tore off some parts of the front of the ship. I was sitting on the sonar and felt like I was going to heave."

He opened the hatch just as a wave came over and knocked him back into the room.

"When it was a choice of getting washed overboard or swallowing, I sat down and swallowed and swallowed and swallowed for an hour, and I never got sick again," Gose said, "and I haven't ever since. That cured me."

The ship escorted convoys from the middle of 1944 until VE Day, the day victory was declared in Europe upon the surrender of German forces. The surrender was signed on May 7, 1945, in Reims, France, and on May 8 in Berlin, Germany.

"In early 1945, we escorted the Queen Mary out of New York as far as Iceland one time, and we ran into a storm, of course, and ice," Gose said. "The ship got top heavy. We got the Queen Mary out far enough that she could go fast enough not to worry about subs."

Most of the ships the PC escorted up and down the coast were tankers.

"We never caught a sub," Gose said. "We heard pings back once and dropped some depth charges, but didn't get anything, not any oil anyway."

During the escorts, the ship was about two miles from shore.

"After VE Day, we headed for the Pacific," Gose said.

Before they left New York, he bought a pair of barber's shears and a comb from his barber.

"We didn't have a barber on the ship," Gose said. "We only had sixty-five men aboard. That's how I learned to cut hair."

When he arrived in San Diego, he bought some more barber equipment. Four patrol crafts were tied up at the dock.

He began giving twenty-five-cent haircuts. Soon, men were flocking over to him for the haircuts.

"I never had to draw another paycheck the whole time I was in the Pacific," Gose said.

The Pacific Ocean, he reported, wasn't anything like the Atlantic, but had "smooth waters."

"We were about 200 miles off Japan when the atomic bomb went off," Gose said. "We were going to be in the group escorting ships to Japan, but we didn't have to do that."

Although they didn't see the bomb blast, "we found out about it on the radio."

"I never got shot at," Gose said. "We were in the Bonin Islands, when the Marines and Army had already run over them."

The ship anchored and went ashore at Yap Island, which had had a lot of Japanese on it.

The ship then followed mine sweepers, and would shoot the mines that came to the surface.

"We did that for about a week or two," Gose said. "When I had enough points, I got off the ship and onto a destroyer. It was like going into a hotel. It was so big and nice, and you had running water."

On the patrol craft, the men took a bath out of the sink because when they were at sea for any length of time, there wasn't enough fresh water for a shower.

He arrived back in Los Angeles, California, and was discharged, as a Sonarman 2nd Class, on January 23, 1946—exactly three years from the time he joined.

"I had a good time in the Navy," Gose said, "but I was glad to get home."

220                                    GOD'S UMBRELLA

# McBride, Dan

## DOB 04/09/1924

Dan McBride, who was a paratrooper in the 101st Airborne, 502nd Parachute Infantry in World War II and landed in Normandy, France, the night before the sea invasion, said "it took four days longer for us to get to Europe than it did for Columbus to find the New World.

"We left the United States in a big convoy on September 5, 1943, and arrived in Liverpool, England, on 19 October," McBride said.

Off the coast of Newfoundland, the British ship carrying about 800 paratroopers and 200 Women's Army Corps personnel was pulled out of the convoy and returned to St. John's, Newfoundland, because the desalinization equipment on board was not working on the salt water that was being carried in the tanks. Then the ship "hit a big rock after we took off again."

"We were a day out of St. John's and taking on water," McBride said.

They returned once again to St. John's and an American ship detoured to pick them up. They had to go to Halifax, Nova Scotia, to resupply and then finally made it to England.

"What was really funny was, when we left New York, a band was playing 'Beer Barrel Polka,'" McBride said.

"When we arrived in Liverpool, a band was playing 'Beer Barrel Polka.'"

When his company departed New York, 119 men were in the group. Only nine returned from the war.

"I'm the only one left," McBride said. "My last buddy died in January."

His company of paratroopers was involved in the jump into Normandy.

"I was a sniper," McBride said. "The gun I had was too long to jump with. I was jumping in third position. I had a bundle with a rifle and I was supposed to hit a button so it would go down with me, but separately. The green light came on for me to jump. Streams of tracers were shooting at us. I rolled to the right and missed the button for the gun. I fell out upside down. I looked up and it was the ground coming at me, because my foot was hung in the suspension line. I hit the ground and it knocked me cold."

The paratroopers jumped about one in the morning. McBride said he had no idea how long he was unconscious. When he came to, he didn't see anyone for hours. Then he was shot at and returned fire with his carbine, which he described as "the most useless thing ever made." He picked up the German's MP-44 and "wrapped the carbine around a tree."

The team members had clickers that sounded like crickets to identify friendly soldiers.

"I clicked mine and another guy clicked back," McBride said. "We almost kissed each other we were so happy to see a friend."

The two ran into a lieutenant with the 82nd Airborne.

"I asked him where we were," McBride said. "He said, 'As close as I can figure, we're someplace in Europe.'"

They were about twelve miles from where they were supposed to be.

About daylight, a 1934 Ford came down the road.

"My buddy shot the driver through the window and I shot the officer that popped out," McBride said. "We put an orange flag on the front, signifying that it was a captured vehicle and drove it down the road."

They went through a little French town that they found out was a German battalion headquarters.

"We didn't see a soul," McBride said.

The 82nd Airborne commandeered the car for a hurt captain. McBride said the next several days' events are confused in his mind.

By June 11, they had arrived at the bridges leading into Carentan, France, where a huge battle took place.

"We lost a lot of men," McBride said. "They made me first scout, so I was the bait hanging out in front. I walked up on a German outpost. He said, 'Was ist?' and both of us fired. He hit me once and I hit maybe thirty times. The bullet went through my left arm right through a tattoo and grooved my chest. They sent me back to England."

On September 17, he jumped into Holland with a British Army group.

"We had seventy-four days of continuous combat," McBride said. "We were attacking Best, Holland, and were suckered into a trap, across a nursery where pine trees were growing. A bullet ricocheted off my jammed machine gun and went through the package of cigarettes in my pocket. I felt the thump and started crawling back. I still thought I'd been hit. The fighting lasted until October 24."

During the battles when he was behind German lines, he said, an artillery shell went over him and hit the guy behind him, but then a machine gun fell across his ankle and broke it.

"That same ankle was busted four times and operated on six times," he said. "A medic put novocaine in it this time and I walked six miles," McBride said.

He was sent to a British hospital in Belgium and then returned to his outfit by hitchhiking, wearing a cast on his leg. He was still a machine gunner when the Germans broke through in the Battle of the Bulge.

"I had one day's worth of K-rations," McBride said. "That's the only thing I had for eight days and the temperature got below zero. I'm from Ohio, so I was used to cold weather. We stuffed newspaper and straw inside our clothes. We were there over a month."

By January 17, 1945, his unit was down to thirteen men and had little left with which to fight the Germans. McBride was down in a hole underneath a pine tree when a shell took off part of a tree and he got a concussion.

His group joined with others in Alsace-Lorraine to stop the Germans from breaking through.

"From then on it was mostly patrolling and sniping through southern Germany," McBride said. "We liberated five prisoner-of-war camps. We took Berchtesgaden the day the war was ending."

McBride said he took up parachuting because he was afraid of heights. When he went to jump school in November 1942, of the 240 who entered, only forty-three made it. Because he loves to fly, McBride got his pilot's license in 1947.

"When I was parachute jumping, I had no feeling of falling, but it was windy as hell," he said.

The paratrooper outfit McBride was in was the first to receive the Presidential Unit Citation for the whole division, he said.

He recounted a story about the group's stay in Alsace.

"We were in an outpost on a swamp," McBride said. "We had three rookies with us who had not yet seen combat. We were in a house with stone walls and had a bottle of schnaps. The rookies got into an argument and said a .45-caliber bullet would not go through the stove. Well, I said it would and it did and it hit Willy Robinson in the butt and gave him a good bruise. After the war, he drove from Oklahoma to Ohio to tell my father how I shot him in the butt."

After the war ended, McBride went to Bar-le-Duc, France, where his father had been in World War I.

"There was a bar where the streets met," McBride said. "When we went in, the Frenchmen all left. Women on the streets grabbed kids and ran into houses. We asked the bartender why and he said the Germans had spread stories that paratroopers were rapists and murderers, and they let us out of prisoner-of-war camps to be parachutists."

McBride received a long list of medals and commendations, including: the Good Conduct Medal; the Distinguished Unit Badge with one oak leaf; the Bronze Star; the Purple Heart with two oak leaf clusters, indicating the three times he was wounded—January 12, 1944, in France, October 26, 1944, in Holland and January 17, 1945, in Belgium; the Europe-Africa-Middle Eastern Campaign Medal with four Bronze Stars; the Combat Infantry Badge; and the Bronze Arrow, indicating he was in the group that spearheaded the Normandy invasion.

GOD'S UMBRELLA

# JONES, BILLY FRANK
## DOB 08/12/1922, DOD 03/04/2012

Billy Frank Jones served with the 1881st Engineer Battalion during World War II.

He entered the service January 25, 1943, in Fort Sill, Oklahoma

"My parents divorced right after I was born," Jones said. "I lived with my father and stepmother. She was a mean woman."

His father worked on the railroad in Muskogee, Oklahoma.

At the age of fourteen years, Jones ran away from home, using his father's railroad pass.

"I was caught," Jones said. "They put me in jail until my father could get there. On the steps of the jail, I told my father I had been beaten with a whip, a belt and a razor strap, and 'you'll never do that again. I'll run away.'

"My father hit me for talking back to him, and the police grabbed him," Jones said. "It tore my father up and changed him. He put me back on the train toward California."

Because the train didn't go all the way to California, Jones got off at the Colorado River and caught a bus to San Diego.

When he arrived in Long Beach, California, he started mowing lawns for twenty-five cents an hour and washing cars for fifty cents a car. Jones spent fifty cents a day on a room he shared with three other young men.

"They made an impression on us that if we didn't have a high school diploma, we could never get a job," Jones said.

"Being determined, I went to the high school and told them what I had done and that I wanted to get a diploma," Jones said. "They told me to fill out a form. I couldn't see it. The dean of students took me to the optometrist and got me glasses. I had flunked a grade and a half in grammar school because I couldn't see, and no one had ever helped me with school work."

When he was still in Oklahoma with his father and stepmother, it took Jones an hour to get to school and an hour back home.

"We had no electricity, but with a car battery, a radio went on Saturday evenings, and then we went to bed," Jones said. "We had flickering oil lamps."

When Jones got to Long Beach, he met a young man of the same age who had run away from his home in Nebraska.

"We became inseparable," Jones said. "Charles 'Chuck' Temple and I are still 'brothers.' He lives in Oregon.

"We graduated from high school together, along with a woman, Wilma Bates, who lives in Taos," Jones continued.

"We still get together two or three times a year for a class reunion."

After high school, Jones worked for a time for the United States Rubber Company, and then enrolled in trade school for ship fitting. When he graduated, he went to work for Bethlehem Steel Corporation at the shipyard on Terminal Island in the Los Angeles area.

"My first day, I went on the ship they were building, and I started to help by following the blueprints," Jones said. "It got quiet. I crawled up the ladder trying to be of help, and the boss said, 'We think maybe you would make an expediter.' They took me to the 'mold,' a big building where the ship's plans are inscribed on the floor. That was where we made patterns. Next, I was a fitter, then in charge of building rudders.

"This is God's gift to me, to be a builder," he said. "Whenever I finish a project, there's another waiting for me."

Temple went into the Marines and Jones's girlfriend went into the Women's Army Corps.

"I had three deferments because I was working on destroyers for the government," Jones said. "I told one of my inspectors that I was going into the Army Engineers. He said: 'We can use you in the Navy. I can get you in as a chief petty officer.'"

Jones took a bus to San Diego, and when he signed up they said he was a seaman.

"I said, 'Adios,' and went back to the draft board. They shifted me to Oklahoma, and I went home to see my father," Jones said. "He came out to see me when I was working. He told me I was making twice as much as he was."

Jones went to boot camp at Fort Sill, then to St. Louis, Missouri, for training. He also trained in Spokane, Washington, and Windover Field, Utah.

He was sent first to Australia and then to Port Moresby, New Guinea.

Jones spent three years in the Army and reached the rank of staff sergeant.

He eventually was in charge of the motor pool of heavy equipment. The battalion constructed roads, airstrips and buildings.

"We were right in the middle of combat," Jones said. "We worked all up and down New Guinea."

His last posting was in Leyte, Philippines.

"I came home to Long Beach, after being discharged on November 25, 1945, at Fort MacArthur, California," Jones said.

His next story of being a building contractor began.

GOD'S UMBRELLA

# JOHNSON, AL

## DOB 08/15/1922 DOD 05/05/2011

Al Johnson volunteered in March 1943 to become a United States Marine.

He lived in Abilene, Texas, at the time, but moved to Silver City in 1949, when he was offered a job to coach football and track at Western High School and at Western New Mexico University.

"I coached for one year at the high school," Johnson said. "Our National Guard was pulled out for the Korean War and the college coach was called up. He stayed in the service, so I went to the college to coach in 1950 and stayed there until I retired in 1985."

His service during World War II took him to San Diego for boot camp and then to Camp Matthews in Oceanside, California, as a rifle instructor.

"I was classified as an expert," Johnson said. "After that I went into the 5th Marine Division and was assigned to artillery in the 13th Marines. I was a surveyor at Camp Pendleton, [California]."

He was then sent to Hawaii for further training, after which his outfit was put on a ship. They were then told they were going to Iwo Jima, "although we pretty much knew where we were going."

"I landed on a beach mid-day February 19, 1945," Johnson said. "We stayed pinned down on the beach for several hours. Our Navy planes had bombed Iwo for days, but because of the underground bunkers, they did no damage. We had been told to prepare for three days to a week."

He reported it was "horrible" when they landed, and they remained there about six weeks.

"I saw the flag being raised," Johnson said. "In our part of the invasion, we were assigned to take the airfield, which was on the opposite end from Mount Surabachi. I could see from a distance the flag being raised. It was encouraging, but there was still some fighting when we left the island."

He returned to Hawaii for some rest and recreation.

"We were shot up so bad, they had to send us there to reorganize," Johnson said. "Like Curtis Maxwell said [in his recounting of combat on Iwo Jima, page 365], the best medal was getting out alive. Our sergeant had seen action on Guadalcanal and he trained us well in what to expect."

After the Hiroshima bombing, he was sent to Japan with the occupying troops.

"Our group was the first to see the results of the bomb," Johnson said. "Everything was really wiped out. The Japanese civilians had run away. We only saw military men. We were sent to destroy Japan's military facilities. We were there for three months getting their military equipment and destroying it."

The Japanese had numerous airplane engines.

"There were caves and caves full of crated engines which we destroyed," Johnson said.

His outfit arrived back in San Diego on Christmas Eve, 1945.

"The war had been over for three months, so there was no one to greet us," Johnson said. "We had gone by way of the Aleutians and hit a major storm, with most of us getting seasick."

He took a delayed thirty-day furlough to Florida where he was discharged. He then returned to Hardin-Simmons University in Texas as a junior to finish his degree.

Johnson has kept in contact with a buddy named Joe Krupa and has visited him several times in Phoenix, Arizona.

"Krupa said, 'Al was the only one at boot camp in good shape,'" Johnson said. "I had been playing football."

He continued to "work hard to stay in shape" by using free weights three days a week at a Silver City gym.

Johnson is not only in the Athletic Hall of Fame at WNMU, but, in 1948, he played in the college All-Star football game in Chicago which pitted the team against the winner of the professional All-Star game—the Chicago Cardinals. He was also drafted by the Philadelphia Eagles, but most of his life, he coached.

# Kirker, Mario

## DOB 11/26/1925

"I volunteered in April 1943," Mario Kirker of Santa Clara said. "I wanted to go into the Navy."

Kirker signed up in Silver City and was sent to Santa Fe, New Mexico, where he was inducted into the Navy.

"My boot training was at Farragut Naval Training Station in Idaho," Kirker said. "Then I got a ten-day leave, but only spent one day at home."

He then reported to Maryland where he trained for two months and was assigned to the amphibious force.

"I trained for [Landing Ship, Tank] 123," Kirker said. "I was trained as a diesel mechanic. They called us the 'Black Gang.'"

LST 123 was built in Evansville, Indiana, and commissioned on September 1, 1943. It was assigned to the Asiatic-Pacific Theater LST Flotilla 5 under the command of Captain G.B. Carter, USN, under Group 15 commanded by Commander V. K. Busck, USN, Division 30.

Kirker said the crew was a friendly group, with mostly engineers and diesel mechanics aboard.

When the ship first arrived in the Pacific Theater, after loading in Guadalcanal, it was in Bougainville, where it got stuck on the sand because the tide was so low.

"Breakfast was at six in the morning, and afterward, I went to the bow of the ship," Kirker said. "I heard a familiar voice. 'Do you have a Kirker aboard?' It was my cousin Utimio Udero. He came aboard and asked if we had anything to eat because he had been on K-rations for a month. I took him down to breakfast, but we did something wrong. You're supposed to salute the flag and ask permission to come aboard, but Mr. Butler welcomed him aboard."

Kirker wished his cousin "all the luck. He was in the Navy on land and that was the last I saw him until the war was over."

Kirker served as the barber for the ship.

"When the captain asked me to cut his hair, I would hide," he said. "He was a big guy and mean. I only had hand clippers. But the stewards would always find me. I used to hide in the two rooms on the bow above the landing ramp."

He was the only one aboard who cut hair. An officer named Dabney "told me, 'You touch my hair, Kirker, you'll never get your rating,' but the captain told me to cut his hair. I never got my rating, but I made more money because I was the barber. I got six dollars and forty cents a month after all deductions, because I was the only support for my family. But, I got fifty cents a head cutting hair. The Marines would give me all their change and money, because they weren't allowed to take it with them when going ashore to battle. Sometimes, I made pretty good money.

"The ship was our home for a little over two years," Kirker said. "When I went in, I was a little kid, just turned eighteen years old when we went into the first battle."

He said the convoy was going to hit Saipan one day and Guam the next, but didn't receive a lot of opposition, so the ship was sent back to their base in New Guinea.

"We had 150 Marines with us and we were running out of water and food," Kirker said. "They rationed us to a gallon of water a day and the food was rationed until we got back to New Guinea, where we started reloading what we needed for the invasion of Guam."

When the troops on the ship went in on the first wave into Guam, "we didn't finish unloading, because we had a lot of opposition."

The following day, provisions were unloaded.

"I sneaked out of the ship, because I wanted a Japanese wristwatch," Kirker said. "I first came upon two American tanks—one had big holes and bits of flesh on it. On the other tank a Marine was standing on top of the tank. He was one of my best friends. He told me to get out of there before I was killed.

"He jumped down and hugged me and started crying," Kirker continued. "He said, 'You remember the Italian boys?' I remembered them because they prayed together every day. Every one of them was killed. Of the 150 Marines who had been aboard our ship, he said, 'Only forty of us are left.'"

Kirker started heading back to the ship.

"I noticed two Army trucks with four-wheelers on the back," Kirker said. "They were filled with dead Marines stacked up like wood. A bulldozer was digging trenches and the dead Marines were being buried six inches apart.

"I sneaked back onto the ship," he continued. "The sights I had seen didn't bother me at the time, but later in life they did."

Tears filled his eyes.

"I forgot about getting a watch," Kirker said.

At sea, the ship was attacked three times by kamikaze pilots. Kirker's battle station was the first gunner's station on the starboard side.

"We got credit for knocking two of them down," he said. "The last time we were attacked was by a torpedo plane. Another ship came alongside us and the torpedo cut it in half. Eighteen sailors died instantly. We were very lucky we never got hit, but we knocked down the torpedo plane."

Their next operation was the Leyte landing in the Philippines, so the ship returned to New Guinea for provisioning. Each time the ship returned, it would pick up Marines or Army men to take to the battles.

"At our first landing in the Philippines, I saw [General Douglas] McArthur," Kirker said. "There was a commotion among the Philippine people.

"We had hundreds of ships and thousands of troops," he said. "Right before my eyes, the transports were hit. The

Japanese threw everything except the kitchen sink at us. It was their last chance."

The crew of the LST 123 received three battle stars for participation in the capture and occupation of Guam in July 1944 and for the Philippine operations—the Leyte landings in October 1944 and the Lingayen Gulf landings in January 1945.

LST 123 typically traveled with ten to twelve other vessels.

"It was always the same ones throughout the war," Kirker said. "I never met the sailors from the other ships until years later at a reunion."

"I was with the ship from the day it launched until it returned to the United States on May 1, 1945," Kirker said. "The second-in-command on the ship got the command of another ship and asked me to go with him. I said, 'No,' because I had been told I was coming home. He was in two more battles."

When Kirker was returning to the United States, the ship went into Pearl Harbor to have work done on it.

"I had my seabags ready to get off the ship," Kirker said. "Then they changed my orders and said the ship would continue to San Francisco, so I stayed on it to go back with it."

Kirker was later assigned to Seattle, Washington, "about to be put on a brand new repair ship, but the war ended," so he was sent to California where he served two days as a shore patrolman and then was discharged.

The Kirker family has been in Grant County since 1824. Mario Kirker's great-great-grandfather, James Kirker of Belfast, Ireland, was in the United States Navy in the War of 1812 and became a prisoner of war of the English. He later moved west.

"I, too, wanted to be in the Navy, like my great-great-grandfather," Kirker said.

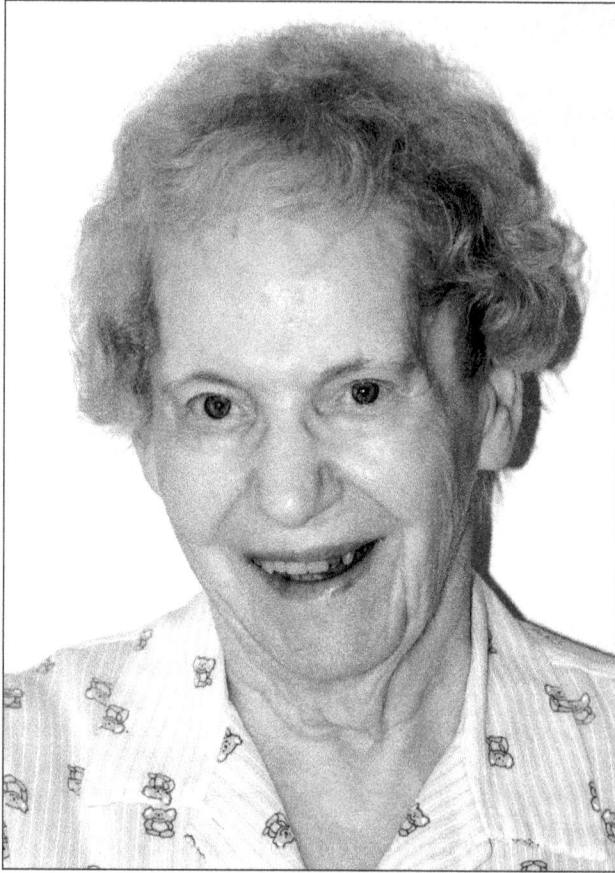

GOD'S UMBRELLA

# Guasco, Dorothy

## DOB 8/11/1922 DOD 1/25/2011

Dorothy Guasco of Silver City joined the Army medics in Albuquerque in 1943.

"I took my basic training at Fort Oglethorpe, Georgia," Guasco said. "Hospital training was in the afternoon."

She was then transferred back to New Mexico.

"I chose Santa Fe—Bruns General Hospital—because my parents lived in Albuquerque," Guasco said. "I was a ward master and I had thirty-six patients. I helped the nurses and doctors. The boys all had tuberculosis (TB)."

The first thing they did, she said, was clean up the place. At that time, everything was put in an autoclave to sterilize items.

"I loved my time in the service," Guasco said. "The boys were about my age. I had one forty-year-old who was in an oxygen tent. You give them a little time and they loved it."

A few of the soldiers were released when they went into remission of tuberculosis. Otherwise, the men didn't go out except to the sun porch to play cards.

"I remember a wedding in the hospital ward one day," Guasco said. "We had a cake and everything."

The soldiers kept themselves busy crocheting and knitting and doing leatherwork. Most of the men had contracted TB in New Guinea and other Pacific islands, she said.

"I helped the doctor give air into the lungs," Guasco said. "We went by the rules. If someone had a cold, we wore a cap and mask. If they weren't sneezing, we didn't."

The men got lotion for backrubs, so the nurses would stay longer. They talked, not so much about the war, but about everything in general, she said.

"I helped the nurses with the charts and had plenty to do," Guasco said. "I had night duty for about two years."

She described her work as a "busy, busy job, but you felt like you had done something when you went to bed at night."

Guasco said she had heard that the barracks have been torn down. The facility served as an Indian School for a time, but none of the buildings remain.

"That's where I married the Guasco," she said. "Ray was a great guy. Everyone had me married to someone else after I got out of high school, but I told my mom I was not ready to get married and that I was going into the medical corps."

She worked in Albuquerque for about five years and then decided to go into the service because of the good benefits.

"I met Ray in the mess hall soon after I arrived in 1944," Guasco said. "He was nice-looking, with big, almost black eyes. He and Anthony 'Red' Santelli, his good friend, asked if they could sit down. It was the beginning of a romance."

Her husband's fingers had been crushed in a loading accident in El Paso, so he had been transferred to the medics.

"He was Italian and would translate for prisoners, but he didn't go to Europe because of the crushed fingers," she said.

She said that when she met him she was still studying from books, because "they had crammed so much in my head during the six weeks of training."

"Ray and I decided to get married," Guasco said. "He got out of the service in April. I didn't get out until November 1946. We got married in December."

Before the wedding, she worked at the NCO Club selling tickets to help pay for her wedding dress.

"We were married for forty-six years until he got cancer and died," Guasco said. "The worst day of my life was when I lost him."

After her husband's death, she decided to return to Silver City, "which I always loved."

Her parents had homesteaded a section of land near Pie Town, New Mexico.

"My cousins were my friends," Guasco said. "The closest doctor was Johnny Warren, a chiropractor in Datil [New Mexico]."

She described her childhood as a life of "no trouble."

GOD'S UMBRELLA

# ALCARÁZ, ANGEL

## DOB 10/20/1925, DOD 07/12/2012

Angel Alcaráz of Silver City, who served during World War II, the Korean War and the Vietnam War, volunteered for each conflict.

"It was all voluntary," Alcaráz said. "I was never drafted."

He joined the Navy in May 1943, when he was seventeen years old.

"I went to basic training in San Diego, California," Alcaráz said. "Three people from here went with me— Ramon Carrillo, William Woods and Ramon Lopez."

After basic, Carrillo and Lopez were sent to a destroyer base, and Alcaráz and Woods went to electrical school in Ames, Iowa. Woods went on to an advanced school for aircraft, and Alcaráz was assigned to the amphibious forces in Solomons, Maryland, and was trained on Landing Craft Infantry (Large), called LCI(L)s.

"I also went to refrigeration school," he said. "I used that training when I got out."

Alcaráz was shipped to Orange, Texas, where the ship was being built.

"We took it for a trial run in the Gulf of Mexico," Alcaráz said. "It was commissioned the LCI(L)-966."

The ship traveled through the Panama Canal up the west coast to Long Beach, California, where it was outfitted and then headed to the South Pacific.

From New Guinea, the ship started its service by landing troops behind enemy lines up and down the coast. Then the crew traveled to Moritai, off the coast of Mindanao, Philippines.

"While we were there, the main invasion force was making a landing in Leyte," Alcaráz said. "We went there and started operating on different landings with American troops or Philippine guerrillas."

The ships were having problems with suicide bombers, he said, and near Okinawa they went through a couple of typhoons, which caused a lot of damage.

While American troops were mustering and getting ready for an invasion of Japan, the Japanese surrendered. At that point, Alcaráz and his unit were dispatched to Shanghai, China, where they transported Chinese nationals from the mainland to the island of Formosa, because the communists were taking over China.

After he left Formosa, Alcaráz was transferred back to the United States and was discharged December 31, 1945.

Alcaráz returned to Silver City and went to work as a miner for United States Smelting, Refining and Mining Company in Vanadium at the Bullfrog Mine.

"I decided to quit and joined the Navy again in 1948," Alcaráz said. "I was sent to Long Beach, where I picked up the oil tanker USS Talluga AO62. We serviced ships in the

Mediterranean, made a run to Japan and dropped off oil at Pearl Harbor."

Other stops included Singapore; Colombo, Ceylon; Bahrain, where they picked up black oil and aviation gas; through the Suez Canal to Italy; and back to Bahrain and Saudi Arabia. The ship returned to the United States by way of Algiers, Tangiers and the Azores.

Alcaráz attended minesweeping school while stationed in Yorktown, Virginia, and then was sent to Japan, where he joined a minesweeper, the USS Chatterer (AMS-40).

The ship's base of operations was Yokosuka, Japan, where it was cleaning up the inland sea of mines laid by the Americans during World War II.

In June 1949, the Korean conflict began, and Alcaráz was sent to Pusan, Korea. The ship went up and down the Korean coast and cleaned up the harbor before landing at Inchon.

"On the Wansan side of the harbor, we could see lights in Russia we were so close," Alcaráz said. "After completing my tour of duty, President [Harry] Truman gave us a one-year involuntary extension. I was discharged June 25, 1952."

He went to work for El Paso Natural Gas Company.

"When they asked me if I wanted to go to Odessa, Texas, I said no," Alcaráz said. "I needed a job, so I hired out as a janitor at Fort Bayard [New Mexico]. I was never too proud, because I needed food on the table."

Through friends at Fort Bayard, he was hired on at Kennecott Copper Corporation as an electrician.

"After fifteen years, the Vietnam War was in full bloom," Alcaráz said. "I volunteered and joined the Seabees, a construction battalion."

At the age of forty-three, he was sent to Gulfport, Mississippi, for basic training and assigned to the Naval Mobile Construction Battalion (NMCB) 40, "the Fighting 40."

"Some of my battalion were sent to Vietnam and some of us went to Diego Garcia," Alcaráz said. "There was nothing there but coconuts, coconut rats and donkeys. We built an airfield, a mess hall, an ice plant, quarters for the officers, an officers' club, quarters and a club for enlisted men, a non-commissioned officers' (NCO) club and a generator station.

"We were busy, and the temperature was hot," Alcaráz continued. "We were relieved by NMCB 71 in November 1971."

Alcaráz came back to work for thirty-two years with Kennecott.

"I got a GI loan to buy a house," he said. "I spent nine and a half years in the service, but I never asked for compensation because I believed I owed my country. My country didn't owe me anything."

He said his years of service were hard on his wife, because he left her with young children.

"I did everything, saw a lot of the world and got my kids educated," Alcaráz said. "I liked what I was doing, and I still do. The Navy trained me and gave me a job by introducing me to the electrical business."

His medals included, for World War II, the American Campaign Medal, Asiatic-Pacific Campaign Medal with four Bronze Stars, National Distinguished Service Medal with one Bronze Star, World War II Victory Medal, Philippine Liberation Ribbon—Foreign with two Bronze Stars, and Philippine Presidential Unit Citation—Foreign, and China Service Medal.

For his service during the Korean War, Alcaráz received the Korean Service Medal with one Silver Star and one Bronze Star, and a Navy Unit Commendation with a "V."

In addition, Alcaráz received a Navy Occupation Service Medal with Asia Clasp and the United Nations Service Medal for his service during the Vietnam War.

GOD'S UMBRELLA

# RANE, TOM

## DOB ABOUT 1926

Tom Rane did not have a birth certificate when he tried to enlist in the Navy in May 1943.

"I had to get one, and I had to have my mom sign for me because I was seventeen," Rane said. "I had good grades; they let me out early and gave me a diploma."

He was born and raised in Grimes Pass, Idaho.

"Three of us boys were in the Navy during the war, in the Pacific. My father and his brother were in World War I in France in the mud and cold," Rane said. "Our dad told us to go Navy."

He completed his basic training at Farragut Naval Training Station in Idaho. In San Diego, California, he received training as a radar operator.

"I shipped out on the USS Gambier Bay, a baby flattop aircraft carrier," Rane said. "It was one of the smallest ones made. It was made to get airplanes within distance of big aircraft carriers and we were picking up Marines along the way."

Fully loaded, the small carrier carried thirty airplanes, twelve of which were Grumman torpedo bomber fighters.

"We also had F6F and F4F planes, known as Hellcats and Wildcats," Rane said. "The F8F was even faster and better armed, but they had to land at a faster speed, which was not good.

"We soon learned that our type of ship was cheap," he continued. "They were putting one out a month. These escort aircraft carriers were called CVEs, and the old-timers told the greenhorns it stood for combustible, vulnerable and expendable."

The ships cruised at twelve knots and had to turn into the wind to allow airplanes to land.

"We could do twenty knots in short spurts," Rane said. "We were assigned to the 7th Fleet, which was made up of a lot faster ships, and we were kind of a drag, but they put up with us."

The ship first went into action in Saipan, Tinian and Guam in June 1944.

"We were part of the Marianas Turkey Shoot [also called the Battle of the Phillippine Sea, which was the Japanese Navy's attempt to hold the Marianas Islands—it became a decisive American victory]," Rane said. "One [Japanese] plane hooked the guard rail, but didn't hit us, so we got out of that one all right."

He said the ship traveled between islands often, "wiping up along the way."

"I had a brother on the USS Langley," Rane said. "One time, when we returned to resupply, his ship was in the harbor. I got permission to board it and spent the day with him."

After other stops, the ship was sent to the Leyte Gulf in the Philippines. The Gambier Bay was part of Taffy 3, the farthest north group.

The Japanese had decoy aircraft carriers, with no airplanes. They pulled Admiral William "Bull" Halsey away, even though he had orders not to leave the Leyte Gulf. Rane's brother was with Halsey.

"He [Halsey] sank the ships, but the Japanese fleet came back toward us," Rane said. "Halsey started back, but he was 400 miles away and the Japanese fleet sneaked back through the San Bernardino Strait."

The Japanese fleet had four battleships, the largest of which was the Yamada, which according to Rane, had 18.5-inch guns.

"Our surface radar was only good for about twenty miles," Rane said. "It was a rainy, squally day. We knew they [the Japanese] were close, because we could hear them talking on the ship-to-ship intercom, but we couldn't pick them up on radar."

A plane was sent out to check the Japanese fleet's whereabouts. The pilot said, "Those are the biggest pagodas I've ever seen."

Most of the Gambier Bay's planes were out on submarine watch or bombing runs.

"We were hit about nine in the morning, while the planes were refueling and getting ready to go again, so we didn't have any air cover," Rane said. "The first shell hit us and went right through the boiler, so we were dead in the water."

He said the rest of the ships in his group "hightailed it south," except for an escort.

"A Japanese cruiser did target practice on us," Rane said. "It was over an hour before we got word to abandon ship. We took over sixty hits.

"The Japanese evidently thought we were first line, and they got cold feet and left, back through the straits," he continued. "They never went into battle again."

"We were sinking, and I couldn't swim," Rane said. "We each had a rubber life belt that we had to blow up. Many of them were old and leaky. The day before the ship went down, I had stopped and patched my belt. It took about an hour. At nine o'clock the next morning, I was floating with it."

The ship was listing to port, and Rane was high up on the starboard side.

"We had knots on a rope to go down," he said. "The guy above me had his head shot off, and he landed on me. It about broke my neck. I was fully dressed, and I went into the water, way down in the water. I didn't have time to take a breath. I was trying to get back to the surface. I'm glad I had a good lung capacity, because a few more seconds and I wouldn't have made it.

"When I came up, I grabbed a rope and blew up my life belt," Rane said. "I knew I had to work my way toward the stern to get away from being pulled down with the ship. I finally cleared the fantail and got on a floater net—a net surrounded by corks. I was sitting almost to my chin in the water. Some life rafts joined together, and we had about 300 guys tied together.

"The captain was there, and he got us organized," Rane continued. "He decided we could paddle our way to land. We were about sixty miles off Samar, which was still a Japanese stronghold."

Many of the men on the rafts died and were given military funerals, with the remaining men reciting the Lord's Prayer and then pushing each body overboard and shoving it away from the raft as far as they could.

"The sharks were terrible—tiger and hammerhead sharks," Rane said. "We lost quite a few people to sharks. It was a horrifying experience.

"One of our planes flew over us and wiggle-waggled its wings, but nothing happened. They were reporting us about 30 miles off the island. The next day was the same, but the captain of a troop landing ship found us. He had lots of cots, unloaded his troops and figured out, with currents and wind drift, about where we should be. He asked and got permission to go into enemy waters to look for us.

"It was early in the morning and still kind of dark," Rane said. "We saw this big thing loom up. We had no idea what it was. A voice came on in English, asking 'What ship are you from?'

"We all screamed, 'the Gambier Bay,' at the same time. When I went down I swallowed so much seawater that I had the hiccups and was spitting blood, plus I was hallucinating.

"I wouldn't have lasted much longer," Rane said. "A buddy—Glen Beckett of West Virginia—got me to the hospital. I couldn't swallow food or water—it felt like I was on fire. I remember I had no clothes on."

Rane was given two shots of morphine.

"They told Glen to 'take him down to a cot until he comes out of it,'" Rane said. "My buddy stuck with me and saved my life. When I woke up, I felt better and could drink and eat little bits."

During this time, the ship got in a small typhoon and it was rough.

Rane's next stop was Hollandia in New Guinea, where the troops were put on the SS Luriline—a luxury cruise ship that had been turned into a troop carrier.

"It had a hospital and could carry 10,000 men, but we were like pancakes," Rane said. "I evidently banged my leg and got blood poisoning. They wanted to put me on sulfa, but earlier they overdosed me on sulfa and that darn near killed me. I was told never to take sulfa again. Penicillin saved my life."

His unit received the Unit Presidential Citation.

He got a thirty-day leave to go home to Idaho for Christmas, but "it was cold, and I had been in the South Pacific. I had shell shock—I didn't realize how bad. I'm good at smothering things."

He was mustered out of the Navy in Washington state in 1945, after a time on the East Coast, including New York City, where he was when the Japanese surrendered, and the war was over.

He said he recently attended a funeral at Fort Bayard, New Mexico. He didn't realize that a gun salute would be part of the ceremony.

"I went over backward in the chair, but somebody caught me," Rane said. "The shot totally unnerved me."

Rane has lived in Grant County for more than thirty years.

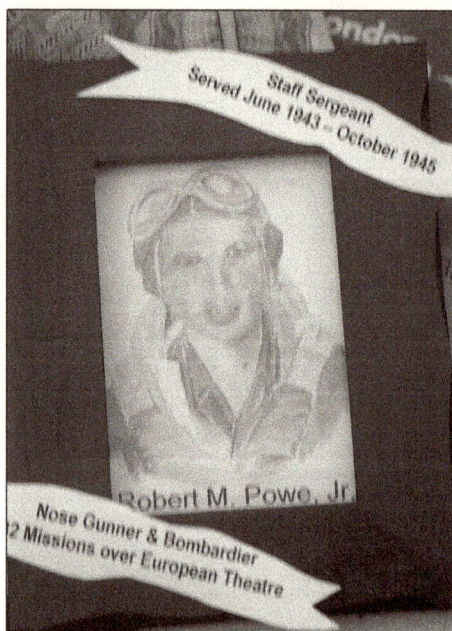

Staff Sergeant
Served June 1943 – October 1945

Robert M. Powe, Jr.

Nose Gunner & Bombardier
2 Missions over European Theatre

# POWE, ROBERT

## DOB 8/16/1923, DOD 7/20/2011

In 1943, Robert "Bob" Powe volunteered for the Army Air Forces, and was inducted on June 3 at Fort Bliss, Texas.

His basic training was in Harlingen, Texas.

"They marched us down the streets," Powe said.

He served with the 446th Bombardment Group as a nose gunner and bombardier in a B-24M airplane. It was the last of the models of the B-24 built for the troops.

Powe reported that one night he and a group of fellows went to a place to eat and go to a party, "but they wouldn't let me in. When they looked at my card, they said, 'Sorry, you can't go in, because you're flying tomorrow.'"

He left the next day to board a ship to travel to England.

"We went over on a ship by a circuitous route because of submarines," Powe said.

The ship traveled down toward South America and across the Atlantic to Africa and up to England.

"I was in the second bunk and there were four or five above me," Powe said. "I didn't think I could stand it. The second day, a guy came in and told us he needed people to help on deck. I said, 'When do you want 'em?' Another guy asked, 'Can I go, too?'"

The two had to clean the deck and slept on the deck at night, "but once a day I had to go to my bunk to show I was there."

He learned "a lot" about ships.

"When I saw the sea up here," Powe gestured above his head, "I knew to grab something.

"It was warm on deck," he continued. "I had never been on such a ship before."

As an airplane gunner, Powe was in charge of twin guns in the nose and also checked the bombs throughout the plane to be sure they wouldn't drop prematurely and blow up the plane. Another man was in the front of the plane below him. He had to drop the bombs.

"On either side of me, I had layers of ammunition on belts that fed into the guns automatically," Powe said.

Stationed in Bungay, England, near Norwich, he said he generally flew out over the North Sea on the thirty-two missions in which he was involved.

"We were always the lead plane," Powe said, "and we had the best pilot in the whole outfit."

He recalled one incident that occurred during a bombing run.

"The plane had been hit and we were ready to jump off," Powe said, "but the pilot said to stay on.

"We landed in England at another base," Powe said. "They installed another engine and we flew back to our own base." He also remembered a sad situation.

"I would have to wake up the other crew members," Powe said. "One small guy didn't want to get up and I had to go back several times."

Later the plane went down and the crew that Powe had awakened was lost.

"It was a bad day for me," Powe said. "I kept thinking the whole time I was in [the service], 'I hope I get back.'"

He reported that often it was so cold in the nose of the plane that he had to break ice out of his oxygen mask.

"One time, the plane got a hit and knocked the glass out of the nose," Powe said. "We had a lot of wind in there and had to block it up. It was the closest I came to getting hit."

He recounted another experience.

"A German had parachuted from the plane I shot down," Powe said. "I could have fired on him, but I didn't fire the second round. None of the American planes fired on him."

When he returned home, he had "three stripes and got a couple of more when I came back."

Although his outfit was scheduled to go to the South Pacific, Japan surrendered and, "we didn't have to go. But I was proud because my pilot wanted me on his crew."

He was sent to Davis-Monthan Base near Tucson, Arizona, to train gunners. Powe was discharged from the service in October 1945.

His commendations include an American Theater Ribbon, the European-African-Middle Eastern Campaign

Medal with two bronze stars, the Good Conduct Medal, the Air Medal, and a certificate for meritorious service.

Powe was a native of Grant County, born in Hurley, New Mexico, and his brother, Henry, served in North Africa and Italy during World War II.

Powe mentioned several friends from the area who did not make it back home from World War II.

Randy Goodwin and Powe grew up together, but Goodwin's plane went down and he parachuted into Holland. According to what Goodwin's mother told Powe, Goodwin was killed by civilians when he landed.

Another friend, Reggie Wiseman, the son of a veterinarian, was on board a ship when he was killed. Donny Lusk was yet another of Powe's friends who were killed in action.

# Ortego, Felipe

## DOB 8/23/26

Felipe Ortego served in the Pacific in World War II.

"When I went to school, my public and documentary name became Philip D. Ortego," he said. "It was my military name and is still on my driver's license. I was about forty before I learned my name was really Felipe. My nom de plume professionally is Felipe de Ortego y Gasca, PhD."

Ortego was born in Illinois. His parents had been picking beets in Minnesota and were on their way back to their home base of San Antonio, Texas, when little Felipe decided to show up early. "Then, after I was born, they continued their journey back to San Antonio."

He said his father told him about his Irish ancestor, John Darragh, who was in the San Patricio Battalion [St. Patrick's Battalion] of Irish soldiers who served in the Mexican-American War and survived. When Mexico surrendered in 1847, and a treaty was completed in 1848, the general hung all the Irishmen, but "my ancestor had changed his name to Juan Dara. The D. in my name is for Darragh."

As for his World War II service, Ortego enlisted in the Marines in August 1943. He had tried to enlist in 1942, but the recruiter realized he was too young." He told me, 'We know you're not seventeen, and besides you have flat feet.' I also tried to enlist in the Navy, but they said I was color blind. I was just seventeen years old in 1943, so I had my guardian sign for me. My parents died when I was ten, and I lived with my father's cousin Ernesto Mendes in San Antonio, Texas. When I enlisted in the Marines, they said 'sign here,' color blind, flat feet and all. At that time I had only one year of high school, because they held me back twice because I was not good in English." The irony of this is that Ortego's PhD is in English and he has taught English at the university level for many years.

After enlisting in the Marines, Ortego did his basic training at Parris Island, South Carolina, and then shipped from Quantico, Virginia, to the Pacific Theater.

From Oahu, Hawaii, Ortego boarded the USS Monrovia to go to Iwo Jima.

"Since I was a machinist, I was on a floating machine shop—a tender," Ortego said. "I was offshore and never part of an assault. I served in the Marine Aircraft Group (MAG) 24 of the 1st Marine Aircraft Wing. We were in the water offshore and could hear what was going on. There was a terrible loss of lives. I was in Iwo Jima in February 1945 and was sent to Okinawa in April 1945. I was on the tender the whole time."

He said he remembered, when they were aboard ship, the Marines were assigned to chip the paint off the sides. They were suspended in scaffolds and ropes. "I never had a fear of falling in. We chipped, but the sailors painted. We had a library of books on board, and I did a lot of reading. I was lucky that I was not in battle."

After the bombs fell on Japan, Ortego said the military magazine, the Stars and Stripes, did not run the story for ten days. "I'm glad [President Harry] Truman made the decision to drop the bombs. Otherwise, there would have been even greater losses of lives."

Following the dropping of the bombs, troops from the European Theater were sent to the Pacific to build up assault forces.

"I did not have enough points to get out of the service, so we went to China as the Army of Liberation," Ortego said. "I was there from September 1945 to August 1946, still with the 1st Marine Aircraft Wing. When we landed in Shanghai, there was a flotilla of ships miles long. By that time, I'm nineteen. We ran races in the streets with the rickshaw drivers. I realized later how superior we were acting. It was not a good time. Later, the experience in China would make me see myself as 'the other' in American society. Yes, I'm an American as part of my heritage. Unfortunately, from my experience, it was the Mexican-Dixon Line."

During his service, he said he loved to play Ping-Pong.

"In China, in April 1946, I was assigned as NCO of the day," Ortego said. "That night, the British compound in Tsingtao caught fire. I dispatched three fire trucks, and I rode with one. We saw the Chinese pumping water by hand, and the water was barely coming out of the hoses. We replaced them and sent in foam spray, which saved the compound. The English women thanked us profusely."

After the war, he took different jobs and received a PhD in English.

GOD'S UMBRELLA

# LEWIS, GENE

## DOB 03/10/1925

Gene Lewis of Silver City served in World War II with the 2nd Armored Amphibian Battalion of the United States Marine Corps. His tour of duty took him to Saipan and Iwo Jima.

"I didn't go to Tinian Island," Lewis said. "The tank I would have gone in hit a mine, and the driver and radio operator were badly injured."

Although he was on Iwo Jima for a month, he did not see the flag being raised. He did, however, turn twenty years old on the island.

"I was quite a ways away from Suribachi where the action was," Lewis said.

He served as a radio operator, sitting next to the driver of amphibian tanks.

"We were in between the final barrage and the tanks that came ashore carrying personnel," Lewis said. "I carried a .30-caliber machine gun, and a .75-millimeter howitzer would be firing overhead as we went in. We did that at Saipan and again at Iwo Jima."

From the time Lewis was eleven or twelve years old, he wanted to be a Marine, he said. His brother went into the Corps in 1936. Lewis turned eighteen in Manhattan,

Kansas, and went to Kansas City to sign up as soon as school was out.

"I was working on the recruiting officers, but I had to wait for the draft because I wanted the Marines," Lewis said. "I went in in August 1943."

He traveled to San Diego, California, for boot camp, then to Camp Pendleton, California

"I was assigned to the 2nd Armored Amphibian Battalion, which was just being made up," Lewis said. "We went to Maui, Hawaii, to get a new type of tank, but we only had ten days to train."

Before leaving for Saipan and Iwo Jima, the unit was in Pearl Harbor.

"It was a Sunday and all the tanks and sailors except for two of us were taken off the ship because civilians were doing welding work," Lewis said. "I was topside in the shade and decided to read a paperback. The other fellow, Ernie Lund, went to take a nap. I went to sleep, too. All of a sudden, there were explosions all around me. The ship was exploding and on fire.

"People were in the water and I was throwing life preservers to them," he continued. "They were calling to me to jump in the water and I finally did. I spent three days in the hospital because I got bunged up pretty bad. A few years ago, I found out it was sabotage on that ship and two others."

He said he begged to get back to his unit and soon headed to Saipan.

"We arrived June 15, 1944," Lewis said. "It was quite a while before the island was secure. I was assigned to the company commander's tank."

The captain went ashore to try to find a place for land tanks to come onto the island.

"He told us to wait in the water, but we refused to leave him," Lewis said. "We found a hole in the sand to duck our heads from the firing. Because the captain needed to be in contact with the ship, I found what we called a portable radio that weighed about fifteen pounds or so."

Lewis received a Bronze Star for his efforts. It was given to him by Major General Clifton B. Cates, who later became Commandant of the United States Marine Corps.

"I didn't think I deserved a medal any more than everyone else," Lewis said.

One fellow, a loader, was known as Herman the German. When their tank, going ashore, got hung up on a stump, a .37-millimeter projectile went right between his legs.

"He was taken away and we didn't see him again," Lewis said. "The armor was not thick, not like a land tank which would sink in the sand. The mechanics welded on one-quarter-inch steel for armor. Going onto Iwo Jima, our tank got torn up, including the radio."

Seabees set down metal roadways for the land tanks, which didn't come ashore until the second day after the ships arrived.

He remembers one special story from Iwo Jima. A replacement Marine, Marion Brown, from Nebraska, was "a big guy, wet behind the ears and out of place. I took him under my wing. When we got to Iwo Jima, he was one of the first ones killed. I wrote to his parents about him. His mother wrote back and thanked me. She was concerned about whether he got baptized. I wrote back and said, 'Yes,' even though I wasn't sure, but I wanted to make them feel better."

Lewis's outfit and the 4th Division arrived on Iwo Jima on February 19, 1945, and left March 19, a few days before the official securing of the island.

"We went back to Maui for training to prepare for Japan," Lewis said, "but we didn't go. Most of us went back to San Diego."

He said the group received a "thundering ovation" when they returned.

"It was so exciting, I almost wanted to sign up again."

He did sign up again in July 1948, serving through the end of June 1950. Although North Korea had invaded South Korea and Lewis reported to San Diego, he "didn't go over. They sent me to officers' screening. I did that but told them I didn't want to be an officer. I was married and had a child and another on the way."

A few years ago, Lewis said he received a letter from a buddy, John Eloff, who had contacted Kansas State University, where Lewis went to school.

"The college wouldn't give him my address but told him that if he sent them a letter, they would mail it to me," Lewis said. "Eloff lived in Sun City, Arizona."

Eloff gave Lewis the phone number of another buddy, Tony Chaidez, "and we've all gotten together every year."

GOD'S UMBRELLA

# Moorehead, Jack

## DOB 5/2/1924, DOD 4/15/2010

Jack Moorehead flew his combat tours in Italy during World War II.

"I was with the 15th Air Force, 450th Bomb Group and the 722nd Squadron," Moorehead said. "We were affectionately known as the 'Cottontails.'"

The name came from the airplane rudders being painted white. The main target of the bombers was Ploesti, Romania, oil fields, which provided ninety percent of the Germans' petroleum reserves.

"It was also the most heavily fortified of the targets," Moorehead said. "Every time we went to bomb Ploesti, they put up a smokescreen and we would bomb into it."

For the job, Moorehead said it required "youth, usually because of a misguided sense of immortality."

He spent sixteen months in combat. A plaque at Wright-Patterson Air Force Base and a duplicate at Holloman Air Force Base commemorate the 1,505 men of the 450th who were killed or missing in action.

"The largest fighting group at a time was 400 men," Moorehead said. "For all practical purposes, we were annihilated four times. It was a slaughterhouse."

He served as a gunner and flew eighteen or nineteen missions with his first crew and then flew with other groups, checking their gunners.

"I volunteered for the service at the ripe old age of eighteen," Moorehead said. "I took and passed the exam for aviation cadet. I had a brush-up with an instructor. On the day my class graduated, I washed out, but that instructor got to go straight to combat. I had already been to gunnery school, so I was just the kid they were looking for."

It was early December 1943 when he "washed out," and was sent to Salt Lake City for crew assignment. In late January 1944, he was sent to Boise, Idaho, for overseas training.

He was stationed near Manduria on Italy's bootheel and flew on B-24s.

"I was extremely fortunate," Moorehead said. "Almost everyone I knew got killed, but thankfully I was never shot down. I had a lot of thrills I didn't want to have, and a couple of times I don't know how the plane made it back, it was shot up so bad."

He went to high school with a fellow named Bill Rice and, when Moorehead arrived in Italy, Rice was there flying combat.

He said the soldiers played a lot of pranks on one aother. He recounted one of the "better ones."

"There were several targets where the German fighters wouldn't come into the flak because it was too heavy,"

Moorehead said. "[We played it on] Ellis Flippo, a tail gunner who was a red-headed Irishman. He said his name was due to the Spanish Armada wrecking on the island. Flippo would ease out of his position a little bit. We were over the Adriatic Sea and would be firing .50-caliber machine guns. Another gunner, Jack Robinson, and I gathered our brass and threw it at him when there was a big boom. Flippo slumped down like he was dead. He and I have had a sixty-four-year friendship."

After the war, Moorehead moved to Lawton, Oklahoma

"I had a good friend who was a first sergeant," Moorehead said. "He came to my store and asked me how old I was and what my rank was. I was a staff sergeant. 'Have I got a deal for you,' he said. I could have gotten a direct assignment as a second lieutenant, but I said, 'I don't think so.' That Christmas I was in Lawton and he was in Korea. My mama didn't raise no nitwit."

Moorehead moved to Silver City in 1967 and said that, the first time he came, "the place really impressed me, plus my allergies cleared up."

He has been self-employed all but two years of his adult life and "I haven't starved yet."

"I'm the happiest man I've ever known, and I never met the man I would trade places with," Moorehead said.

# Duran, John

## DOB 1926

John Duran a native of Silver City, said that when he was sixteen years old, he would go to the movies at the El Sol Theater.

"I would see ships loaded with soldiers going overseas," Duran said. "When I was seventeen, I told my mom and dad I wanted to join the Navy. Tears ran down their faces, because my brother was already overseas. I was a seventeen-year-old who didn't know what he was getting into."

It was 1943, and he and his dad went down to the Grant County Courthouse to sign papers. Duran was sent to El Paso, Texas, for a physical and then to San Diego Naval Training Station for boot camp, where he was taught to march, swim and shoot rifles.

"One day they told us to put on gas masks," Duran said. "They put us in a large building, closed the door, then turned the gas on. Then they opened the door and told us to take our gas masks off, so we would know what gas smelled like."

He had a short leave at home before he was sent to Treasure Island, California.

"They told us we were shipping out and put us on barges and took us to ships that were waiting at sea,"

Duran said. "We were given a mattress, a pillow, a life jacket and soap that would work with salt water."

They would wash their clothes and hang them on a rope over the side of the ship to dry.

"I lost two pairs of pants and a shirt," Duran laughed.

The men slept below deck, but it was so hot they would often take their mattresses to the deck.

"The rain would wake us up, and we'd go back below and sleep in a wet blanket," Duran said.

One day an announcement was made that a submarine had been spotted.

"They told us to go below, so we wouldn't be in the way of the gunners," Duran said. "We were packed like sardines. I could see a torpedo coming. If it had hit us, there would have been no survivors."

He said his grandson asked him if he was ever scared.

"I can't remember being scared the whole time I was in the service, maybe on account of my age," Duran said. "I was always wondering what was going to happen next."

During the day, the ship zigzagged, hoping any torpedo would miss. At night, the ship was blacked out. One night, strong winds hit the convoy and separated the ships. They couldn't send signals, because they didn't want the enemy to know where they were.

They got together again and landed in New Caledonia. Next the ship was sent to the Solomon Islands.

"The chaplain told us if you know how to pray, now is the time," Duran said. "The majority of us sailors knelt on the back of the ship and prayed. We didn't know what to expect, but by the time we landed on the islands, they had been taken away from the enemy. A lot of men died on those islands."

Later, he was assigned to the amphibious force. He was sent to Nissan Island, which means Green Island. He said it had a beautiful big lagoon, but it wasn't deep enough to take the ships. The landing crafts ferried the supplies—food, bombs and medicine—to the island.

"We had a bomber base, a Seabee base and a torpedo boat base," Duran said. "The Seabees also put up a big screen. They cut down coconut trees for us to sit on to watch movies."

One afternoon, the crew was going to the movies, and "I didn't go. The captain asked me why and I told him I was studying for the petty officer second-class test. He told me not to worry about it, but I thought it looked pretty hard."

Whoever was on watch when the ship was set to go out to sea would secure the landing crafts to the ships while supplies were loaded.

"One day I was on watch [on the landing craft] and the supplies had been loaded," Duran said. "The lines had been secured, when I got a message that the captain was aboard the ship and not aboard the landing craft. I waited until we knew he was aboard [the landing craft]. When I landed, the captain came over to me and said I had received my second-class petty officer rating. I was told that the captain could have been in trouble or embarrassed if he wasn't on the craft."

He spent about two years in the area.

"I was getting bored," Duran said, "but then I heard ships were being sunk. That got rid of my boredom, and I decided I was lucky to be where I was."

After the war was over, he was still there.

"The captain told me to get my seabag together, because I was going to the states," Duran said. "It was like a heavy weight was lifted."

After boarding a ship, the troops traveled through the Panama Canal.

"As we got near the states, we were told to throw our mattresses overboard," Duran said. "But when I got back to the states, I was told I didn't have enough points, so they assigned me to an aircraft carrier. I was one sad person."

He was on the USS Attu, named after an island taken from the Japanese.

"The Navy had rules about not drinking alcohol aboard ship, but they had a lovely little island, with chairs and tables for that purpose," Duran said. "The ship would drop anchor, and they would take the crew down there to drink beer or Cokes or whatever we wanted, but they didn't let us stay too long. They didn't want us to get too happy."

He said the aircraft carrier had much better food and had movies and doctors.

"I think they were trying to get us to stay in the Navy," Duran said. "The food on the smaller ships was terrible."

The ship cruised around, because the war was over. They stayed in Australia for a while and then returned to the states through the Panama Canal again.

"The ship was so huge, it was scraping the sides," Duran said. "You could see scratches."

He was taken where he was supposed to receive his discharge papers in 1946.

"An officer told me that if I stayed in, they'd make me a first-class petty officer," Duran said. "I told him I hadn't seen my mother, my father or my brother for three years, and I just wanted to go home."

He related a story about when the ship crossed the equator the first time. Those who hadn't been initiated lined up and ran through two lines of sailors who had rubber hoses with which they lightly hit the uninitiated.

"Then they put us on a platform in a rocking chair," Duran said. "They would drip salt water in your nose or mouth. Then they would tip the chair backward and we'd fall into a bucket of garbage. We got a certificate, so we didn't have to go through it again."

Referring to his time in the service, Duran said: "It was some adventure."

# JAURE, DEMETRIO

## DOB 06/10/1925, DOD 03/14/2014

Demetrio "Mike" Jaure said he enlisted in the Marines before he was eighteen, but was inducted October 4, 1943, after he had achieved the milestone.

Born in Las Vegas, New Mexico, he moved south to Silver City in 1942.

Jaure served in the Pacific Theater of World War II in 1944 and 1945. He saw action in Saipan, Tinian in the Marianas Islands and Iwo Jima. He was an amphibious tractor crewman in Company B of the 5th Amphibious Battalion. The tractors carried troops ashore from their ships.

He recounted when he and a Lieutenant Haas started unloading ammunition from one of the amphibious tractors.

"A Zero [a Japanese fighter plane] was strafing one of our transports," Jaure said. "Haas yelled at him to get away from our ship. The plane turned and came at me. I curled up and he flew up right before he got me."

He said the worst battle he experienced was in Saipan.

"I got close to getting killed," Jaure said. "We were going onto Red Beach 1 and got hit by pretty big fire. The cab of the tractor got hit. A Japanese .37 [millimeter gun] went through and killed the operator and radioman, who was named Griffin. We couldn't get in on the beach, so we went in on Red Beach 2. Another man was killed and everybody jumped out, including me. The Amtrak was full of holes."

He said one "big boy" went out of his mind and took a Japanese bayonet and was running around.

"I wasn't scared," Jaure said. "We just went after him. We had to tie him up.

"Why did we take chances?" he asked rhetorically. "I was scared going into Iwo Jima, so I found an Italian priest and confessed. Once I got onto the island, I wasn't scared anymore."

When he was in Iwo Jima, he said, he didn't get to see the flag-raising, because "we were hiding out on one side of the volcano."

He took an Amtrak onto Blue Beach.

"The beach was covered with dead Marines," Jaure said.

[At this point in the interview, he began crying and covered his face before he could speak again.]

Later, he said he still has nightmares about when he drove onto beaches where there were bodies. He feared that some might have still been alive, but he was under orders to take the troops ashore.

He and his unit stayed on Iwo Jima for thirty days.

"At the end, we were trying to clean out the snipers," Jaure said. "They were Japanese soldiers shooting from caves."

Coming to one of the islands, he was on a Landing Ship, Tank (LST), which carried vehicles, cargo and troops. He said the LST was hit by a shell and was sent back for repair.

"My seabag was left with the ship," Jaure said. "I got it back about a year after I got out. The only thing left was a Japanese flag and a picture of my girlfriend."

He said the flags had the history of what Japanese soldiers did.

When he got out of the Marines, he was asked if he wanted to enlist again, but he told them he wanted to go home.

"After a month, I missed the Marine Corps," Jaure said.

He said that most of the time he wasn't afraid of anything.

"Except once at Saipan, when I went into a store," Jaure said. "I had my .45 in my hand, and I heard a little noise. I picked up a violin and took it with me. Later I wondered why the hell I did that by myself. I later sold the violin to a guy for fifteen dollars."

Also, in Saipan, he and his "best buddy," John Norman Upsted, split up to try to get someone to surrender.

"A guy came out with his hands up and said, 'Yo soy something.' I don't remember his name," Jaure said, "but there were a lot of Spanish-speaking people there. It was a beautiful island with lots of fruit, papayas, bananas, oranges, lemons and a few coconuts. When the trees were knocked down, they grew back fast."

He also remembered an event in Iwo Jima, when the American soldiers were fighting for the airport.

"We went up there," Jaure said. "We had no business being there. There were snipers with machine guns. We jumped in a hole. Gravel hit me in the leg. That was real close. No more souvenir hunting—we learned."

He said he still has nightmares, and sometimes jumps at night because he is scared of the night.

"The night belongs to the enemy," he said.

Although Jaure said he doesn't want to talk about a lot of the things that happened, he remembers the funny stories, such as when it rained hard.

The soldiers took soap and stood out in the rain until they felt "cleaned up."

He recounted when he and members of his unit traded some souvenirs for a can of pork and beans, a couple of eggs and an onion.

"We cooked them in a helmet," Jaure said. "It made us sick. I will never again make pork and beans with eggs and onion."

Jaure said he got dengue fever [a mosquito-borne illness] in Saipan.

"After I got out and went to Denver, I got the fever again," he said. "The doctor thought I had malaria, but he checked and said I didn't. At that point, I was getting a little bit of benefits, but they were taken away from me."

Since then he has been denied veterans's compensation for his years of service.

# ARRINGTON, LLOYD

## DOB 06/16/1924, DOD 12/25/2015

Lloyd Arrington of Hurley volunteered for World War II in October 1943.

"I was living in North Carolina," Arrington said. "I was sent to Camp Croft, South Carolina, for induction and then to Camp Shelby in Mississippi for basic training."

He said he didn't get much training because he was in the hospital for about two months with a hernia that he had when he was inducted. He rejoined his outfit at the end of basic training and was assigned to an anti-tank company in the 65th Infantry Division.

"From there we were shipped out as replacements in Europe," Arrington said. "Our first stop was Marseilles, France."

His outfit was put in a replacement depot for a few days before being shipped out again to Naples, Italy.

"I volunteered for the 1st Special Service Force USA-Canada," Arrington said. "We were sent to Santa Maria, Italy, for advanced training and rappelling. I was young then—full of spit and vinegar—and I thought I could do it all."

The outfit was commanded by Colonel Robert T. Frederick, and the troops were sent to the Po Valley, where the river was called the "River of Blood" because of all the Allied and German casualties.

By the time the troops arrived, the valley had been secured, but Germans were holed up in the mountains. Back the troops went to France.

"In Menton, France, we were issued battle gear and trucked to the base of the Maritime Alps," he said. "We dismounted the vehicles to march on foot and were told that we were under enemy observation from now on. 'Stay behind each other and stay on the sides of the roads,' they said."

When he arrived at his new unit, he was met by a Canadian first sergeant with a goatee and handlebar mustache.

"He welcomed me in. 'Hi, Kid, come on over and I'll introduce you to your new platoon and squad leader,'" Arrington said. "Those Canadian and American guys were all rough-and-tumble son-of-a-guns. I was only eighteen and the youngest one there."

The squad was bunked out in a cellar, with .30-caliber machine gun emplacements all around it. The troops were assigned two hours on and four hours off on the machine guns.

"I stuck with the older guys because I knew they knew the ropes, and I was full of questions," Arrington said. "That evening one plane came over. I was told, 'That's Midnight Charlie, checking out our positions. We try to keep ourselves camouflaged so well they can't spot us.'"

He said that once in a while, German planes firing 88s—a form of German anti-tank artillery—flew over their encampment.

"'As long as you can hear the screaming, you're fine,'" Arrington said he was told. "They let me get oriented and adjusted to that type of life, then one evening the sergeant said, 'OK, Kid, a squad of us is going out on patrol.' I went out with them. We were behind each other and went up the mountain to where we thought the Germans were. We had to keep as quiet as possible, with no smoking or coughing. 'We're just checking them out to see where they are, and we'll come back later,' I was told when we went back to our bunks just before daybreak. That evening the Germans really lay down the fire.

"We were dug in, and the 88s were cutting trees down around us, but as far as I know, no one got hit," Arrington continued.

The troops spent about three months in the area, and then were sent back to France and were replaced by the 10th Mountain Division. The troops were billeted at the Continental Hotel in Menton. Arrington described it as a fancy tourist hotel up against a mountain. He said the city was "torn all to crap, and they still threw fire at us."

"It wasn't exactly rest and relaxation, because we had to pull guard duty at night," Arrington said. "After three days of R&R, we were sent to Nice [France], where we camped on the ground in pup tents."

His outfit was broken up, but some members stayed in the same group, which was renamed the 474th Infantry. In

1945, the troops went into Germany and "hooked up with the British outfits, the Criminal Investigation Command and the Secret Intelligence Service."

"We were told we were going to be the cleanup outfit," Arrington said.

They went through apartments in Aachen, Germany, and confiscated any Nazi military equipment they found. He carried a duffel bag of souvenirs all the way to his next posting in Berlin, where he was assigned to a military police battalion at Wansee Lake outside the city.

"I was there when Berlin became a divided city among the French, Americans, British and Russians," Arrington said.

After about two months, he had enough points to rotate back to the United States, where he was discharged at Fort Bragg, Georgia

He said no jobs were to be had, so, in 1947, Arrington rejoined the Army, as an infantryman.

"I was sent to Fort Gordon, Georgia, which I did not like," he said. "They kept sending me to swamps, so I kept volunteering for overseas assignments."

He was sent to Korea, but before he got there, he was pulled off the ship to serve with the military police in Yokohama, Japan. He spent about three years there.

"I was in the honor squad for the dead coming out of Korea," Arrington said. "I saw no action, except for police action," Arrington said.

When he returned to the United States, he was sent again to Fort Gordon, so he again volunteered for an overseas assignment.

Arrington was sent to Vienna, Austria, where he spent fifty-two months in a military police battalion.

When he returned once again to the United States and while he was on leave, he received orders.

"I couldn't pronounce the name of the post," Arrington laughed.

He drove toward Arizona and Fort Huachuca. Intending to travel to Tucson, Arizona, he stopped in Benson, Arizona, for fuel.

"I happened to ask how to get to Fort Huachuca," Arrington said. "The fellow told me to turn left on that highway and that forty miles down the road would be Fort Huachuca. I had never seen the desert before. There was nothing out there."

When he arrived at Fort Huachuca, he pulled up to the main gate, where the military police met him.

"I was sent to the desk sergeant, who was my old friend Sergeant Schell," Arrington said. "I had served with him in Vienna. I was placed in his unit and spent about four years there."

He and Schell had a cabin in Ash Canyon. They spent weekends there, where Schell looked for gold.

"He finally got maybe an ounce," Arrington laughed.

Arrington met his wife, Hope Acuña of Tyrone, at Fort Huachuca, where she worked for the Civil Service.

"Fort Huachuca was a good post," Arrington said. "Thirty days after [Hope and I] were married, I was sent to Korea again."

This time he made it to the Asian country and spent about thirteen months as a sergeant first class.

His next overseas assignment was with the 3rd Infantry Division in Schweinfurt, Germany. Because of his rank, he was allowed to bring his wife with him. He spent most of his time in training during this stint of about a year.

Arrington's last assignment was with the 2nd Armored Division at Fort Hood, Texas, where he spent eighteen months. Part of the time he was acting sergeant major with the 2nd Armored, 41st Infantry. He was discharged in 1963.

Arrington and his wife relocated to Grant County, where Arrington served as chief of police of Hurley, New Mexico, for thirteen years.

"I have lots of good friends and neighbors here," Arrington said. "I love this little town."

GOD'S UMBRELLA

# HENSLEY, RALPH

## DOB 06/03/1926  DOD 08/07/2016

"Two buddies and I went to volunteer for the Marines," Ralph Hensley said, "but I was color-blind. They would not take me and told me to go to the Seabees, because 'they'll take almost anyone.'"

He said he went home and ate a lot of carrots, but "it didn't change a thing."

Hensley was living in Reed, West Virginia, when he left high school in the "eleventh and a half grade" to work for shipbuilders in Newport News, Virginia.

"I came home at seventeen to volunteer for the military," Hensley said.

His two buddies ended up on Iwo Jima with the Marines and Hensley was on Saipan, "running a road grader, building a temporary hospital."

One of his friends was taken to the hospital, but Hensley didn't find out about it until after the war when they got together and shared stories.

He said his first year in the service was "pretty easy," on the island of Maui, Hawaii.

"At the end of that year, my unit joined with the Marines for training for the invasion of the Marianas," Hensley said. "We went to Saipan, where the Marines went in and secured everything. About a month later or less, we went in to enlarge the Japanese airstrip to make it possible for our B-29s to come in."

The Seabees worked from daylight to dark, he said.

"A lot of Japanese were up in the hills," Hensley said. "Even after the war was over, they were still in caves up in the hills."

While the Seabees were expanding the airstrip, they were susceptible to Japanese air strikes.

"The one I remember most got pretty close to us," Hensley said. "I got under a truck, and an older man told me in no uncertain terms in rather specific language to get out from under the truck and over into a ditch. I said to myself: 'God, if you get me out of this, I'll serve you the rest of my life.'

"Those words had an effect on everything I've ever done in life," Hensley said. He, too, believed that God held an umbrella over him during World War II and ever since.

He said the words didn't stick with him during the war, because he got in with the older guys in the Seabees and there was lots of drinking.

After the war, he went to work in construction, but "kept hearing those words."

"I decided to go to Davis and Elkins College from 1949-53," Hensley said, but because he couldn't afford more school, he worked for Goodyear Atomic Corporation from 1954-58.

In 1958, Hensley went to the Louisville Presbyterian Theological Seminary in Louisville, Kentucky. By that time, he and his wife, Mary, had four children.

"I had learned one thing in the Seabees—the motto was 'Can Do,'" Hensley said. "I would not quit. It's been a part of our life's story. We have had some pretty good struggles, but we managed to get through them and keep a-goin'."

He said that just after the war, his unit was shipped to Hawaii. He got a new dollar bill that was printed in Hawaii and got a bunch of buddies to sign it.

"When I was in seminary, we were totally broke," Hensley said. "I took that dollar bill to the grocery store and asked the grocer if he would hold it for me until I could pay him. I got a few things in exchange."

The nearly three years in the Seabees, he said, taught him that "you can endure, can go on, can make it and not to give up. Struggles make you tougher."

In 1961, the Hensleys moved from the seminary in Kentucky to Silver City in a tent camper that he had made. Hensley served as a Presbyterian pastor in Cliff and Animas, New Mexico, and served as a Sunday school minister in Silver City.

Hensley rejoined the service as a chaplain in the Marine Corps in 1968.

"I felt if we were sending young men to die in Vietnam, there should be people going with them that could be supportive in spiritual ways," Hensley said. "I wanted to be a Marine's Marine, in the sense that I would be in the field with the men."

In a report that Hensley made to the chief chaplain in Da Nang following Operation Meade River, Hensley described a day in which he held services from eight in the morning to late in the evening and some of the problems that were going on.

"It was raining and muddy, and when I returned that night, my commanding officer wanted to know 'Where the hell have you been?'" Hensley said. "He knew where I was, but he said, 'From now on you'll be called Muddy Boots.'"

When he was in the Seabees during World War II, although the battalion had a chaplain, Hensley said he didn't see the chaplain in the two and a half years Hensley was there.

"I decided I would be available to the men (in Vietnam)," he said. "I would pull a trailer behind the Jeep loaded down with soft drinks, beer and ice, and everybody got one drink of their choice. Then I'd have a short service, three or four a day, as many as fifteen a week."

He used crackers and whatever drinks were left over for communion.

He was transferred out of the infantry into a reconnaissance outfit in Da Nang and would fly out for services.

One Easter Sunday, the news services were looking for a chaplain who was going to do a sunrise service.

"I was the only one they could find who was going to do an Easter sunrise service," Hensley said. "Out of that, they took a few pictures and it was broadcast on the Today Show."

Mary Hensley said she had people calling her from Ohio to say they had seen her husband on television.

He said that, with the recon battalion, he had the opportunity to learn rappelling and, "I don't know what it was called, but I rode on a rope ladder along with several other guys hanging outside of a helicopter going over Da Nang."

"The last four months were kind of relaxed," Hensley said. "I had an office and a chapel. On Sundays, all day long, they would serve shrimp, lobster and steak."

The cooks had traded with General William Westmoreland's cooks, according to Hensley.

"I feel even today it's so important we support our troops, through writing letters, [saying] prayers or giving verbal support," Hensley said.

GOD'S UMBRELLA

# MARKS, RICHARD

## DOB 11/15/1925  DOD 11/23/2017

Richard Marks of Pleasanton, New Mexico, served in the Army Air Forces during World War II.

"It's the group that won the war," Marks said.

He volunteered for the service in October 1943, in Cedar Rapids, Iowa, and took his primary pilot training in King City, California. Basic training was in Bakersfield, California, and Luke Field, Arizona, was the site for his advanced flying training. He went to Mather Field, California, after being commissioned and getting his wings.

"I flew B-25s," Marks said. "When we were at Luke Field, all the single guys were assigned to P-61 night fighters and the married ones to B-25s," supposedly because night fighting was more dangerous, but that was not the case, according to Marks.

He took overseas training at Greenville, South Carolina, and then went to the Pacific Theater, serving in the 345th Bomber Group, 499th Bomber Squadron. He was stationed first at San Marcelino in the Philippines and later at Clark Field near Manila.

"We were the first ones to fly minimum-altitude missions," Marks said. "Those guys in the night fighters were lucky."

He said the tips of the B-25 propellers were green.

"If a pilot didn't have green prop tips, he was flying too high," Marks said. "He got the green prop tips from flying through the trees. Over a target, we were down as far as we could get, and once in a while we hit the top of a tree."

He recounted a tale told by one of his friends who, before a mission over Hong Kong, flew over the city earlier in the day to check out the weather.

"When he landed, I asked him about the antenna that sticks out below the plane," Marks said. "It was bent at about a forty-five-degree angle. He told me he hit it on a locomotive smokestack over Hong Kong. That's how low we flew.

"We [flying the B-25s] were the first strafe bombers," he continued. "We had more guns than any other plane in the Air Force. We had eighteen .50-caliber machine guns, and we'd usually carry four 500-pound bombs. Sometimes we carried parafrag bombs—a whole bunch of them. They had a little parachute on them. They were small bombs and they would fragment."

He said troops on the ground "can see what they're doing and what they did, but we could never see what we accomplished."

Marks recounted his first mission. The Army requested that his plane go to Luzon in the Philippines and bomb and strafe the last Japanese troops on the island.

"The next day, the Army gave us a report, and I guess there were no survivors," Marks said. "We didn't see a thing. All we saw was treetops. I'm kind of glad of that. That happened at other similar times, too."

He flew thirty-seven missions. He said he remembers seeing a movie on television about B-29s flying the last mission of World War II.

"The last mission I flew on was the last mission of the war," Marks said. "They [B-29 pilots] didn't fly the last mission of World War II because they were back in their sacks and snoozing, when we [B-25 pilots] were flying up the west coast of Kyushu, looking for any Japanese ships out of harbor. We were prepared to strafe 'em, bomb 'em and sink 'em. It was the fifteenth of August 1945. We were flying and we got the message from our base: 'Hostilities have ceased. Return to base immediately.' The war was over when we turned around."

The planes hauled their ammunition and bombs back to the base.

"It may have been the fourteenth of August over here, but the war ended on the fifteenth in Japan," Marks said.

The first mission he said he remembers overseas was one that he wasn't on. During a flight to Hainan Island off South China, an American plane went down and ditched in the bay.

"The next day, I flew co-pilot for the lead plane," Marks said. "We found the four guys in a raft. One of our submarines was coming to pick them up, but six Japanese fighters showed up and strafed the sub, until we got closer to the sub, and the fighters couldn't get to it. We had six guns that would fire backwards. We circled the sub and the raft and kept the fighters away. Once the sub picked up the guys, the fighters went back to their base."

On a training mission over Clark Field, he was flying co-pilot with his friend, Mo.

We wanted to put the wheels down to land and the hydraulic system went out," Marks said. "The engineer had to pump them down by hand, probably the flaps, too. We didn't have any brakes."

The engineer and the pilot fumbled over the manual release of the brakes, which had two applications of air and "it's gone."

"We went off the end of the runway over a bunch of Japanese planes that were stored there," Marks said. "We ended up ninety degrees to the runway on top of the planes. I think all three of us went out the hatch at the same time."

Although their plane didn't burn, the engineer told him that when they hit the Japanese planes, a chunk of metal from one of the planes came through the window and traveled "behind me and in front of (the engineer's) face. I didn't know about it, so it didn't bother me, but it sure scared him."

Marks' wife of sixty-two years, Lois, said once she hadn't heard from him in a long time. She was returning from the store and her mother was running toward her and told her, "You gotta get home. There's a telegram. I thought, 'oh, no,' but when I read the telegram it said,

'Happy Birthday.' I received it more than a month after my birthday."

Her husband said he was sure he had sent it on her birthday.

On one trip Marks took on a C-47, the plane encountered turbulence over New Guinea.

"We were flying to Biak, off the north coast (of New Guinea)," Marks said. "Not bad when we left, but it was solid overcast ahead of us. The pilot wanted to turn around, but it was solid overcast behind us, to the east of us and to the west of us. So [the pilot] headed to the ocean off the northeast coast."

They ended up in a thundercloud and the wind took them straight up in altitude and, then, all of a sudden, they were upside down and slammed against the ceiling.

"We didn't know the pilot was knocked out until after we landed," Marks said. The co-pilot had taken over.

The turbulence twice more slammed them against the ceiling and back to the floor. Those manning the controls headed toward an airstrip on the coast.

"Then, we saw a little island offshore where a couple of ships were tied up," Marks said. "They were American ships, so we landed on Wadke Island. The Americans told us that it was a good thing we didn't land at the airstrip, because the Japanese were cannibals. They hadn't had supplies in so long that they were eating whatever they could subdue.

"Before we landed, my navigator and I were sitting right over the wing at the back engine of the left wing and we saw rivets popping out of the engine cowling," Marks said. "The next morning, we got on the plane to continue to Biak and we remembered about the rivets. We told the pilot and he went back to Wadke. I guess the plane is still there. They sent a plane from Biak to get us."

Marks returned home on January 18, 1946. The officers were the last to come home.

"The pilots' first job after the war was over was to drive the big personnel carriers to haul the enlisted men to ships," Marks said.

The Army Air Forces changed its name to the United States Air Force in 1947. Marks remained in the Reserves until he retired in 1963.

He went on an Honor Flight of the first thirty-six World War II veterans from southern New Mexico to be transported, as a reward for their service, to Washington, D.C. They saw the monuments and spent the most time at the World War II Memorial, according to Marks.

"In the hotel, I could look out the window and see the Air Force Memorial," he said.

GOD'S UMBRELLA

# COSPER, EDWARD THOMAS

## DOB 11/30/24  DOD 01/05/2018

Edward Thomas Cosper grew up on a ranch "north of Clifton, AZ, in the boondocks," the younger son of Jim and Katie Cosper.

"My grandfather, Frederick Fritz, an immigrant from Germany was called the Little Kaiser on the Blue ([River])," Cosper said. "During the war, they weren't sure about his loyalties. He was almost killed by one of the last grizzlies in the area. My family homesteaded in that country."

He said he went through school in a one-room schoolhouse, where, when he was in fourth grade, he was moved to fifth grade, so the teacher would have two students in the class. "I've always regretted that. I became a college freshman at sixteen years of age. I spent a year at Arizona State University and a year in Fort Collins, Colorado, at what was then called Colorado A & M University. I studied range management."

Cosper said his father was alone on the ranch, because Cosper's older brother Phil was serving in the Pacific Theater.

"I got a deferment after my third year in college to go home and help Dad on the ranch," Cosper said. "I was grieving that I couldn't be in the military, too. I had to go before the draft board to relieve me of the deferment. They asked my dad if he could manage the ranch alone. He said, 'If I have to I'll work day and night. I'll not miss one bit of production.'"

"I went to Phoenix to enlist in the Air Corps," Cosper continued. "I applied for cadet status. They were overwhelmed with pilot applications. It was an extraordinarily difficult test, but I made it."

After three months of basic training and three months of advanced training, he was officially a pilot.

"But I spent two years trying to get a flying job," Cosper said. "I was moved from one air field to another, at least half a dozen air fields scattered throughout the county. Mostly we were working on planes, not flying them."

He finally began his three months of pilot training, with more live training. "I was just finishing the advanced training when the war ended. I got mustered out before I got to fly B-51s, which is what I trained for."

"My older brother, Phil, was a Navy captain on some kind of boat," Cosper said. "He fought a tough war, but he made it through. Our dearest friend, Emil Kiehne, was serving in the Pacific. I roomed with Emil at Fort Collins. He went into the Marines and was in Tokyo. He knew the name of the ship that Phil was captain of. When he heard it had come into harbor, he put on his dress uniform and got on the ship. He told the deckhands to tell the captain 'to get up here. I'm gonna throw his ass in the water.'" They had a happy reunion.

When Cosper was given his medical exam on discharge, the doctor asked him, "What have you been doing in the

Air Corps? I hope you weren't flying. You have a systolic heart murmur."

"Either they missed itwhen I went in or I developed it while I was training," Cosper said.

Although he kept a diary during his service, he said, "It was totally routine."

Cosper's daughter, Deborah Cosper-Hughs, said he had been told by her grandmother, who was a very devout Christian, "God will bring you home."

After he was mustered out, he returned to the ranch to help his dad. "I met Mary. I chased her down and corralled her. We worked four years in Morenci for Phelps Dodge." Mary worked as secretary to the general manager and Cosper served a four-year apprenticeship as an electrician. "I went back to college and got a degree in education. I was in education the rest of my career."

"We moved to Silver City about thirty years ago, because Deb lived here," Cosper said. He noted that his mother and grandmother always called him Edward Thomas.

He and Mary were married for seventy years.

GOD'S UMBRELLA

# Youngs, Richard

## DOB 1926

Richard Youngs volunteered for the Navy in World War II.

On Oct. 20, 1943, Richard Youngs reported to boot camp at Camp Sampson, N.Y., after volunteering for the Navy.

When he was 16 years old, he said the song "There's a Star-Spangled Banner Waving Somewhere," sung by Elton Britt, "got me fired up to join the Navy."

After basic training, Youngs was assigned to the armed guard as part of the gun crew to ride in merchant ships.

"I was checking the bulletin board and saw I had been assigned to the USS Missouri, which was still being constructed," Youngs said. "A day or so later, I was on my way to New Orleans to be put on the Landing Ship Tank 290."

The LST hit a log in the Mississippi River and had to be sent to dry dock to have a bent shaft repaired.

"My folks rode from Pennsylvania to see me," Youngs said. "I got to see them for 20 minutes, because we were pulling out."

During a trip around Florida to Cape Hatteras, N.C., in heavy fog, the ship was rammed by another ship.

"We had watertight compartments and they kept us afloat," Youngs said. "The next morning, we saw the hole that had cut my bunk and five others in half. It was a good thing we weren't in them."

After another stint in dry dock, the ship headed to New York to take on equipment.

"I was taken off at Halifax, Nova Scotia, to have a hernia repaired that I had received in the collision," Youngs said. "I was discharged after 28 days and spent three weeks at home."

The ship left for Slapping Sands, England, without Youngs.

"While I was home, my mother received a telegram that I had been killed in action," he said. "I never made it to England, but my records were on the ship."

He said nine German torpedo boats had caught the convoy.

"One ship went down and it had all the records from my group," Youngs said. "The ones of us they couldn't find were reported as killed in action."

He said the captain of LST 515, Joe McCain, went back to pick up survivors, but there were so many bodies he was afraid to start the engines. Seven hundred thirty-six Navy and Army personnel were killed. Fifty years after the disaster, one of the officers brought the information to light.

"These guys are my heroes, along with a bunch of others who didn't come back," Youngs said.

"I spent two months at Camp Bradford, Virginia, and wasn't getting paid," Youngs said. "They finally told me I was killed in action. The third month, I was put on the crew of the LST 947, where I spent the rest of my Navy days."

The ship headed to the Pacific Theater through the Panama Canal and spent a month at Pearl Harbor, Hawaii, for instruction on "what the group was headed into," he said.

The LST 947 was assigned to "moving troops around" among New Caledonia, Guadalcanal and Tulagi in the Solomon Islands. The crew also picked up and carried 17 LVTs — Landing Vehicle Tracked.

"To launch an LVT, which was large enough to carry five tanks, we put a list on the ship and the LVT slid right into the ocean from the main deck," Youngs said.

He was in a Landing Craft, Vehicle, Personnel radio boat that was the first onto Red Beach in Okinawa.

"When we first went in, there was very little firing from the Japanese," Youngs said. "We stood off the beach until 2 or 3 in the morning, and spent 20 hours hauling the wounded and the ones who had cracked up to the hospital ship."

He said the troops spent seven days fighting off suicide planes.

"On the sixth day, the battleship Utah was struck," Youngs said. "I was a pointer for the 20-millimeter gun on the LST. I had headphones on and a plane was headed toward us. I fired a few shells, but wasn't coming close. I stopped until it was closer, pulled the trigger and it jammed."

He said the captain told them later that a shell had hit the plane just as "it was upon us. (The pilot) veered and the only piece left on the deck was his wing."

"If we hadn't hit him, we would have sunk," Youngs said. "It's another case where I was lucky."

He said one of the officers, "who we really liked because he entertained us on the guitar, was a black man named Webster, whose first name I don't remember. He was on the port side. The ship was hit on the starboard side and afterward we couldn't find Webster. He had jumped off the side and was hanging by the cord on his earphones. He was OK, but we laugh about it now."

Although Youngs sent home a box of souvenirs, including a piece of the plane and the pilot's flag, it never arrived.

The LSTs carried food, ammunition, vehicles, troops and equipment. Winston Churchill, England's prime minister during World War II, described the ship as "the ugliest ship that won the war."

After Okinawa, LST 947 went to Leyte, Philippines, to get ready for the invasion of Japan.

"We were a happy bunch of sailors when we found out the war was over," Youngs said. "Then we were sent to Tokyo Bay as some of the first occupation troops."

After gathering snow-removal equipment, the ship was sent to Hokkaido Island, where Youngs pulled shore duty.

"We were riding around on top of about 8 feet of snow," he said. "About the middle of April, I decided to come home. I started to volunteer to go on the LST with a mine sweeper, but decided it was time to go home."

He was discharged in mid-May 1946.

"I have three loves I speak of," Youngs said. "They are love of country, love of freedom and love of family. I'd still go to preserve our freedom."

GOD'S UMBRELLA

# CHAPTER 8

☙

## DRAFTED IN 1943

# Lloyd, Joseph P.

## DOB 03/03/1922

Joseph P. Lloyd said he tried to volunteer for the Air Force, but "they didn't want me, so I got drafted into the Army in Washington, DC, on March 12, 1943, and I was immediately sent across the country to the West Coast."

Lloyd spent four years in the 1st Army, 3rd Division, 981st Battalion, with a very short stint in the 3rd Army. He reached the rank of corporal.

He was put into a battery of six-inch rifles when it was split in half to make two batteries. "They filled in the half with us young guys. The men who trained us were interested in making us good buddies, but the trainers took great delight in beating us up. However, it makes a difference if they train you, so you can depend on one another."

"I had one year of college and had a math background before I went in," Lloyd said. "In those days, you didn't have computers, so I had paper and pencil to add numbers together."

His first training was on the West Coast, with some of it taking place in the Mojave Desert, because they were training the soldiers for duty in Africa. "By the time they got us trained, the African war was over. So, they sent us back to New York and shipped us across to England, where we built our own camp along the coast around the first of the year, 1944."

"We went into Normandy on D-Day, June 6, 1944, on Utah Beach, the same day as the main invasion onto Omaha Beach, where they got clobbered so bad," Lloyd said. "When I went ashore with my gun, the infantry had already wiped out the defenses, so we didn't even get shot at going ashore.

"Our guns could shoot seventeen miles, and we figured we would always be about five miles behind the lines," he continued. "But that's not the way the generals saw it. They found out we could [in our trucks] run as fast as the tanks could, so they made us run with the tanks. With our guns, we were usually well in front of the infantry, because we could take out fortifications the tanks couldn't knock out."

The evening they got ashore on D-Day, "the first thing we did was dig a foxhole," Lloyd said. "One fellow had gotten his foxhole dug, so he got in it and lay down on his back to sleep. This frog came along, and, after all these rumors about how the Germans would sneak up on you and cut your throat, this frog jumped in and landed on the guy's face. You never heard of a guy getting out of a foxhole as fast as he did. That's the humorous part."

He said the unit, which was a mobile unit assigned wherever it was needed, didn't move inland until enough troops were on shore after the invasion to form a large force.

"We always slept in a foxhole," he said, "unless you were confined to a better structure and most of them were blown to hell."

He explained that the whole army was motorized. "No one marched. That was World War I."

He said the Air Force was going to drop bombs in front of where his unit was advancing. "But they dropped them five miles from where they should have been, so we had no cover from the bomb craters. The infantry had to fight through. We had the infantry in front of us. We were the advancers. At least up until the Battle of the Bulge. Then we temporarily got clobbered."

"As we rode along, a guy was riding on a fender of one of the vehicles with his carbine loaded, cocked and ready to go," Lloyd said. "We were worried about whether snipers were going to shoot at us. All of a sudden, the guy falls off. He had shot himself in the foot."

He said by this time winter had set in. "They didn't have any winter clothes for us. So, I borrowed a needle and thread, a shelter half and a blanket. I cut and made my own gloves, a helmet and very thick booties to keep my feet warm."

Lloyd noted that even in combat areas, "most of the time we were doing nothing. Only now and then was there some real action."

The Battle of the Bulge took place from December 16, 1944, through January 25, 1945. It was over Christmas. He was asked what they did for Christmas. "We tried to stay warm. We were out in the boonies," he chuckled. "On

Christmas Day, the skies cleared, so our Air Force could see something to shoot at, which they did a whole lot of."

He told the story of an American who got stopped at a roadblock. The Americans had tried to figure out questions that Germans couldn't answer. "They asked him where he was from. He said he was a little Okie, so that got him passed."

He said that, during the Battle of Bulge, "my outfit was on the northern flank, and we had just received a new kind of fuse for our shells. They were called proximity fuses. When you shot them, they would explode 30 feet above the ground. So, they were then 10 times more effective than shells that had to hit the ground. That was one of the advantages we had for the Battle of the Bulge. They made us much more effective. One of the men caught, a German, said he had never experienced anything like that with the shrapnel coming down on him."

It was cold and wet, and they often made fires to warm themselves. "We could always find something to burn. There were blown up buildings all around."

"We moved awful fast," Lloyd said. "I don't remember actually being shot at. We were always moving, and we did the shooting."

He said the thing to do was to capture a bridge. "When we got up in the vicinity of the Rhine, a handful of men managed to get across the bridge and took out the near defenses. So, the rest of us galloped across. The Germans tried to bomb the bridge, but they couldn't hit it and lost a lot of aircraft trying. By the time they managed to damage the bridge, we had other ways to get across the river. By the time we got across, the fighting was almost over."

To a question about whether his unit ever captured any Germans, he said, "I don't remember my unit capturing anyone. We weren't in that business. That was for the infantry."

Lloyd remembered the beautiful young ladies who "were brought to Europe to entertain us. Ones like Dinah Shore. We liberated a lot of food and found a cognac once in a while. I enjoyed Spam during the war. It was a perfectly good food. We sometimes got only stuff left over from World War I. The meat, vegetables and biscuits survived. When you're hungry enough, you'll eat almost anything. Our kitchen and crew always found what we needed. The most important man in the outfit was the sergeant in charge of food."

Lloyd said, at the end of the war, most of the soldiers liked the Germans better than the French, whom they found arrogant.

He recalled one incident in a town during the fighting where the building was surrounded by heavy stone fencing. "The opening was not big enough for us to get through, so we took a sledgehammer to it and opened it up. When we lived in Europe in the 1960s, I went back to the town and the fence had been rebuilt."

"The war was suddenly over," Lloyd said. "The word got around real fast. It came by radio."

After the war, four of the men from his unit had a furlough in Paris. "We found all kinds of trouble. We hit the first joint where we could buy whiskey. We each bought a bottle of French cognac. After the fourth bottle, we were sozzled. We could read the street signs, but we couldn't read the map. How we found our way home, I don't know, but we did find our way back to quarters."

They also went to the coastline of France. "I didn't have any swimming trunks, so I found a parachute and some needle and thread, and I manufactured my own swimming shorts. I got properly burned, because it was hot there."

Every battery had four six-inch rifles with twenty-foot barrels, each of which could lob a hundred-pound shell up to seventeen miles. "A good crew could get off two a minute. We were a top-flight crew and were going to be sent to Japan after we returned to the United States. I'm very happy for the atomic bomb."

"When the war was over, they sent all the soldiers with families home first," Lloyd said, "so we sat with nothing to do."

He served in the Ground Observer Corps during the Cuban Missile Crisis. "We were in Houston watching the Soviets come into Cuba."

Lloyd then served in the Civilian Air Corps . "I have a background in physics, so my outfit chose to go see the atomic tests at the Trinity site in the 1950s."

"The GI Bill put me through college," he said. "When I got back to the States, I went back to college in Kansas City [Missouri]. I went to Rockhurst one year, where I got no math or science. They were training me to be a priest, so I deliberately flunked out."

He received his bachelor's degree and went straight through to a PhD in physics at Washington University in St. Louis, Missouri.

As of this writing, Lloyd lives in Silver City, New Mexico, having been brought to the area by his daughter.

GOD'S UMBRELLA

# Leyba, Manuel R.

## DOB 6/10/1925

Manuel R. Leyba was drafted in March 1943, but was given a choice of which branch of service he wanted. He chose the Navy and was sent to Farragut, Idaho, for training.

"I applied for carpenter's mate," Leyba said.

He traveled to his first stint overseas on the USS Howell Lykes, a large transport ship. He spent about one year in the Admiralty Islands. Although he had been fishing in the Pacific Ocean off Long Beach, California, when visiting family, he had never been out on the ocean in a ship.

"I did not get seasick, but a lot of my mates couldn't even eat, they were so sick," Leyba said. "On our way to Biak, we stopped in Guadalcanal for refueling."

On the small island of Biak, his company was assigned to build living quarters, such as Quonset huts, for the Naval Air Transport Service.

"Most of the time on base, my duty was to fill airplanes to haul troops and cargo," Leyba said.

Sometimes the troops had a chance to go out to the other islands in the archipelago.

"About three or four of us carpenters built a sailboat and sailed it to the other islands," Leyba said.

Fighter planes were commonly seen on the base, where sailors would repair them and send them back into battle.

"We saw the destruction," Leyba said, "but I was willing to serve my country any place they put me."

Leyba remembers the fun that the troops had.

"On the island [which was made of coral] they dug a big hole to take the coral for the runways," he said. "[It filled with water and] we made a diving board and would jump in. It was deep."

Sometimes the sailors would watch the natives from the other islands when they fished.

"Mama would be in the boat and the boys, probably twelve to fourteen years old, dove into the ocean," Leyba said. "They would come back with a fish held in the teeth and one in each hand. It was fun watching them. Mama would cut the fish up and later they would dry them."

Recreation for the troops included boxing, "which I tried, but I didn't like it. I landed one punch on a colored guy, and he landed on the floor. When he got up, he said, 'No more.'"

Movies were brought in for the troops and shown on an outside screen, where the sailors sat on benches made of coconut trees.

"I remember when Bob Hope and Frances Langford visited us," Leyba said. "We used to be happy to see people from back home. We also liked it when we got mail from home. Somebody would get cookies, and we would share them with our buddies, and the cookies would disappear. We would have to wait until the next cookies."

Later he was sent to Samar and Manila in the Philippines, where he was stationed when it was "my time to come home."

The troops left Manila on a small ship, one used to repair large ships.

"After five or six hours, it got dark, and the ocean started getting wild," he said. "That's when I got scared. We went down the big waves and up to the top of the next. Sometimes we would get hit from the side. Things would slide. I liked the large ships better."

The ship stopped at one small island and picked up a few troops. They landed at a naval air station in California.

From there he was sent to Washington, D.C., Maryland, then to Miami, Florida, for about six months.

"After that I came home on furlough, went back to Miami, and they sent me to Terminal Island in California, where I was discharged [in 1946]," Leyba said. "Then I flew back home [to Grant County]."

Following the war, Leyba worked at Fort Bayard Medical Center, New Mexico, in construction and then as an attendant. Then he spent thirty-two years at the Santa Rita Mine in Santa Rita, New Mexico, most of the time as a driver of the large ore-hauling trucks.

After returning from the service, he married Christina Legarda in 1948. Their two sons, David and Clemente, were born in Santa Rita, and their two daughters, Drusilla and Christina, in Silver City. After thirty-one years of marriage, Leyba's wife died. He later married Esther Pino, to whom he has been married for twenty-six years.

"She's a beautiful woman," he said.

GOD'S UMBRELLA

# CLARK, FREDERICK JAMES

## DOB 10/12/23, DOD 06/02/2017

On October 12, 1923, Frederick James "Fred" Clark was born at his grandparents' house at 610 12th Street, across from today's Harlan Hall on the Western New Mexico University (WNMU) campus in Silver City. "My grandmother was Phoebe Estelle Fleming Clark," Fred said. "Her brother was Colonel John Fleming, who donated the first twenty acres for the college."

In the spring of 1943, after graduating from high school in 1942, he was drafted.

"Three of us were drafted from here together: Benny Perrault from Mimbres and Tiny Young and I from Silver City," Clark said. "Tiny was a state policeman.

"I was wanting to get into the Army engineers, because I ran a bulldozer," he continued. "Old Tiny said engineers were in the Marines, so the fellow in El Paso enlisted all three of us in the Marines."

Their next stop was San Diego, California, for boot camp. "After we had a little bit of drilling, we were sent to Camp Matthews for rifle training. When I got out of boot camp, I went to Camp Pendleton, where I stayed for about six months. After that I went to Maui, because we were setting up for the first invasion of the Marshall Islands."

He served as a private first class in the 4th Marine Division and carried a Browning automatic rifle.

Clark reported that, in the Marshall Islands, there was a causeway between the islands of Roi and Namur. One of the islands had an airport.

Clark trained on a Higgins boat, which he described as having a big gate up front and, when the boat bumped up on the sand, the gate would come down. After a week of training, they went back to Hawaii. He said the boats were kind of like a floating tractor with tracks. "We would travel on the water and then we would go over the side."

The next stop was Saipan.

"I was wounded on the beach at Saipan," Clark continued. "Our vehicle was bringing us in and got hit about 500 yards out. We had to bail out and walk onto the beach. We got part way in and a shell hit behind me. It hit mostly my backpack, which had the pick and a carton of cigarettes. Whatever hit me, bent the pick on my pack and the point went into me.

"I was in the water and when I got to shore, I couldn't walk. My legs wouldn't go. They put me in an amphib and sent me back out to the ship."

Clark was put on the hospital ship to Hawaii and then sent to the hospital in Honolulu.

"When we came back from the Marshalls, our company was kept there [in Hawaii] to clean up the ship," Clark said. "Where we were docked was right next to Dole Pineapple."

The company stole $3,000 worth of cans of pineapple. "We ate and ate. I still don't eat pineapple to this day."

"I was then in the hospital for three or four months in San Diego [Balboa] Naval Hospital," Clark said. "While I was in the hospital, Walter and Ellen Ward, who lived there, but were from Silver City, would get me out of the hospital on weekends.

"I received the Purple Heart, was discharged and came back to Silver," he said.

He still has the cane that he came home with.

In September 1945, he met the woman, Millie, who was to become his wife. "He was still using the cane," Millie reported.

Clark decided to use the GI Bill, and started college at what is now WNMU in the summer of 1946. They lived in barracks that had been turned into apartments. "I got $105 a month on the GI Bill. Rent was twenty-one dollars a month. I graduated in the summer of 1949, having majored in business."

He put his business degree to good use, managing and owning several businesses around Silver City before retiring in 1978.

GOD'S UMBRELLA

# HUGHES, BOB

## DOB 3/2/1925, DOD 8/31/2009

During World War II, Bob Hughes served as a gunner aboard a B-26 airplane, which had five turrets with five gunners, a pilot, a co-pilot and a bombardier, he said.

In the first part of July 1943, Hughes was drafted and went into the United States Army Air Forces from his home in Gallup, New Mexico.

"They put me on a train to El Paso, me and the rest of the Indians," Hughes said. "They cut our hair and gave us shots. Many of the Indians had braids and they didn't like having their hair cut."

He had only six weeks of training at Lake Ponchartrain near Baton Rouge, Louisiana, "then they loaded us on a ship. I was seasick every minute of the time."

On a train on his way to the ship, Hughes said he was sitting behind an officer.

"I was a country boy and I didn't know squat," he said. "He asked me how I liked the service, and I said I didn't like it worth a damn. He just looked at me and could tell I was country. I didn't salute him because I had so little training. All they did was boss me around."

After landing in England, he received training as a gunner.

"When I started flying, we were still bombing France," Hughes said. "Then we got an air base in France and we flew from there into Germany."

He was in Europe during 1944 and 1945.

"The first part of 1945, the Germans shot us down and I was a prisoner of war for 15 months," Hughes said. "They kept changing where they had us. They would load us in boxcars or make us walk ten to fifteen miles to the next place."

He said the meals were "bad—that old black bread and some old meat."

They relieved themselves in "honey buckets." They then had to carry them to dump the contents on the Germans' gardens for fertilizer.

"We would go through towns and they would spit on us, kick us, and throw rotten eggs or tomatoes at us," Hughes said.

He reported that a German woman, "Axis Sally," would take those prisoners with tattoos, kill them, skin them and make lampshades out of the skin.

"They would also fill us with propaganda that they had bombed New York and that President [Franklin D.] Roosevelt was dead," Hughes said. "We had no baths, except when we came on a creek or river. We got to swim to put bombs on bridges to keep the Americans out."

While he was a prisoner, he and another soldier escaped at night, but they didn't know where they were going. They ended up in the basement of a castle with barrels of wine.

"The Germans were upstairs partying," Hughes said. "I was inside a barrel for three days and nights. I was scared they would tap my barrel. I finally got out on my own."

German ground soldiers soon recaptured the prisoners and took them back to the camp, where they "beat us, starved us and worked us until late at night."

When the war was over, the German guards disappeared, and the Americans loaded the prisoners into trucks. The former POWs went to England and then on to New York. Hughes weighed only ninety pounds.

"At the end of 1946, I got back home," Hughes said. "There was no way I wanted to stay in the service."

He said the German people were very clean, and "I always said I was going back to Germany, but I haven't."

His wife, Betty, had a brother, Thomas H. Mann, who was in the Bataan Death March and was imprisoned in Japan.

"He was seventeen years old," Betty Hughes said. "He joined in 1940 from Albuquerque. Jobs were hard to find."

She said her sister has a letter from their brother begging his folks to get him out of the Philippines, because he was homesick and hated the humidity.

"I think it haunted my folks," she said. "My other brother, Donald, went in while Thomas was a prisoner. He was drafted. He served in the tank corps."

Betty Hughes said that once the Bataan survivors came home, they were kept in isolation in Santa Fe and were fed to gain weight before their families could see them.

"It was exciting to get V mail even with words censored and blacked out," she said. "We would gather around to hear the news."

She remembers gathering scrap metal during the war and saving bacon grease.

"We would take the team and wagon to gather the metal for the war effort," she said. "We would all sit close to the radio to get the news over the static. We were not allowed to be noisy when the news was on."

Betty was ten years old when Pearl Harbor was attacked. She said everyone was patriotic.

"We didn't grumble and were glad to do our part," she said. "It was a different America then."

She also remembers blackouts with curtains over the windows. She sold war bonds and stamps.

"I would work hard for a ten-cent stamp to put in a book," Betty Hughes said.

Meat, sugar and shoes were rationed. She said some people hoarded sugar and sold it on the black market, but for one family it backfired when the basement flooded and ruined hundreds of pounds of sugar.

"When Mom died, she still had some food stamps from World War II," Betty Hughes reported.

"I was a little girl when a neighbor came over to get me to tell me the 'war is over,'" she said. "We went to town and were really celebrating. Every serviceman was kissing the women, cars were honking, confetti was coming out of every window, [and] flags were waving. It was quite a celebration."

# ROGERS, FRANK

## DOB 01/03/1925

Frank Rogers, a Wisconsin native who has lived in Silver City since 1989, is a veteran of World War II.

"The story about Mr. Magdaleno Leyba's wartime experiences in Saturday's Daily Press was of special interest to me," Rogers said. "I knew Stalag IXB and Bad Orb from the outside, while he had the unfortunate experience to know it on the inside."

Rogers served in the 103rd Infantry Division as messenger and radio operator and, when the communication chief was killed, he was promoted to that position.

"We began our frontline experience in the Vosges Mountains of France, and the last place we took was Innsbruck, Austria," Rogers said. "The rifle company I was in, Company G, 409th Infantry Regiment, had the duty of occupying Bad Orb a few days after another unit had taken it. Stalag IXB was part of our territory."

Rogers had the responsibility of providing communication among the platoons, an added platoon from another company, the battalion headquarters, and the acting commandant of the stalag, who was a British Army major and had been a prisoner there.

The units were connected by wire to a German ten-drop switchboard, which "we had 'liberated' during our travels southward as the front moved. One of my runner/radio operators was just a few credits short of an engineering degree and he made up a headset with mike and earphone which we had taken from a Maginot Line supply building along the way," he said.

"I remember one day visiting the stalag," Rogers said. "It was one of the most disgusting, nauseating sights I have ever experienced. To think that anyone was forced to exist—'live' doesn't sound quite right—under such conditions is almost beyond belief."

Another part of Bad Orb included seven hospitals. The town was, before the war and after, a place where vacationers and those with certain kinds of illnesses came to "take the baths," and the hospitals were there to house those who needed that kind of care.

"When we arrived, they were filled with wounded German soldiers, who then became the responsibility of the Allies," Rogers said. "German doctors, still in their German army uniforms were allowed to move about the town, caring for their wounded, with supplies provided by our side. It took a while for us to understand that they were not 'escaped prisoners of war.'"

He said that, after having tramped through France and Germany, the days they spent there before moving on south were almost idyllic—safe from frontline hazards, and with far less primitive conditions.

"We actually slept in beds," Rogers said.

He was drafted into the Army, although he was given a deferment to finish a semester of college, before leaving his home in Madison, Wisconsin, in July 1943. He said they stayed in France until spring came, as they awaited a spring offensive.

Rogers and his fellow radioman received a pass to Nancy, France.

"We missed the Rhine Offensive," he said. "My buddy volunteered us to move a few miles back from the front. We went to another town and slept in a house with the first sergeant of a mule company. In the morning, we were assigned to move mules."

He said he started with five mules.

"I don't speak horse or mule," Rogers said, "so I lost some. One of the quartermasters on horseback took my mules and I got to walk back to headquarters."

His unit approached the Siegfried Line, where Germans were 700 yards on one side of them, and about 1,500 yards on the other.

"They were unaware of us when we moved in," Rogers said. "But, then, every morning we had a firefight. We would win and they would go back down the mountain."

He said he remembers the funny stuff and tries "not to recall the bad stuff."

One time, when Rogers was on the switchboard, "Bed Check Charlie began strafing a convoy," he said. "I practically strangled myself trying to get out of my headset to get under the table."

Rogers said he was returning to the United States with the 45th Division and was slated to go to the Pacific front, but "halfway across France, the war in the Far East was over."

When he returned to the United States, he still had time to serve because he "didn't have enough points to be discharged," so he became a counselor of discharges and filled out the back of discharge papers.

"I filled out my own and got out on January 12, 1946," Rogers said.

GOD'S UMBRELLA

# Maxwell, Curtis Lile

## DOB 07/11/1924, DOD 09/13/2016

Curtis Lile Maxwell said he was called to serve his country right after he got out of high school. He arrived in El Paso, Texas, on July 7, 1943, to take his physical. They asked him what he wanted, and he said, "the Marine Corps, and they said, 'OK.'"

"I told my mom that I would be back that evening but ended up on a train to San Diego [California]," Maxwell said. "The next morning, I woke up in Yuma, Arizona."

He spent two months in boot camp and then was sent to communications school, where, he said, he made high grades.

"The 5th Division was just starting to form, so I was sent to Camp Pendleton with the 5th," Maxwell said. "They wanted me to be on the telephone for regional communications."

His next stop was Camp Tarawa, Hawaii. He stayed there until he was sent to Iwo Jima, where he arrived on February 19, 1945. His outfit landed on Red Beach 2, but "no place on the island was safe. It was all caves and pillboxes. It was nothing to hear a bullet go right by your ear. You were afraid, but you got to where you were numb."

Now when he thinks about something that is "too great to bear, my mind shuts off. I'll think something, but I'll erase it real quick."

"We had trained real hard all that time and knew what was going on because we were getting news," Maxwell said. "We were told it would take six to eight days to clear the island of Japanese troops, but we knew better because we could see no buildings on top of the ground."

He said the Japanese had facilities up to seven stories down.

"We bombed them time and again, but killed hardly anyone," Maxwell said. "I went in with the 2nd Platoon late in the evening. The first day we missed the bombing, but the second day we didn't. We were there thirty-six days. I saw when they raised the first flag and the second flag on February 23."

The first American flag on Iwo Jima was a small one raised by a different group. Because a larger flag was wanted, a bigger one was raised at the same time the smaller one was taken down.

"On Iwo Jima, it was horrible," Maxwell said. "That's the reason I never talked about it. My kids didn't know about it until they were grown.

"When we were taken off Iwo Jima at night on the thirty-sixth day, they gave us a big meal and we ate," he continued. "We were all sick, and I was never so seasick, because we hadn't eaten during the battle for the island."

He knew and worked with the Navajo Code Talkers and said he has attended a few of their reunions.

"One of their top sergeants, Sandoval, died this year," Maxwell said.

Maxwell ran the division headquarters with the general and "I knew who was there. It aggravates me when someone tries to tell me something that isn't true."

"When I first got on the beach at Iwo Jima, I had my breath taken away by the bombs," Maxwell said. "People ask me why I didn't get a medal. I got a medal—my life."

He said he never saw a Marine slack off and not do what he was supposed to do.

"In training, a lot [of men] got left behind because they knew they wouldn't fit the bill [for battle]," Maxwell said. "They say 6,000 were killed, but what hurts is when they are maimed, and their life is ruined."

He often attends reunions of the 5th Division, where the survivors talk about the pranks they pulled on one another.

After the war, he was sent to Bepo, Japan, for the occupation. The troops were staying in a "big old barracks. I had just gotten off the midnight shift and got in bed in my mummy bag. I saw the sergeant get up. I was almost asleep when he tied up my bag, leaving just a little hole for me to breathe. I couldn't have gotten out of it if I had to. He untied me the next morning, and I played innocent."

A couple of mornings later, the sergeant set out his clothes on his bed and then he hung them up when he got in the shower.

"I took his clothes and towel and spread them out nice on his bed," Maxwell said. "He was a good sport. We loved each other, all of us did. We never did anything mean."

During the occupation, he said a Japanese woman wanted to paint a portrait of him because of his blond hair. She and her mother came in for eight or ten nights and she created the painting.

"It was like I was looking in the mirror," Maxwell said. "I wondered how much I could pay her for it, but I never saw her again."

He said the Japanese treated the American soldiers well and would invite them into their houses for tea.

"We also treated them well," Maxwell said.

Maxwell was discharged on April 10, 1946.

"I don't remember much at all about that trip," Maxwell said. "I do remember when we pulled up in San Diego. Gals in uniform were dancing. It was good to see them."

He said that after his daughter found out that her father was in the Marine Corps, "she would dig and call up the others I served with. She's still finding them and sending me things."

He said the Marine Corps offered to put him through school if he stayed in the service, but he told them he wanted to go home.

"I've been here all my life, except when I was a baby and when I was in the Marines," Maxwell said. "I grew up out at Buckhorn and Cliff and went to high school in Silver City."

His best friend in the Marines was Kendall Cobalt. When Maxwell's daughter was traveling with the youth theater company, Jeremiah People, she went to Sioux Falls, South Dakota, where Cobalt lived, and he walked right up to her and introduced himself.

"All of us had a high respect for each other and we talk and laugh, but never talked about things we saw there," Maxwell said. "When you were in a bloodbath like I was, you don't talk; you don't say things."

GOD'S UMBRELLA

# Soto, Henry G.

## DOB 06/06/1924, DOD 04/22/2013

Henry G. Soto of Silver City celebrated his twentieth birthday during the Normandy invasion that took soldiers into France in World War II.

"Of course, I was afraid," he said. "I remember the birthday because we were still on the ship. At five in the morning, we transferred [to landing ship tanks] and went onto the Omaha Beach. We were lucky because we had a Ranger battalion on our right flank that made the landing before us. They dropped rope ladders for us."

He said the 82nd and 101st Airborne Divisions had dropped into France the night before, but, because the weather was so bad, "they didn't land where they were supposed to. We met up with the paratroopers four or five days later."

Soto met two friends from Grant County—Raul Salcido and George Barela—in a hospital in Le Mans, France.

"Barela was a paratrooper, and he was shot in both ankles when his parachute landed in a tree," Soto said.

Soto served with the 29th Infantry Division, 175th Regiment, Company A of the 1st Battalion.

"I was a platoon runner," Soto said. "Three days into the invasion, they made me a company runner. The outfit picked guys who were small and fast."

He also served as a radio operator during the invasion. While he was a runner, he was wounded in the left leg, foot and elbow, when artillery was firing "left and right and a shell exploded in front of the captain. I was about ten to fifteen feet behind him. Medics treated me and sent me to a field hospital on June 17, 1944."

The following day he was flown back to England lying on a bunk in a C-47.

"I was strapped in, so I wouldn't fall off," Soto said.

He spent about two months in England and saw President Theodore Roosevelt, General Dwight D. Eisenhower and English Prime Minister Winston Churchill when they went through the hospital.

After rehabilitation, Soto was sent back to France.

"Saint Lo was the center of operations," Soto said. "When we got off the ship that time, it was quiet. They loaded us into trucks and sorted us. I still remember my serial number—384411589. You never forget it."

A lieutenant colonel would call out names.

"This one was from Doña Ana, and he sent me to his headquarters and I was reassigned to a service company," Soto said. "After that, I drove a Jeep, carrying a captain, lieutenant or second lieutenant. There were always two of us. We had a .50-caliber machine gun on the Jeep, so we could fire back. I was lucky, because most of the guys who went to France went with infantry companies.

"Several times, I had to drive a captain to Paris," Soto said. "I saw General [George] Patton once and used to see General [Omar] Bradley a lot."

One time, the soldiers put their names in a hat and those drawn got to spend seven days in Paris. Soto was one of the lucky ones.

His medals include the Purple Heart, Bronze Star, Combat Infantry Badge, Good Conduct Medal, Presidential Unit Citation, American Campaign Medal, European-African-Middle-Eastern Campaign Medal with one Bronze Service Star with Arrowhead, World War II Victory Medal, Combat Infantryman Badge and Honorable Service Lapel Button World War II.

Soto was drafted into the Army in 1943 when he was eighteen. Although he was supposed to receive twenty-two weeks of basic training at Camp Waller, Texas, he said he had only thirteen weeks of training when he was sent to Camp Shanks, New York, before going overseas.

"They were replacing the old guys with new recruits," Soto said.

Soldiers would carry rations for three days, but "once in a while, when we were close to the front line, they would take hot dinners to Company A."

It took six men to support one infantryman at the front, according to Soto.

He said Germany's mistake was opening two fronts—on the west toward the rest of Europe and the east toward Russia—"or we would have had a heck of a time."

When the war in Europe was over on May 8, 1945, he was in Mannheim, Germany, still with a service unit.

"Then I got a job at the headquarters in Stuttgart and made the mail run to Mannheim," Soto said. "It was 100 miles, so I left on Monday and came back on Tuesday with mail and supplies."

After the war was over in the Pacific, he left Europe in 1946, and landed in Norfolk, Virginia, where the troops stayed on the ship for three days for medical inspections. After a forty-five-day leave, he had to report to Fort Bliss, Texas, and was discharged February 4, 1946.

# Muñoz, Santiago "Jimmy"

## DOB 11/27/1925

Santiago "Jimmy" Muñoz of Silver City was drafted in 1943.

"I was eighteen years old and still going to school in Cliff [New Mexico]," Muñoz said. "I was born and raised on the Gila River."

He went to Fort Bliss, Texas, where he asked to join the Army, but "they gave me the Navy." He was inducted on April 4, 1943.

"Three hundred of us left here in three loaded buses," Muñoz said. "I asked for the Army, so I'd be with friends."

After his physical, he was put on a train.

"I didn't know where we were going," Muñoz said. "First, we went to Richmond, Virginia."

His next stop was Camp Perry, Virginia, for boot camp. He was placed in Seabee training and learned to run heavy equipment, such as bulldozers, graders and cranes. When he finished training, he was assigned to break in new recruits.

Muñoz was given a thirty-day furlough to go home before being sent overseas.

"It took almost five days to get here by train," he reported.

When he had returned from furlough, his unit was sent to Washington, D.C., to a receiving station, then to Indian Head, Maryland, where captured bombs were being shipped to be disarmed.

"At Indian Head, I saw the Potomac River," Muñoz said. "It was part of the ocean and I saw big ships go by. It was the first time I had seen the ocean."

He said about 150 sailors, twenty-five Marines and thirty WAVES (women's branch of the Naval Reserve) stayed at the base.

His crew was assigned to unload the bombs from the flatbed cars of trains.

"My friend and I set them in a restricted area of a warehouse," Muñoz said. "We also brought out the empty shells and put them on trains where they were taken I don't know where. That's what I did for most of my three years there."

At one point, he was sent to Norfolk, Virginia, and, along with other troops, was put aboard a ship.

"After we were loaded, we got word that the war was over," Muñoz said, "and we didn't get to go. I was pretty happy about that."

He said only one accident happened during his years of handling loaded ordnance.

"One boy got hurt when he was stripping shells," Muñoz said. "They told him not to do it, but he did and blew himself up."

Another time the sailors were rousted out of bed to try to rescue a captain, a WAC and another passenger from a plane whose engine quit over the Potomac and the aircraft landed in the river.

"We couldn't find them that night," Muñoz said. "We found the bodies the next day when they washed to the shore."

During his time in Maryland, he got into a scrape.

"A colored guy, who had finished boot training, would come and push his way into the chow line," Muñoz said. "He pushed me and my buddy out of the way. I told him to move to the back of the line, but he said, 'Nah, I've been doing this all the time.' I got mad, picked up a cup and hit him with it right between the eyes. It knocked him out and I thought I had killed him."

The cook, a good friend of Muñoz, poured ice water over the bully and brought him back to consciousness. The military police took Muñoz.

"I was told to report to the captain's office," Muñoz said. "He told me, 'I'm not going to do anything to you, because he's been pulling that all the time.' The bully was put on restricted orders. He was about seven feet tall and weighed a lot. I don't remember his name, but he was restricted to barracks or sent somewhere else. I didn't see him again. It's the only time I got in trouble, but I guess I did the right thing."

Muñoz was discharged as a seaman first class on February 8, 1946, in San Pedro, California. He returned to

Grant County and began dating Betty Marquez. They were married in September that year.

"I've been ranching ever since I got out of the service," Muñoz said. "I worked for the 2C Cattle Company as the foreman for ten years. Then, I worked for the John Starks Ranch at Whitewater [New Mexico] for thirty-seven and a half years. I was running it when I retired in January 2003. It's been a good life."

# SALAS, JOSÉ

## DOB 04/18/1925, DOD 04/09/2016

José "Pepe" Salas of Bayard served in World War II and became a prisoner of the Germans.

"My poor mother was in the hospital for three weeks when someone told her I had been wounded and had both legs chopped off," Salas said. "Then the government told her that I was a prisoner of war."

Born in Santa Rita, Salas was one of four brothers, who all were in the service. His older brother, Felix, was a prisoner of the Japanese at the same time as José was a POW in Europe. Both came home, because of God's umbrella over them.

Salas was drafted August 9, 1943.

"I passed the test to go to cadet school, so I chose the Army Air Corps," Salas said.

He was trained as a tail gunner on a B-24 Liberator. Salas had his basic training at Shepherd Field, Texas, then went to gunnery school in Harlingen, Texas. In Salt Lake City, Utah, the crew was formed. Overseas training took place at Biggs Field in El Paso, Texas.

He has a photo of the crew taken in Topeka, Kansas.

"They had ten planes in Topeka," Salas said. "Our crew didn't get an airplane, so they took us to Norfolk,

Virginia, and put us on a boat. There were about 3,000 infantry troops and ninety crews on board."

Sixteen days later, after a stop in North Africa, they disembarked in Naples, Italy, where they were put on a train to Foggia, Italy.

"I was put in the 65th Bomb Squadron, 764th Bomb Group of the 15th Air Force," Salas said. "I got there around July 23, 1944. I had been there a couple of days when I was woken early one morning and told to fly."

He said the crew's tail gunner had finished his assignment, so a replacement was needed.

"It wasn't my original group," Salas said. "Richard Freeman was the pilot. On July 25, we were sent to bomb Linz, Austria. Shrapnel started hitting us. I heard someone yell, 'Fighters at six o'clock.' There were five fighters shooting at us from a Fokker 190. I had two direct hits to my turret. I passed out a while and when I woke up my turret was on fire. The side gunner was walking around in circles. I pulled him down and tried to get oxygen on him, but the lines were cut."

Salas said a parachute was put on him, but backward.

"I pushed myself out of the airplane," Salas said, "but the parachute didn't open.

"When I was taking parachute lessons, they told me that if the parachute didn't open to go back to the airplane and get another one," he laughed. "I started pulling parts of the chute out of the bag and it opened. I was coming down over trees, so I pulled the parachute and managed to miss the trees by about twenty feet. I tried to pull myself up on my right leg, but it buckled. The bones in my left leg stuck out. I passed out for a while."

He had landed near a house, but the people closed the door when he called to them.

"Two kids, German soldiers, came up to me and asked me if I had a pistol," Salas said.

They checked him and found he didn't, so they wrapped him in his parachute and carried him on a ladder to the house. A "big redheaded German" spoke to him in English and asked him lots of questions, but Salas gave him his name and rank.

"I did tell him I was from New Mexico," Salas said. "'We're not at war with Mexico,' he told me."

After trips by train and truck, Salas was in a hospital. When he woke up, a Frenchman was talking to him in Spanish. When asked how he knew Salas spoke Spanish, he laughed and told him that Salas had been "cussing" at him in Spanish.

A piece of bone was cut from his leg and he was put in traction for twenty-two days and then into a full-leg cast. While he was in the hospital, Hitler's niece visited him.

"She was very nice to me," Salas said. "Just before Christmas, I started walking on crutches. They gave us a very nice meal and took us to midnight Mass."

He and another POW, Reece Stephenson, who was up to his neck in a body cast, became friends.

"They took us to Vienna, where they used us as guinea pigs, putting nails in our bones to help them heal," Salas said. "Two Red Cross ladies gave us two biscuits. Stephenson warned me not to eat them because they might be poisoned. I ate mine and then pretended I was choking and being poisoned. Then I ate his. He was mad at me."

They were taken to Wells, Austria, and then to Wörsdorf, Germany, to a "beautiful two-story building."

"We were receiving a Red Cross parcel every week," Salas said. "We would take out the candy and cigarettes, and give the food to the cooks, who made nice meals. I gained back the weight I had lost. I was down to eighty pounds but weighed about 150 when we were liberated."

He said they had a "really mean nurse," but she completely changed after she fell in love with an American POW.

An Austrian doctor gave the prisoners information about how the war was going until he was relieved of duty and a German doctor took over.

"They used to let us walk along a beautiful river," Salas said. "The old doctor would come and talk to us and tell us that the war was almost over."

Once when he was allowed to take a bath, he said he almost drowned because he still had a cast on his leg and couldn't get out of the tub. Finally, someone rescued him.

One morning a member of Hitler Youth, an officer, came to the building and said he was going to kill the prisoners.

"The old doctor stood in front of us," Salas said. "Then we heard a big noise. It was an American tank going by. The German soldier took off and we heard that he wrecked his bicycle and ended up in the hospital. We went through the hospital and got all the guns and liquor and got drunk. We started shooting inside the building. It's a wonder we didn't kill ourselves."

Salas said he was given a Swiss watch, which he brought home with him, along with a pistol.

He and Stephenson were separated and sent to different hospitals. He said he slept a lot, and one day when he was talking to a man in a hospital in Germany, the man said: "You speak English! We were about ready to move you to India."

With stops in England, Scotland, Newfoundland and New York, Salas was finally sent to El Paso to Beaumont Army Hospital.

"I called home and I started talking to my sister," Salas said. "We were so emotional, we couldn't talk, but the next day, we talked for two or three hours."

His leg was operated on again and he was put in another cast, but he received a leave to go home.

On July 16, 1945, his brother called from the mine where he was working and asked him if he heard a loud noise.

"It was the day they tested the atomic bomb [at the Trinity Site, White Sands, New Mexico]," Salas said. "I didn't hear it because somebody was giving mañanitas [a Mexican birthday song] to my neighbor."

He had more operations on his leg, but the wound wouldn't heal, until his mother put hierba del indio [a tradional Mexican herbal medicine] on it. The leg healed. In 1996, the wounds opened up again and doctors wanted to amputate, but Salas said, "No."

"I can't stand up, but I can walk with a cane or walker, thanks to God," Salas said.

His and Felix's brother Manuel fought in the Aleutians against the Japanese and in the Battle of the Bulge against the Germans. Their brother Eusebio was drafted right after the war and served in the Army during the occupation of Japan.

"The crew I was with thought I had been killed," Salas said. "In 1995, I heard from one of them when he called me and said, 'You're supposed to be dead.'"

The last reunion he went to was in 1990 in Tucson, Arizona. Salas said he is the last of his crew; his buddy died in 2008.

GOD'S UMBRELLA

# HUFF, MELVIN

## DOB 02/07/1919, DOD 06/29/2013

Melvin Huff was drafted into World War II, although his two older brothers who were physicians went into the service by volunteering.

"Billie Beth [Huff's wife] and I came home [from Las Cruces] to take care of Ma," Huff said. "I went to work at Kennecott—until 1943 when they took the copper workers off the protected list."

He was drafted in November 1943.

"If they had just waited a few months, I would have been old enough they wouldn't have gotten to me," Huff said.

His first stop was Fort Bliss, Texas, followed by Camp Hood, Texas, for basic training.

"Basic was cut short by two weeks, because the Germans made a big push," Huff said.

"Before I left Hood, a couple of boys—I was quite a bit older—asked me to go with them to San Antonio. We got four-day passes," Huff said. "I supported myself on poker in those days. I'd just made a killing that weekend."

The soldiers went to Macy's. Huff saw a pantsuit in the display window that he wanted to buy for his wife. He went inside and asked one of the salesgirls to try it on to see if it would fit her. She said yes.

"I thought it would fit Billie Beth, so I bought it and sent it home. It fit her like a glove."

Huff's mother-in-law was a good tailor.

"They were amazed that it fit so well, just by my looking at it," Huff said, "so I did quite a bit of the shopping for Billie Beth after that."

He was sent to Fort Benning, Georgia, as an officers' training cadet.

"I washed out in the latter part of training," Huff said. "I was waiting for reassignment.

"I went in for a physical and a captain was sitting there, and he had the insignia of a doctor. I said, 'Doctor, they called me in for a physical.' He said, 'I'm a captain.' And I said, 'If that means more to you than your degree, it's fine with me.'"

The captain did no examination, but said Huff was "fit for overseas duty and that was my physical."

"I had a choice of a radar outfit or experimental recoilless rifle duty," Huff said. "Several of us found out the radar fellows had to carry a thirty-five- to thirty-nine-pound pack, so we went with the rifle."

He said that, although the rifle was quite accurate, it "did not catch on because the flare when it was fired was too visible."

"We stayed at Benning, instructing officer candidates in the use of the rifle for about six months," Huff said.

Seven men and an officer made up a team. Four of the teams were sent to Camp Swift near Bastrop, Texas.

"We stayed on base," Huff said. "We were training the 2nd Division in [the use of] the recoilless rifle."

He said he took the medical orderly job for the rifle teams. He would fill out the daily reports and sign them and send them

"I only had trouble one time," Huff said.

One of the officers came in and saw the report that Huff had just completed. The officer grabbed it up and signed it.

"I asked him why he did that, because I'd have to do it all over again," Huff said.

The officer told him to send it in, so Huff did so. Sure enough, it was returned, and he had to redo it.

"We didn't see our officers much when we were at Camp Swift," Huff said. "I don't know where they were and what they were doing, but we were all sergeants and we knew what to do."

Shortly before Christmas 1944, Huff said, because he was clerk of the teams, he was trying to figure out how many had vacation time.

"A major came in who was attached to us," Huff said. "I told him I was trying to find out how many of the men I could let go for Christmas. He asked me how many were of the same intelligence quotient. I said, 'Pretty much all of them.' He said, 'Then we'll have to absorb you.' I don't know what happened or how many were absorbed [into another unit]. And only some of us got leave."

It was a "long time before they gave up on the recoilless rifle," according to Huff. The rifle was a .57-millimeter-caliber gun with a .75-millimeter casing that had holes drilled around it. It had enough powder to propel the .57-millimeter shell. The rifle would exhaust out the rear. They also had a .75-millimeter rifle in a .155-millimeter casing on a tripod.

"It had a fix on the back of it to keep it balanced, so there would be no movement, so it could be fired from the shoulder, although it was a little heavy," Huff said.

"We would put on a good show," he said. "One time at night, I was doing the lecturing and called for a piece to be fired and the piece took off, too."

The captain wanted to know what happened and Huff said he didn't know, but he would find out.

"I don't know how the kid had put it together in the dark, and I don't know how it fired," Huff said.

Fortunately, no one was hurt.

Another time, the teams had to demonstrate the rifle for General Mark Clark.

"I went out with the boys, and I was standing in the background," Huff said. "A boy was shooting the rifle and laying phosphorous shells in a trench a good quarter of a mile away. The general asked me how many of the team could do that. I said, 'All of them.'"

General Clark asked why the troops had not had the rifles for combat. Huff explained that the rifle was experimental.

"We're the only ones that know about it," Huff said. "He said he wished he'd had them in Europe."

Huff was in the Army for fifteen months. He said he contacted the Red Cross, and the organization helped him get out of the service. He returned to Silver City around the first of March 1945.

"I stayed [at Camp Swift] until they let me out to come home," Huff said. "I only accepted five dollars out of each paycheck and the rest came to Billie Beth for her and the two kids. I wanted to come home and take care of them. I was always looking for somebody to fire me, but they never did."

At Fort Bliss, where Huff was discharged, he was asked if he wanted to be in the reserves.

"I said, 'No,'" Huff said. "I came on home, and was quite relieved, and I went to work."

GOD'S UMBRELLA

# Osmer, Louis

## DOB 10/26/1924 DOD 03/06/2018

Louis Osmer of Silver City was drafted into the United States Army in 1943.

According to Osmer, Virgil Cosby, who made his living hauling sand, drove "a bunch of us who were drafted" to El Paso to be inducted.

"We were put in tents with Army cots in each corner," Osmer said. "It was gravelly and there was a lot of dust at Fort Bliss. We used our clothes for pillows and had no pad or anything to sleep on. The chow was abominable. I didn't think much of the Army, so, in my civvies, I went over the fence, hailed a taxi and asked the driver to take me to the nearest Marine recruiter."

He passed the test and physical to become a Marine. He was inducted in August 1943. After two weeks at home, he was "escorted and entrained, where we enjoyed a coal-burning train to San Diego, California."

The barracks had double bunks with pads.

Osmer was assigned to Platoon 580. At four in the morning, the Marines were arranged according to height and walked to the chow hall.

"We had to eat everything," Osmer said. "We had gravy on toast for breakfast, as well as fruit cocktail and lots of milk in pitchers."

They were taken back for orientation and the next day they were issued clothing—white T-shirts, white skivvies, dungarees and field boots.

"We had to make the boots shine, spit-shine," Osmer said.

The recruits were marched early in the morning to the drill field for calisthenics in time to music.

"Shortly, we were given our khakis—trousers without hip pockets, a khaki shirt and a foraging cap, which turned into a bag for foraging," Osmer said. "Then we got our dress greens and they were lumpy and wrinkled. Then another set of khakis, a green overcoat and a green foraging cap, as well as a sea bag to hold it all."

The Marines were taught how to make a bed with hospital corners so tight that a quarter had to bounce. If it didn't, the bed had to be remade.

Their two field packs made an eighty-pound pack, with straps and buckles and "puzzling appurtenances." The Marines were issued scrub brushes and GI soap, which was yellow, with which they scrubbed themselves and their huts.

"A lieutenant would come around and look for dust with his white gloves," Osmer said. "He would find it."

They were issued rifles, but no ammunition at first, and taught how to clean their rifle bore with hot soapy water and ramrods.

"The Marine Corps is still a rifle outfit," Osmer said.

He wrote to his mother to ask for a steam iron and starch, which she sent.

"I would get five dollars a piece because I had the only iron in the platoon," Osmer said.

"We were beginning to learn to march while singing a cadence," Osmer said. "Pretty soon we were a marching platoon. The sound of all those boots striking at the same time invoked pride."

On graduation day, the men received their private first class stripes.

"That first stripe means a lot," Osmer said.

He was sent to Camp Mathews, California, which was a rifle camp. The Marines first learned how to fire while down on their stomachs, then in a sitting position, then kneeling, and finally from a standing position.

"I fired and made a perfect bull's-eye," Osmer said. "I did the same thing over and over. They asked me if I wanted to be a coach and I said, 'No.'"

There were three grades of riflemen—rifleman, marksman and expert.

"I was a marksman," Osmer said. "The reason I didn't make expert was that I made a bet with a Marine named Burke from North Carolina. He broke a tooth out of my rifle sight with a Bowie knife, so it had a hole in it and he won the bet that I wouldn't make expert."

At Camp Mathews, he reported there were no mattress pads, just boards to sleep on.

"I got to where it was acceptable, and I could sleep," Osmer said.

Next, for training in hand grenades, semaphore and Morse code, was Camp Pendleton, California, and then they went to Miramar, California, where the Marines awaited their assignments.

"I passed the test for aviation ordnance—bombs, torpedoes, mines, guns and small arms," Osmer said.

He also was trained on Thompson machine guns and Browning Automatic .45-caliber Colts.

He was shipped to Norman, Oklahoma, for "fast training."

"For instance, here's a bomb fuse," Osmer said. "You better be able to set it correctly or it was going to detonate. I survived the training and was shipped to Cherry Point, North Carolina, for aerial gunnery training. The instructors were lady Marines, who were dedicated and effective."

A photo of an aircraft would be flashed for one-tenth of a second.

"Soon, we knew every Japanese airship and every Kraut [German] one," Osmer said. "By the time they were showing a silhouette for one-forty-fifth of a second, it was easy to tell whose plane it was."

He was assigned to Parris Island, South Carolina, where we "engaged with pilots for strafing and bombing runs," using targets. He remembered one red-headed pilot who later became an ace and got six kills in combat.

Osmer boarded a troop ship, with 3,000 other troops, in San Diego and "headed west."

"We hit a becalmed sea, as flat as anything, like glass," he said. "It traveled at two knots for about five days. It was hot from the sun, but we saw two waterspouts, sperm whales, flying fish and porpoises alongside. We also could see, at night, phosphorescence in the bow wave."

The ship entered Buckner Bay on Okinawa and formed a landing party on a Landing Craft, Vehicle, Personnel (LCVP).

"We learned to dig rapidly when the Japs fired on us," Osmer said. "Here came a battalion of Seabees. There was a big old kid with a helmet on top of his seabag. It was my brother, so I knew he was on the island."

Osmer was in Marine Air Group 31, Squadron 224, and later Squadron 311, when things "calmed down." He said while things were "quietening down," the ship did scouting and patrolling and "had some engagements with Japanese troops and old ladies with hand grenades. They were more dangerous than the soldiers."

It was on Okinawa that Osmer got to chat briefly with war correspondent Ernie Pyle, who sought out New Mexicans. Pyle was later killed on Ie Shima, a small island off Okinawa.

The troops endured two typhoons while on Okinawa. When a typhoon was approaching, Osmer told a "scrounge" named Wallace to get some rope.

"We roped the tent down, so it looked like a spider web," Osmer said, "but it was the only one standing after the blow."

After Japan had surrendered, Osmer was about to board the USS Alcoa Polaris, when his brother "came by for a visit."

"He handed me my rifle as I climbed up the rope," Osmer said. "We sailed into another storm—a really serious one. The ship was shuddering with the waves, but the captain kept it headed into the storm and the ship held together. When the wind and seas abated, we had six days of fog."

When the ship was steaming slowly into Tokyo Bay, a Landing Ship, Tank (LST) cut in front of it. Osmer said the "skipper rang 'all reverse,' and we avoided a collision by feet."

The troops were sent to Yokosuka, where they occupied wooden Japanese bunkers fitted with steel turnbuckles. When an earthquake would hit, the building would shake, but not fall apart.

Underground hangars had been built where the Japanese constructed and built aircraft before flying them out of a tunnel.

"They had an upper-wing monoplane with enough fuel tanks to bomb Washington, D.C.," Osmer said.

The troops had orders to disable all aircraft by cutting the propeller shafts and dropping them in front of the aircraft. They also repatriated thousands of Japanese troops from China and "helped preserve what is now China. The Japanese had aircraft in China, but didn't have enough fuel to get them back to Japan."

Two American hospital ships—the USS Bountiful and the USS Benevolence—were in Tokyo Bay at the same time Osmer's ship was there.

"One of the nurses was from Silver City," he said.

According to Osmer, the bombs that landed on Japan and caused the country to surrender "saved hundreds of thousands of American lives, and probably millions, counting the Japanese."

He served in Japan during the occupation until he had enough points to return home. He described the citizens as "gentle people."

Osmer returned to San Diego Harbor on the USS War Hawk.

"When we got ashore, ladies had beverages for us," he said. "Ninety percent of the guys chose milk."

He said he "made buck sergeant in the field and received an honorable discharge."

"I was so damn green, I enjoyed the whole damn war," Osmer concluded.

GOD'S UMBRELLA

# Leyba, Jr., Magdaleno H.

## DOB 7/24/1925, DOD 6/23/2011

Magdaleno H. "Nano" Leyba Jr. of Silver City was drafted into the United States Army in 1943. He was inducted into the Army on October 4, 1943, and was honorably discharged December 7, 1945, at Fort Bliss, Texas, where he had entered the service. He served as a military policeman in the 75th Infantry Division.

"When I was drafted I only spoke a little English," Leyba said. "In the Army, I started learning more and read pocketbooks so I could understand better."

His wife, Nellie, said he now reads more than she does. He also likes to work on jigsaw puzzles, several of which were laid out on a table at his house. Leyba recounted some of his commentary in English and most in Spanish through a family friend—Robert Polanco, a Vietnam veteran—who served as a translator.

Leyba was only twenty years old when he was taken prisoner by the Germans. He spent 180 days as a prisoner of war in 1945.

He lived in three POW camps but could remember the names of only two—Stalag XIIA in Limburg, Germany, and Stalag IXB in Bad Orb.

According to Leyba, the men slept sometimes on straw and often on the floor or ground, with one blanket.

Leyba was by himself when a sergeant and nine men came to where he was at one of the POW camps. The Germans soon arrived and asked them to surrender. The eleven men were taken to a building, where they were put in a sheep corral.

"The next day we moved to a warehouse where there were lots of American soldier POWs," Leyba said. "There was a lot of snow and it was so cold our blankets froze to the ground."

When prisoners died, shovels and pickaxes had to be used to pry their frozen bodies from the ground, so they could be buried.

He described the food as bread with sawdust mixed in with the little bit of flour.

"I remember the sticks in the sawdust," Leyba said. "On Sundays we got a soup made of water and rice."

Once when the prisoners were being marched to another site, they came upon a German truck stuck in the mud. They were ordered to push it out, but the men were so weak that they couldn't push it.

"One of the Americans said, 'Give us something to eat and we'll move the truck,'" Leyba said. "The Germans said, 'No.'"

He said the group spent two weeks in Limburg and did no work.

The prisoners were given their ration and locked into a boxcar to be moved.

"We were packed in like sardines, and no air was moving in the car until an American broke a window," Leyba said. "It was amazing that only one prisoner died."

In the next prison camp, Americans were joined by Frenchmen, Russians and Indians with turbans who were also POWs, according to Leyba.

"The Russians were put by themselves because when a guard took them food, they killed him," Leyba said.

He said the guards were not nice to the POWs.

"One afternoon, I was sent to get water," Leyba said. "I had been given a bone to chew. I dipped it in the water to try to get a scrap of meat off it. I was busy chewing on it when a German guard yelled at me. I didn't hear him, so he came up behind me and knocked me into the ditch with his rifle butt."

At one POW camp, the prisoners were taken out at night to clear roads that American bombing raids had damaged.

"On one of the trips, we came upon a hill of dirt where the Germans had hidden beets and potatoes," Leyba said. "Some of the POWs kept an eye on the guards while others of us rushed to get the potatoes. Those potatoes were delicious."

In the afternoons, he said, it was often terrible when the American P-38s were coming in, but the good thing was that C-rations were often dropped to them from the planes.

The 3rd Armored Division liberated the prisoners in 1945.

"We were so weak that some of us had to be carried into the truck to take us to France," Leyba said. "The Red Cross gave us food and goodies before we were sent back to the United States."

Before he was captured, Leyba said, he weighed about 150 pounds, but when he was liberated, probably about seventy-five pounds.

Nellie said that, when she first met him, he told her he would never again be hungry, because he would keep peanut butter and jelly in the car.

"When we were first married, in 1946, he would have nightmares or get out of bed and try to hide," she said. "With psychiatric care he got better, but he was very depressed."

Former soldiers have a bond, like a brotherhood, Polanco said.

"We experienced things that only other soldiers will believe," he said. "Even if we serve in different wars, we still have a bond."

"He hopes none of his grandkids have to go to war," Nellie said.

Polanco said, "A lot of Hispanics served in World War II. He [Leyba] wants his story told, because many people think not many Hispanics served."

In a touch of irony, Leyba at one point, before he was drafted, guarded German POWS who were held at Fort Bayard in Grant County.

He said he treated them well and sometimes gave them food.

According to Polanco, many of the German POWS, once the war was over, did not return to their homeland, but stayed in New Mexico.

Leyba was a corporal when he was discharged, having received the Combat Infantryman Badge, and decorations and citations, including those for serving in the American Theater and the European-African-Middle-Eastern Theater. He also was awarded the Good Conduct and Victory medals.

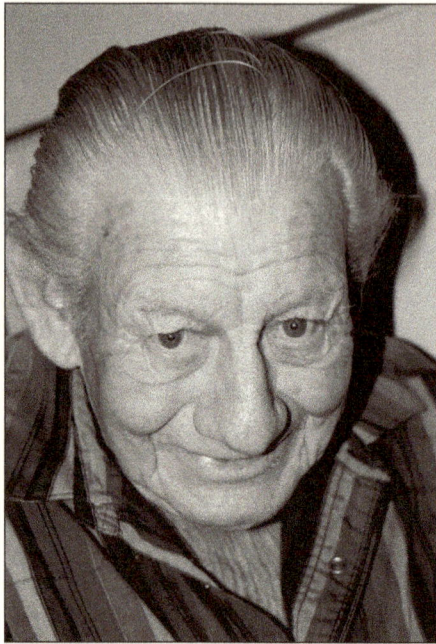

# SCHLIM, MARTIN

## DOB 6/25/1925, DOD 10/27/2009

Martin Schlim of Hurley, New Mexico, was living in Kansas when he turned eighteen years old and was drafted into the United States Army in 1943. He did not attend high school because he had to help his father at their farm.

He served in Europe in the artillery under General George S. Patton in the Third United States Army. It was known as "Patton's own."

"I served under Patton at first in heavy artillery in southern France," Schlim said. "We also went to Cologne, Germany."

He fired howitzer cannons, which he estimated could hit targets up to thirty miles away.

He saw a lot of action, but "I could write a letter while the shells were going off," he said. "Shells were falling not too far away. They would light up and the moon was up. I was writing letters to Mom and Dad and my friends."

Schlim arrived in Europe in November 1943 and remained there until he returned to the United States in June 1946.

Toward the end of the war in 1945, he guarded German prisoners of war in Germany.

"I was never wounded," Schlim said. "They couldn't shoot very good. I was always shooting at somebody, and they were shooting back at me."

Schlim was in basic training at Camp Roberts, California, in the same outfit as the entertainer Red Skelton.

"We were in the kitchen peeling potatoes one day and Red said, 'That's good enough' and threw the potato in the pile," Schlim said. "The cook said, 'Glad when the day's over with you two.'"

During the war, Schlim served as a private, but made staff sergeant when he signed up for more service.

He remained in the Army until 1955. In 1956, he joined the Marine Corps.

While still in the Army, he served in the Korean War. He took part in two major battles—Heartbreak Ridge and Bloody Ridge.

Heartbreak Ridge was a month-long battle from September 13 to October 15, 1951. The battle site is in the hills of North Korea a few miles north of the 38th parallel north, the prewar boundary between Korea and South Korea, near Chorwon.

Bloody Ridge was a ground combat battle that took place from August 18 to September 5, 1951. Located in hills north of the 38th parallel north in the central Korean mountain range, the battle was fought between the North Korean forces of the Korean People's Army and the United Nations forces consisting of the Republic of Korea Army units and the United States 2nd Infantry Divison.

After Schlim got out of the Army, he spent two years in Hawaii and a year in Okinawa with the Marines.

He was in Okinawa when a typhoon hit.

"We had twenty-four inches of rain in twenty-four hours, then a tidal wave about ten or eleven o'clock that night," Schlim said. "Water was coming in the mess hall. We opened the door and shoved it out."

He served as a cook during his stint with the Marines.

"I could make forty-seven pies in two and a half hours," Schlim said. "That was when I was in Okinawa."

GOD'S UMBRELLA

# WILT, BILL

## DOB 1923, DOD 05/05/2012

"I wanted to volunteer for World War II," Bill Wilt, a Grant County resident, said, "but my mother wouldn't let me, so I was drafted."

He was born in West Virginia but was living in Ohio because "there was no work in West Virginia. We had relatives in Ohio, so I went there."

Wilt had served in the Civilian Conservation Corps, and said he had to fill out a questionnaire when he went into the Army in 1943. The United States was trying to make up an Army as quickly as possible.

"I was sent to Santa Anita, California, and trained in ordnance," Wilt said. "They were contemplating a war similar to World War I, where the troops were right next to each other."

They were trained to use the enemy's ordnance, as well.

"If we were retreating, we were supposed to destroy everything we left, so the enemy couldn't use it," Wilt said. "In Patton's Third Army, we didn't move like that. Some days we moved seventy miles. Patton believed if we gave the enemy time to dig in, we would need to outnumber them by seven to one because we would lose a lot of people, so we didn't let them dig in."

One morning, the officers called for volunteers for the infantry.

"Since I wasn't getting any action, I put my hand up," Wilt said. "I was the only one in the company that did that."

When he transferred from ordnance to infantry, no position existed that was comparable to his ordnance rank, "so I became a 'private no class' soldier for a while until I got my first stripe back."

He said he didn't pay much attention to where he was because he thought it was going to be a long war.

"I was in all five major battles from Normandy on to the end," Wilt said. "We ended up down in Czechoslovakia in Pilsen, where Pilsner beer came from. The people there were kind of holding their breath because the Russians were about to move in and they didn't know what to expect."

Russia and China were allies of the United States.

"We weren't exactly friendly," Wilt said. "We just had a common enemy."

The last battle he fought in was the Battle of the Bulge.

"That was a battle," Wilt said. "The Germans had been hammering at our lines trying to find the soft spot. They broke through on our way to Antwerp, Belgium, to resupply."

His company had been given rest and recreation (R & R) in Luxembourg.

"We never got to see it," Wilt said. "We pulled in after dark, and the Battle of the Bulge started. We loaded back up and went back to the front line."

He said in the movie Silent Night, he knew the story was true, because "I was there."

An American squad got lost and stopped at a house and asked to spend the night. The woman said, "yes." When a German squad asked to stay, she said, "yes." She took the arms away from both so they wouldn't shoot up her house. Through the night the troops became friendly.

Shortly after landing in Normandy, Wilt said a sign went up on the latrine that it was closed. It was covered by a mound of dirt. Most of the French were happy to see Americans.

"Little girls came from the town and put flowers on it," Wilt laughed. "They had a priest bless it, too."

He said that everywhere the GIs went, they loved the little kids.

"They made out like bandits, because we gave them gum and candy," Wilt said. "That was a bright spot in the war."

At Ardennes, France, Wilt said Patton wanted to attack from the rear, but wasn't allowed to.

"That would have been a wise move," Wilt said.

During a stint in Paris, Wilt had a picture of himself painted on silk by a sidewalk artist. He sent the picture to his mother, and when he returned home he asked her about it.

"'I burned it,' she told me," Wilt said. "She said, 'It didn't look like you.' I had lost weight. I liked it, but she didn't.

"At the start of the war, I was gung-ho," Wilt said. "Around about the time I went in, I found out that not only the enemy used propaganda, but we did, too.

"I decided I would only shoot at a German if I had to," Wilt said. "The regular German soldiers didn't want to fight, either."

After Wilt and his wife, Mary Ellen, moved to Grant County in 1992, he became friends with Heinz Neumann, a former German soldier.

"He was wounded in Normandy and didn't get to see the rest of the war," Wilt said. "I told him he didn't miss a thing. We fought in the same battles on opposite sides."

Wilt had two brothers, David and Lawrence, who also served in World War II and were in the Navy.

Although he was offered a bonus and a promotion, "when the war ended, all I wanted out of the Army was me," Wilt said.

He retired with sergeant's stripes.

"They were in a hurry back then," Wilt said. "In peace-time, it would have taken about nine years to get them."

Wilt received the Good Conduct Medal, Combat Infantry Badge, the World War II Victory Medal and the Europe-Africa-Middle Eastern Campaign Medal with five Bronze Stars for the five battles, which became a Silver Star.

Wilt fought in Normandy, Northern France, Rhineland, Ardennes and Central Europe battles—the five major campaigns of the European Theater.

GOD'S UMBRELLA

# MANNING, WAYNE ADRIAN

## DOB ABOUT 1921

Wayne Adrian Manning was twenty-two years old when he was drafted into the service while living in Albuquerque.

His brother, Rance, who was one year and ten months younger, preceded him into the service.

"He told me that when he finished his physical in Santa Fe, he was asked by a chief what service he wanted," Manning said. "Rance told him he wanted the Coast Guard. The chief said, 'You're in the Navy.' I got the same chief and I told him I wanted Navy, because I hoped to see my brother once in a while. The chief told me, 'You're in the Coast Guard.'"

Manning was sent to Alameda, California, to Coast Guard Island for boot camp.

"I finished on September 28, 1943, and went aboard the USS Sausalito, a brand-new patrol frigate with 127 men aboard," Manning said. "The library in the town of Sausalito gave us a library of 3,000 to 4,000 books. We had plenty to read."

He was then sent to San Diego, where the ship had a six-week shakedown cruise.

While aboard the Sausalito in the South Pacific for about six months, Manning traveled to Iwo Jima, but never went ashore. The Sausalito was fired upon by Japanese troops near Iwo Jima and near the Solomon Islands.

"One time we dropped a depth charge on a submarine, but I don't know if we got it," Manning said. "When we set it off, it made the ship raise up and go 'yoing, yoing, yoing.' It cracked the ship, but only one compartment."

The Sausalito had to return to the Bethlehem Steel yard near Oakland, California, for repairs.

"On our way back to dry dock, I was 'feeding the fish,'" Manning said. "I was seasick a lot. They gave me pills, but they didn't do much good. I was told later that the 'all-purpose capsules' were given for everything. Three others and I got taken off the ship for chronic seasickness."

He said the ship was later given to the Russians.

"I wish they'd given it to them before I got on it," Manning said. "I was miserable the whole time I was at sea. I slept on the top deck on top of vent covers. A fellow told me to eat a lemon and it would cure me. Baloney! It was sour when it came up. [A buddy, James] Ramos was sick right along with me."

After three weeks back at Coast Guard Island, Manning and Ramos, who were together throughout their entire service, were sent to Front Royal, Virginia, where Manning started training with war dogs as part of the K-9 Corps at the Army post.

"As long as I was there, I wore Army fatigues," Manning said. "Then James and I were shipped to Edenton, North Carolina, for six months. We were the last two of our group to go there. It was a Marine air base and we would load planes with ammunition."

The ammo dump was guarded twenty-four hours a day, seven days a week, with eight-hour shifts. During Manning's stint on guard duty, a German who had disembarked from a submarine was caught attempting to blow up the ammo dump. Manning said he and Ramos didn't like the guard duty nor the town for liberty and threatened "to go over the hill." Two weeks later, they were sent to Baltimore for advanced canine school.

"There were forty of us in the class with 800 dogs," Manning said. "People throughout the United States would send dogs to us. There were all kinds, but we mostly used the German shepherds and Doberman pinschers. We liked the shepherds the best, because the Dobermans were too high-strung."

The dogs were taught to work off leash and were used overseas to sniff out the enemy.

"I was trained as a dog handler," Manning said. "If the war had lasted two more weeks, I would have been overseas. We were ready to go and just waiting for orders. Then we had to detrain the dogs and send them back to the owners if they wanted them."

He said some dogs had become too fierce and had to be euthanized.

Manning recounted a dog story his brother, Rance, told him.

When Rance was on liberty before shipping out, he and the other sailors were warned not to bring a cat or dog aboard or they would be court-martialed.

They were on the USS Yarnell and sixty miles at sea when a dog came "rolling down the deck." Although the captain asked the person who brought the dog aboard to "report to the bridge," no one did. After the third request, the captain took liberty privileges away from everyone, but still no one confessed.

The dog became their lifesaver, because whenever a Japanese kamikaze plane was approaching, before the humans could hear the hum, the dog would start running in circles and whining. The captain would call "General Quarters" (an order to man the battle stations) and the guns aboard would be ready for the planes when they came out of the direct sunlight.

"Rance said the [kamikaze] pilot was so close, he could see him ready for impact," Manning said. "A tracer bullet blew him up and bits of the Japanese and the plane landed all over the deck. If the dog hadn't warned them, it would have hit midships and killed at least 100 men. No one ever did admit to bringing the dog aboard."

Manning was discharged in St. Louis, Missouri, on September. 5, 1945.

# CHAPTER 9

༄

## VOLUNTEERED IN 1944

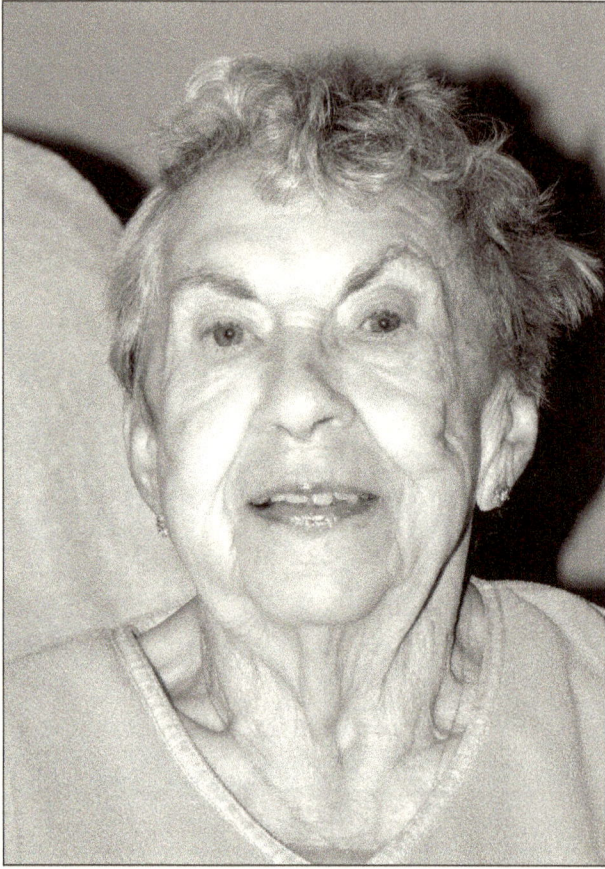

GOD'S UMBRELLA

# WILLIAMS, MARIAN

## DOB 07/08/1927, DOD 02/09/2015

Marian Williams of Silver City joined the Army when she graduated from high school in 1944. The military paid for her four years in nursing school with the Sisters of the Sorrowful Mother in Marshfield, Wisconsin.

"The military paid for my uniforms and tuition," Williams said. "We started out as student nurses and were considered cadets after we took the oath [of military service]."

The war was still on and "they needed nurses. That was the reason for the program," she said.

"When the war got over, I remember the hullabaloo of celebration," she said.

When she graduated from nursing school, she was sent to St. Joseph's Hospital in Madison, Wisconsin, to take a three-day test certifying her as a registered nurse.

"The military planned to send me somewhere when I graduated," Williams said. "They sent me to Fort Bayard, New Mexico. My folks brought me out in the summer of 1948 in a 1948 Chevy. It was a carryall, like a van."

She said two other classmates were also sent to Fort Bayard, a Veterans Administration (VA) hospital.

"We lived in the Nurses Quarters," Williams said. "We treated soldiers with tuberculosis, who had been discharged from the service."

Although she had asthma, once she moved to New Mexico, she said she never had it again.

When Williams was in nursing school, she and the other students received a vaccine for tuberculosis.

"When I got to Fort Bayard, I got the shot again," Williams said. "At Fort Bayard we handed out streptomycin, and penicillin shots in the rear end."

The nurses wore cloth masks to prevent their contracting tuberculosis.

"We would wash them and put them back on," Williams said.

Her retirement is a combination of military benefits and VA benefits through the state, because the Fort Bayard hospital was transferred from the VA to the state of New Mexico.

"I never moved from job to job," Williams said. "I stayed at Fort Bayard for my whole career. If I were to write a job résumé, I could get it all on one sheet of paper. My career is one-line long."

Williams continues to belong to the American Nurses Association, of which she has been a member for fifty-two years.

Williams met and married her first husband, Wayne Toney, in Grant County. Their four children still live in the area. Toney served in Japan, and his father worked transporting soldiers to Fort Bayard from the Bayard railroad station.

After Toney's death, she married Tom Williams, who worked for the Kennecott Copper Corporation in its smelter for forty-three years.

# GARCIA, PEDRO

## DOB 1/31/1921, DOD 5/26/2011

Pedro "Pete" Garcia was born in Santa Rita, New Mexico. He volunteered for the Marines and on June 5, 1944, went to El Paso to be inducted.

Altogether he had five weeks of basic training at the San Diego Marine Corps Base, California, and training as a Browning automatic rifleman at Camp Pendleton, California. The Browning Automatic Rifle (BAR) was the first of the big automatic rifles, he said.

When Garcia was sent to Guadalcanal in the fall of 1944, the island was already secured.

He was then shipped to Okinawa with the 6th Marine Division.

"It was April 1, 1945," Garcia said, "and when I got there, they were still fighting."

They landed at Bolo Point and traveled to Kadena and Yontan airfields, which were soon secured.

"When we landed, there were no Japanese around," Garcia said. "Their strategy was to let us land, so for several days we didn't seen any Japanese."

The group headed southward. The first line of the Japanese defense was the Shuri Line, with the heaviest fighting and bloodiest battles at Sugarloaf. According to

Garcia's son Roberto, the Japanese drew the American troops to the south away from Japan, because they knew their days were numbered. On the south of the island were thousands of caves where the Japanese troops could hide.

"Soon after we landed, a Japanese pilot landed at the airfield," Garcia said. "There's always some guy who doesn't get the word, but we didn't kill him."

During his time in Okinawa, he was on the Ryukyu Islands chain and le Shima Island, where the journalist Ernie Pyle was killed by a sniper on April 18, 1945.

"We went in and out of Iwo Jima, too," Garcia said.

While in Okinawa, he reported that the troops came upon a schoolhouse.

"I saw writing in Spanish on the blackboard," Garcia said. "I asked the teacher who wrote it. She said she did. She was from South America and was on vacation when the war started, so she was stuck there and decided to teach the kids." Garcia had been speaking with the teacher in Spanish.

When they came to another place, a man came out speaking Japanese.

"My buddy, Mike Prisnik, said, 'Hey, Pete, come here,'" Garcia laughed. "I said, 'How am I supposed to understand them? I don't speak Japanese. That was Spanish at the school.'"

Prisknik asked him one day who Siria was.

"I told him she was my wife," Garcia said. "He told me I talked to her all night."

Garcia said he and Prisnik, who was from New York, wrote back and forth for years, especially at Christmas. One year, the card Garcia sent came back. So he sent another card, but it also came back, "so evidently he died or something happened to him."

"I was in Okinawa until I was wounded on May 19 at Sugarloaf," Garcia continued. "I went up Sugarloaf twice. They ran us out the first time; we went back a second time.

"They sent me to Guam to the hospital," Garcia continued. "I never knew how I got there, but evidently they flew me."

He was wounded in the back.

"The doctor told me, 'Son, a quarter of an inch more and you would have never been able to walk,'" Garcia said.

He said that once he could get up and walk a little bit, some of the other troops there told him that the Japanese had been sneaking in and taking food, because they were no longer receiving supplies.

"I ended up in the San Diego Hospital after a stop in Hawaii," he said.

He stayed there several months, and his wife, Siria, with the two older children, lived there until he was better.

On October 11, 1945, Garcia received the Purple Heart medal while he was still in the hospital. He served as a private first class.

While in the service, he also received a sharpshooter award.

His time in the Pacific Theater encompassed a bit more than seven months. He arrived in Guadalcanal on November 10, 1944, and left Guam on June 17, 1945.

When Garcia arrived home, he had a reenlistment offer, but he was still recuperating.

He said his children, Horace, who was about five or six years old, and Gogi, who was two or three, didn't know who he was. The family had been staying with Garcia's father, and they thought he was "Daddy."

"It's been a good life," Garcia said. "When I came home, I went back to work for Kennecott [Copper Corporation] as a painter. I spent forty-one and a half years with Kennecott."

Now that he is retired, he makes canes that look like gunstocks.

"I wrote down who I've given them to," Garcia said. "I've made seventy-two of them."

438                    GOD'S UMBRELLA

# WHATLEY, JAMES

## DOB ABOUT 1926

James Whatley, who used to live in Silver City and now resides in Deming, New Mexico, said he patrolled the autobahn in Germany.

"I was in riot control," Whatley said. "Fortunately, we never had to stop one."

He volunteered for the Army on October 24, 1944, but "I was listed as a draftee," he said.

"By the time I got to Italy, the war was pretty much over," Whatley said. "I wanted to get my hands on Hitler's guys for what they did to the Jewish people."

He served in the 1st Army, "the first one that landed on the European continent," according to Whatley. His unit was under General Mark Clark. Whatley described him and General George Patton as rebels.

Clark's philosophy was that tanks were expendable, but not men, unlike some other generals, Whatley said.

The 1st Army was slated to take Rome, Italy, but the country surrendered in April and Germany surrendered in May 1945.

"I wanted to see Pompeii, but I didn't get to," Whatley said. "I never saw Columbus's home in Genoa, but Venice was beautiful with water all around."

He also said he didn't much care for Italian pasta.

Whatley was going through China-Burma-India training in June 1945 when he received a message to deploy to Rome for travel through the Suez Canal to the Indian Ocean to the island of Diego Garcia to be part of the third or fourth wave into Japan. That didn't happen because, in August, the United States dropped the atomic bombs on Japan and the country surrendered.

"I thought I would get to go home, but I didn't have enough points," Whatley said.

After the end of the war, he reenlisted for three years.

He was assigned to the 533rd Military Police, but Whatley said he complained because he didn't want to be in the police.

"I wanted to be in the Quartermaster Corps, so they put me in it," Whatley said.

He was in the 6th Regiment of the Combat Constabulary Regiment of the 227th Constabulary Squadron.

"I was at headquarters for the regiment and drove a six-by-six CKW Model 253 truck," Whatley said. "It had a long wheel base. I was driving for General Ernest Harmon in Heidelberg, Germany."

He met his first wife in Heidelberg.

"I was checking identifications one morning in early April," Whatley said. "This beautiful woman came walking out of the fog. She worked for my boss, the provost marshal."

Whatley has studied military history and knew about many of the major battles of the war, not only in Europe, but in the Pacific Theater.

"They should have had the same size ammunition for everything," Whatley said.

He also remarked on the Sherman tanks, on which the troops relied and thought were good.

"The German Tiger tanks would hit the Shermans and blow them up," according to Whatley. "It really got to me how our guys burned up in them. I'm glad I was infantry, because I could run. I wanted to be a tail gunner, but I got turned down because I was told they didn't need any more."

He also talked about Gordon Ely, a fourth cousin to the Silver City Daily Press owner, publisher and editor-in-chief, Tina Ely.

Gordon Ely flew in a B-24 Liberator to bomb the Ploiesti, Romania, oil fields, the primary source of fuel for the German forces.

Whatley also talked about his family. Two of his cousins, James A. Murphy and George Molton, also served during World War II. Murphy was killed in Manchuria and Molton survived the Bataan Death March in the Philippines.

# CHAPTER 10

☙

## DRAFTED IN 1944

GOD'S UMBRELLA

# Nuñez, Simon R.

## DOB 09/29/1924, DOD 9/14/2009

Simon R. Nuñez of Santa Clara was drafted for World War II in 1944 but wanted to go into the Navy.

He was working at the mine in the village of Santa Rita, New Mexico, where he was born, and received a deferment for a time because his father had died, and he was supporting his mother.

"That gave me a little more time, but then I was drafted," Nuñez said.

He was sent to boot camp in San Diego, California, where he said the sailors were not allowed to go into town during their training. During boot camp, he made friends with Santiago Padilla of San Antonio, New Mexico. After they finished their training, they went to a bar. Padilla had one beer, but Nuñez was too young.

They served together on the same ship. Nuñez remembered that, when the ship crossed the equator, the new sailors were initiated by having to bend over and have "crap" put on their faces. When the ship next crossed the equator, the already initiated "got someone else who was new."

"I was shipped overseas as a regular seaman," Nuñez said. "I was nineteen (years old) when we went into the invasion of the Philippines, into the Lingayen Gulf."

The USS Warwick, to which he was assigned, was a cargo ship. Nuñez was a deckhand on a patrol boat that, with each trip from the USS Warwick, delivered about thirty fully equipped soldiers to the beach.

"We took in regular soldiers all day long," Nuñez said. "We hit the beach, and then we went and got some more troops."

After that, the ship was sent to Iwo Jima.

A large crane lowered the patrol boat into the water from the attack ship.

"We'd circle the boat and then take [the soldiers] in," Nuñez said. "That's what happened in the Philippines and Iwo Jima.

"I was on the ship when they raised the flag for the soldiers on the island," he said. "After Iwo Jima, we made a couple of trips to Japan, after the war ended, after the bombs were dropped."

On one of the trips to Japan, the ship went to the mainland, and, on the second trip, to an island "up north. That's when they told us we were going home, after a couple of years."

In Japan, the sailors went into the country only in groups, "because they wouldn't let us go by ourselves," he said.

Padilla was discharged before Nuñez, who had to stay another thirty days in the Navy in the Oakland/Vallejo area of California.

The day Nuñez was discharged in February 1946, he found three friends from Santa Rita who were being discharged the same day. They were Charlie Martinez, Francisco Flores and Florencio Flores.

"In the morning when we went to breakfast, all of a sudden everyone saw each other," Nuñez said.

While he was still in the Pacific Theater, he said one of his buddies, Daniel Marrujo, called him from the Philippines. Marrujo was a radioman, also from Santa Rita.

"When we went into the service, there was a busload of us who went from Santa Rita to Fort Bliss, Texas," Nuñez said. "Then we all split up. Joe Salas [who served in Europe during World War II and became a prisoner of war] and I were buddies in high school in Hurley."

At age eighteen, Nuñez had quit high school to work at the Santa Rita mine.

"After I came back from the war, I finished my schooling and became a diesel mechanic," he said. "I worked on the big trucks and bulldozers. I worked at the mine for forty-three years."

Nuñez kept up with Padilla after the war. When Padilla died, his son visited Nuñez and continued to call him and visit frequently.

Nuñez and his wife, Carmen, also from Santa Rita, have been married more than sixty years. They met after the war. They have two sons and two daughters.

When asked to recount more war experiences, Nunez said: "I don't want to remember a lot. I was too young."

GOD'S UMBRELLA

# RENNER, DALE

## DOB ABOUT 1924

Dale Renner said he has never talked much about the war.

"In World War II, you knew where the enemy was, what kind of equipment he had and what kind of war you were going to fight," Renner said. "Today's wars are completely different and a tremendous challenge."

When Renner was eighteen years old, he tried to volunteer for the Marines and the Seabees, but because of a broken arm that he cannot straighten, the Marines would not take him and neither would the Seabees.

"My only alternative was to wait for the draft," Renner said. "Nine months later, I was drafted into the Army and sent to Fort Sill, Oklahoma, for basic."

He became a part of the artillery section, as a gunner on a 105-millimeter howitzer.

"At that time, the Japanese were being successful in the Pacific," Renner said. "I went to a short training in parachute jumping."

The Germans were also doing well in North Africa, so his training changed to make him part of a tactical amphibious assault team on DUKWs, pronounced "ducks." The D indicated a vehicle designed in 1942, the U meant utility amphibious, the K indicated all-wheel drive and the W indicated two powered rear axles.

The land-sea vehicle could be used on the water and then driven directly onto beaches and onward over land.

Renner was sent to train for the invasion of southern France.

"We were part of a transport group of 113 ships," he said. "It was the first major transport that attempted to go into the Mediterranean [Sea]) without air cover."

The Germans attacked the convoy with submarines and Messerschmitt Schwalbes—dive bombers. The attacks usually came from the left rear side by submarine.

"Thirteen of our ships sank," Renner said. "My ship was the next in line. I was part of a deck gunner crew. My job was to get ammunition to the gunner. He was hit, but I didn't know it until he quit shooting. Our convoy was turned around to Africa and we landed in Oran, Algeria."

The troops were transported from Oran to Algiers in railcars called "40 and 8s," because they carried forty men and eight horses during World War I.

"We had no conveniences for several days," Renner said.

His next stop was Italy to become part of the invasion force into France.

"My assignment was to go in before the landing craft," Renner said. "We had three and one-half tons of TNT on the DUKW. Our job was to blow up the anti-landing emplacements."

A German aircraft shot down a barrage balloon [placed to support netting to stop low-flying aircraft] directly in front of the DUKW carrying Renner, Corporal Frank Kirby from Memphis, Tennessee, and the platoon leader, Lieutenant Earl E. Walker. The DUKW's propeller became entangled, which killed the motor. Then mortar fire began to hit the vehicle from shore.

"The first one was short; the second one long," Renner reported. "The French Army on shore knocked out the pillbox that was firing on us, so we got to shore and unloaded our dynamite. The Germans were expecting us to land in a different place.

"That's how my Bronze Star [award] came to be," he said.

In a letter written to Renner's mother, Lieutenant Walker tells her that he has recommended her son be sent to Officer Candidate School in Paris.

"Within ninety days, if he makes good up there, and I am sure that he will, he will be commissioned a lieutenant in the United States Army," Walker wrote. "...he has performed his duties in an excellent manner, both as a soldier and as a man. Many times, Dale has proved by his actions and intelligence that he would make an excellent officer. In Africa, Italy and now in France, I certainly wish I had more sergeants like him. I will hate to lose him as a sergeant, but I know that he will make some outfit a good officer."

Walker recounted that Renner and Kirby dived off the entangled DUKW, and "with shells falling very close in the water, they freed the DUKW and we proceeded to shore and accomplished our mission. If a shell had hit the DUKW with three and one-half tons of TNT… well, I would not be writing you this letter and Dale would not be going to school. … I think you have a son to be proud of, Mrs. Renner, and all the luck in the world to him when he goes to school."

Renner attended school in Fontainebleau, France, and was commissioned as a second lieutenant.

"I was sent to join the 36th Infantry Texas Division," Renner said. "By the time I got to the front line, the war was actually won and Germany was still surrendering. Since I was a new lieutenant, I had fewer points for discharge, so for a year I was part of the occupation forces in Germany."

While in Germany, Renner was stationed in Blaubeuren near Heidenheim, the hometown of the "Desert Fox" General Erwin Rommel, who was noted for his military exploits in North Africa. Rommel was accused of plotting to assassinate Adolf Hitler, and was shot and killed near Blaubeuren by the Waffen-SS shortly before Renner and his outfit arrived in the area.

The town was a training center for German youths.

"The reason we were put there was because there was a large swimming pool and a recreation center," Renner said. "It was a beautiful small town in a lovely part of Germany."

He was at Dachau concentration camp when the Jews were being released.

"I had some photos of wagonloads of dead Jewish prisoners," Renner said. "I gave them to a Jewish woman in Texas."

At that point, he stopped talking about his time at war and didn't talk more about his life afterward either.

# ATCHLEY, DONALD

## DOB 08/24/1923, DOD 12/2011

Donald Atchley who was often called Reverend Don because he served as a minister for forty-seven years after his time in the service, received his "greetings" from the draft board. Because he preferred not to go into the Army, he joined the Navy and was sent to El Paso, Texas, in May 1944.

He was sent to Camp Wallace, Texas—an Army base—for training, but because he got boils all over his legs, he didn't get much training.

While the ship to which he was assigned was being built in California, Atchley was sent to Miami, Florida, to wait to go overseas.

His wife, Johnnie, spent four days on the bus to go to see him. She arrived at one in the morning and found a note from her husband at the bus station to go to the hotel where he was staying. The hotel manager wouldn't take her upstairs, because he said, "How do I know you're married?" He finally took her up to her husband's room.

On Friday of the same week, Atchley was informed that he would be leaving for California to board a ship to head overseas to the fighting zone.

Because the train to California was so slow, the ship had left without him, so he was sent to San Diego, California, and assigned to PT 1401, a Patrol Torpedo boat, to travel the coast from Mexico to Canada.

He didn't see action, and said his time in the service was easy, with only stints on watch.

One time, a Russian submarine was spotted, but because it was beyond where the PT could go, they had no contact.

"I had to pay attention when I was on watch," Atchley said.

The Atchelys rented a room in La Jolla and Johnnie Atchley stayed there and worked while her husband patrolled. He came back to the room Friday evenings and had to reboard the ship early every Sunday morning.

They shared one bathroom and a kitchen with six other couples in the house where the room was rented.

According to his wife, Atchley liked to cook, so he spent time in the galley on the boat.

"I made biscuits, cake, even doughnuts," he said. "I did it for pastime."

The ship sailed up and down the coast some distance off the land.

"The whales were bigger than [some of] our ships," Atchley said. "Our boat was so small, something large like that could have damaged it."

Servicemen were assigned to each PT boat and the ships traveled together, with the larger ships farther off the coast. The only time they had to wear uniforms, he said, was when they would have company from other ships.

His rank was fireman first class.

The men did their own laundry. They lay their clothes under their bunk mattresses to press them.

Atchley said his first experience with guns and ammunition was when he joined the service.

"[The service] drew out of you the real you and what you believed," he said.

He spent two years with Company 49, Battalion 6, patrolling the coast until he was discharged on February 14, 1946.

The couple had a daughter, but because no one would rent to a couple with children or pets, their daughter lived in Dexter, New Mexico, with Johnnie's parents.

When Atchley got out of the service, he went to work for a time in the oil fields, but then became a preacher. He started new churches in Carlsbad, New Mexico, and Odessa, Texas.

In 1972, the family moved to Silver City for Atchley to answer a pastoral call at Bible Baptist Church, where he remained until he retired in 2001 because of his health.

GOD'S UMBRELLA

# Benavidez, Ubaldo

## DOB 8/29/1922, DOD 6/20/2013

Ubaldo Benavidez, born near Hatch, New Mexico, was drafted while he was living in Los Angeles, California, and trained at Fort McArthur, California.

He joined an Army airborne unit and went to train in Georgia, but on a training jump he broke his left ankle on the tower.

"I couldn't keep up, so when I got well, they sent me to the 3rd Infantry," Benavidez said.

He served under the command of General Alexander Patch, and "started combat in Anzio, Italy. We fought all the way to Rome."

While in Anzio, the troops were fired upon by Germans from Monte Cassino, Italy.

"We used to call the gun we used the railroad gun, because it would explode, but without many fragments. It would just open up," Benavidez said. "Then they had a mortar that would fire six rockets. We called it the 'Screaming Mimi,' because of the sound when it started."

He said the Germans' machine guns were much more rapid than those of the American troops, and the shells were larger, with the German shells being .88 millimeter and the Americans' largest at .70 millimeter. He also said the German tanks were superior to the Americans' tanks. The German tanks ran on rubber treads and were silent. The metal treads of American tanks could be heard from a distance.

After the troops took Rome, he trained for the invasion of southern France.

"I was a demolition man," Benavidez said.

He arrived in France on a Landing Craft Infantry.

"I was the first one to get off, because I had to cut the concertina wire with a Bangalore torpedo," Benavidez said.

A Bangalore torpedo was an explosive charge placed on the end of a long, extendible tube. The type of explosive was created by the British for use in India—hence the name—and has been used to clear beaches of wire and explosives since World War I.

"The tank next to us got hit and killed twelve men [during the invasion of France], so I said to myself, 'I'm going to be the first one off,'" Benavidez said. "The captain said, 'Benavidez, are you ready?' I was headed out by the time the ramp was down. I had a safety belt. Going out I happened to half-inflate it. It saved me because I could barely touch the bottom of the sea with my toes."

He blasted the concertina wire.

"We got on shore," Benavidez said. "The captain told us to take a break. We got four cigarettes in our K-rations. As we moved on, here comes a German fighter plane. He wagged his wings at us and we all hit the ground."

But the plane's pilot just waved and kept going.

"I guess he didn't have any ammunition," Benavidez said.

The captain told Benavidez to bring up the rear when they moved on.

"I heard someone yell, 'Comrade.' I looked, and it was a German soldier with a white flag. He wanted to surrender," Benavidez said. "I yelled, 'Enemy in sight.'"

About 150 Germans were in a pillbox and they all wanted to surrender, so the American troops took them in and put them in the middle of the ranks.

"We had to close ranks to keep the French off the Germans. They were beating them," Benavidez said. "I guess the Germans must have treated them pretty bad."

After the invasion, he traveled with his unit to Alsace-Lorraine, which he described as beautiful, on the northeastern side of France. He came upon Hitler's headquarters, where Hitler lived when he was in the region.

"It was so clean you could eat off anything," Benavidez said. "A lady was coming in from a farm with a basket of goodies."

He said he picked up languages—Italian and French—easily, because of his knowledge of Spanish, so he asked the woman what the place was. She told him that it was Hitler's headquarters.

Benavidez said he saw a "kid nearby with both arms cut off."

Benavidez asked him what happened and was told that the Germans had cut the youth's arms off because he wouldn't join the German Army.

In France, Benavidez was twice shot at by snipers.

"Once, I heard the bullet go by my ear," Benavidez said.

The American troops were told they were going to meet the Schutzstaffel, the elite German combat units better known as the SS. It was said that the troops would fight to the death.

"We captured about 100 of them," Benavidez said. "They didn't want to fight."

He said there were "a lot of Germans in France—a lot. They controlled everything."

Everyone wanted to capture Hitler, according to Benavidez, but Hitler committed suicide.

"You should have heard those GIs, saying he was chicken," he said. "We captured Mussolini in Italy. I don't think the Italians wanted to fight, but they had no choice and had to join the Germans."

Benavidez and his buddy Russell, whose last name he couldn't remember, used to team up often and they captured seven men, one of whom was an Italian. Russell was a fellow New Mexican from Tatum.

"We went through a lot in France," Benavidez said, "but we had to fight a war, and that's all there was to it."

On his last day of combat, a German tank approached him, and he thought he was done for, he said, but the

German got out and in perfect English said he wanted to surrender.

Benavidez marched the German to battalion headquarters through a snowstorm with about a couple of feet of snow on the ground. Benavidez's feet were soaked in his leather boots. The sergeant took him to supply to get new boots, but when Benavidez took the boots off his feet swelled up so much that supply had no boots to fit him.

He was sent to Paris to the hospital and the doctor told him to rub them constantly to get the circulation back in his feet.

"By George, I saved them," Benavidez said. "When I was at Fort Carson, Colorado, [where he was sent after Paris] there were a lot of guys with frozen toes and feet like mine, but they didn't rub them. They lost toes and half their feet, but I saved mine."

He was told he would stay there until he could walk well and then he could have a thirty-day furlough.

"So, I kept rubbing my feet," Benavidez said. "I came back and got married. It was March and my wife told me she wanted to be a June bride, but I told her that if she wanted to wait until June, she'd have to find another guy. So, we got married."

Benavidez said his mother prayed for him every day that he was in the war.

"I wrote to my dad in Spanish to get by the censors," he said. "They always knew where I was."

He spent one year exactly to the day in front-line combat.

"I was happy to fight for my country and glad I came out of it," Benavidez said.

When he returned to Hatch after he was discharged, "there were so many people waiting for me. The day before, my high school buddy named Lytle had come back and he told me he had a crowd, too."

Benavidez then went to work for Kennecott Copper Corporation, becoming one of four generations of his family who worked in mining. He would spend ten days at the mine and then spend four days on his family's farm, selling the chiles they raised.

# Diaz, David

## DOB 1924 DOD 02/24/2018

David Diaz of Hurley, New Mexico, went into the service on May 8, 1944. He was born in Hurley and went to school there.

"I went to El Paso, then to basic training," Diaz said. "They shipped me to Louisiana and then overseas. First, I went to Belgium and then into Germany just as they surrendered."

He said his job in Hurley had been as a railroad supervisor for the Atchison, Topeka and Santa Fe Railway, covering the area from Hurley to Hatch to Deming, New Mexico, so he was placed in a railway operating battalion, for when the Army had railway accessibility in Europe to provide services to the troops.

"We worked to improve facilities in England and Belgium," Diaz said. "I wasn't there very long. No more than ten months. I saw England, France, Belgium and Germany. They kept us moving around. There was bombing around us, but we never had any direct hits."

"In Germany, we tried to get the transportation of food, arms and ammo to the troops," Diaz said. "We stayed a while after the surrender until things normalized, then they started sending us back."

He was discharged on November 7, 1945 at Camp Joseph T. Robinson in Arkansas.

"I was proud to serve in World War II and do my part," Diaz said. "I congratulate all the men and women in the military. It proves that America always does the right thing."

Diaz said he was lucky that he saw no action during his stint in the service at the tail end of the war.

"I was hoping I would get in and was glad when they called me and put me in," Diaz said. "I was hoping to go overseas and was glad I got sent to Europe and that I got to do the same work I was doing at home.

"After I returned, I took flying lessons because I always wanted to fly," he said. "I have taught the majority of people around here how to fly."

Diaz spent his career with the Atchison, Topeka and Santa Fe Railway from 1942 to 1984—excepting his years in the service—forty-one years and nine months.

For the railroad, he said he went from laborer to supervisor. The train was still coming to Hurley in 1984, hauling ore from the mines.

Diaz also served as mayor of Hurley for thirty-four years, from 1962 to 2006.

"When the town of Hurley was incorporated, the main road used to come through town," Diaz said. "When the commission gave the road to the town after the new highway was built, I was pleased to have it named Diaz Avenue after me."

# PEÑA, RAUL D.

## DOB 05/14/1926, DOD 09/26/2015

Raul D. Peña of Silver City was drafted into the Army in August 1944.

"When I was drafted, we were living in Fierro [New Mexico]," Peña said. "My parents, Luís and Virginia, had immigrated from Mexico. My three brothers, Luís, Antonio and Rodolfo, were already serving. My mother went to the general at Fort Bliss and pleaded to let me come home, but I said, 'No.'"

Peña was almost eighteen years old at the time. Rodolfo, the first to go into the service, was in the Army Air Forces. He and Antonio received Purple Heart medals. Their brother Eduardo later served in the Korean War in the United States Air Force.

"All of us came home," Peña said.

The youngest brother, Miguel, was drafted, but was not taken into the service because his brothers had served.

Peña was inducted into the Army at Fort Bliss, Texas, and completed his basic training as an infantryman at Fort Hood, Texas.

His next assignment was Fort Ord, California, from where he was sent to Camp Knight in Oakland, California, then put on a ship overseas.

"We went straight to Hollandia, New Guinea," Peña said. "We spent about three weeks there, then they put us on a ship again, and we went to Leyte, Philippines."

The next stop was Luzon, Philippines, where the troops were sent to take the hills.

"We were in combat during that time," Peña said. "After about twenty days, we came down to take a rest and get replacements."

Peña was in the 1st battalion, 127th Infantry of the 32nd Division. The division, the so-called "Red Arrow" Division, headed up the Villa Verde Trail at the end of January 1945.

"We began at San Nicolas, where a memorial to the division stands," Peña said.

The 32nd logged a total of 654 days of combat—more than any other United States Army Division—during World War II from its arrival in Australia on May 14, 1942, through February 1946, when it was inactivated.

Peña described the Villa Verde Trail as a "wide trail—like a Snake Hill [a curving steep hill in Silver City, New Mexico]." It was about twenty miles long.

"We were sent clear up to Yamashita Ridge," Peña said. "The Japanese were under the command of General [Tomoyuki] Yamashita, the one who led the Bataan Death March.

"We were clear up at the top for twenty-some odd days, fighting the whole time," Peña continued. "After we came to a certain point, another regiment took over. We had to rest. We—the United States Army 6th, 32nd and 37th Divisions—took Yamashita Ridge on August 15 [1945]."

That was the day that General Yamashita surrendered to the 32nd Division. The Japanese troops had been living in caves.

"After the surrender, which we couldn't really see, because we were kind of far away, but we knew what was happening," Peña said, "we were loaded on trucks near Santa Fe [Philippines].

"We were taken to an airfield, where we were kind of spread out and resting," Peña said. "Loud speakers on the trucks announced that they wanted fifteen or twenty men. I said to myself, 'They're not going to call me.' I was the fifth guy they called. They called me Pena without the ñ."

The men were taken to another airfield, where "we got a shower, the first in thirty days. We ate dinner, and then they put us on a C-47 airplane."

"I saw the ocean full of ships heading to Japan," Peña said. "We ended up on Iwo Jima, where there was still a lot of fighting in the hills."

The fifteen or twenty men were unloaded and put in tents.

"We were the only Army troops," Peña said. "The rest were Marines."

A "kind of a big plane" landed at the airfield.

"It was a B-25 bomber and the bombs were unloaded," Peña said. "The next day they put us on the plane. We were like sardines in the bomb bay. There were machine guns in front and in the turret. We took off and several hours later, we landed at Kyushu Island, Japan.

"We started patrolling the airfield, which was empty of troops," he continued. "More American Navy planes were coming in with troops needing rest.

"We met a bunch of Japanese farmers, some of whom could speak English," Peña stopped to regain his composure. "They told us some prisoners were working in a mine. We took out Chinese, Australian and American prisoners. I thought later I should have asked if any were from New Mexico."

The former prisoners were loaded into ships at Sasebo on Kyushu Island.

"The Chinese were saying thank you to us," Peña said. "We thought we were going on the ship, too, but the captain told us to keep patrolling."

A few days later the troops were loaded onto a Landing Ship, Tank and transported to Nagoya, Japan.

"We were supposed to get another airfield, but the Seabees were already there cleaning it up," Peña said. "It was full of brand-new Japanese planes. The Seabees took bulldozers and pushed them into the ocean."

A few days later, the men could hear a large plane coming in, and a few days later heard another big noise, which turned out to be a hurricane.

"We were notified it was going to hit the bay, and we helped tie down all the Navy planes using anchors, except for the big plane," Peña said. "The hurricane hit and took all the small planes and the anchors, but not the big plane. We stayed in caves during the storm."

At Fukuoka, Japan, Peña was transferred from the 32nd Division to the 24th.

"I was at headquarters," Peña said. "No more infantryman."

He stayed there for about four or five months, and then took a thirty-day furlough.

"Japan was beautiful," Peña said. "We stayed for a time at a hotel called the Evergreen Hotel.

"When I came back to camp from furlough, I was told I would be discharged," he said.

The train to Yokohama for discharge traveled close to where one of the atomic bombs had landed and "everything was empty." Peña was then sent to Seattle, Washington, and to Camp Beale, California, where he was officially discharged.

In Los Angeles, California, Peña boarded a bus and arrived in Lordsburg, New Mexico, at about eleven o'clock at night.

"I called and called [home] and no one answered," he said, "so I called the Copper Inn Bar. They answered, and one of the guys reported that I was in Lordsburg but didn't tell my folks until the next day.

"My mother and father came to get me," Peña said. "My mother made molé for my welcome-home dinner. There must have been 100 relatives there."

While overseas, he said he sometimes wrote letters, sometimes love letters, for men who couldn't write.

"One time I got a letter from my mother, but I couldn't read it, because it was mostly in Spanish," Peña said. "A sergeant Gigivich from Pennsylvania—he was Polish and I'm not sure how to spell his name—treated me nice. He knew five languages, so he read the letter to me.

"While I was overseas," Peña said, "I kept in touch with my brother Antonio. He was wounded in Europe. Rodolfo was in Europe, too, and Luís, in the Navy, was also in the Pacific."

The brothers also had three sisters: Teresa and Rosa Peña and Alma Dimm.

"After I got home, I met Genevieve and married her," Peña said. "She worked in the mine during the war."

"My sister Florence and I worked in the mine for about a year," Genevieve Peña said, "because all the men were gone.

"We've been married fifty-seven years," she said.

Peña received several military citations, including: the Bronze Star; Good Conduct Medal; Asiatic Camp Medal and Bronze Star attachment; World War II Victory Medal; Army of Occupation Medal and Japan Clasp; Combat Infantryman Badge; Philippine Liberation Ribbon and Bronze Star with attachment (single); and Honorable Service Lapel Button World War II.

Peña lost the originals in a fire, but his family had them replaced.

GOD'S UMBRELLA

# CHAPTER II

&

## VOLUNTEERED IN 1945

GOD'S UMBRELLA

# STAILEY, GENE HERBERT

## DOB 04/24/24

Gene Stailey, who was born at the home of his grand-parents, Franch and Clara Lee, in the Gila Valley, New Mexico, continues to live in the region.

His parents were Ethlyn Lee and Charlie Stailey.

Stailey wanted to drop out of school to go into the service, but, because he had started school a year early and had skipped a grade, he was the youngest in his class, and his parents would not sign for him to join.

"I graduated in May 1944, worked for a while at the old Gila Fluorspar Mill until January 1945," Stailey said. "I was going to be eighteen in April, so I convinced my parents to let me join the Navy. Russell Roberts and I joined together."

They were sent to Santa Fe, New Mexico, for a physical.

"We went by Parrish Stageline," Stailey said. "It was a long-base '40 or '41 Chevy that looked like a limo. We went over the Black Range [mountains] on the unpaved road and caught a bus—I think it was Trailways— in Hot Springs, which is now Truth or Consequences [New Mexico]. Between Albuquerque and Santa Fe [New Mexico], we would stop, and an Indian would get on or off, but we couldn't see their villages."

Roberts did not pass the Navy physical, but later served in the Army, according to Stailey.

The new recruit Stailey returned home for a couple of days and then headed back to Santa Fe, where he and others were sent to Lamy, New Mexico, to catch a bus westward-bound to San Diego, California, for boot camp.

"We got in late at night," Stailey said. "At four in the morning, the lights came on, and a loud-mouthed guy shouted, 'Hit the deck.' I soon learned he meant business."

Calisthenics was the first order of business every morning.

"I decided I didn't want to do push-ups," Stailey said. "I thought I could just lie there and not get caught. Well, I was still doing push-ups when everyone else had gone to chow."

One day, Stailey was "squared off in a boxing match against an Oriental fellow, who wasn't more than five feet or five feet one inch tall. I couldn't lay a punch he didn't block. It turned out he was a professional boxer from San Francisco."

After boot camp, Stailey returned home for a short leave and then headed to Camp Elliott near San Diego.

"One day at muster, the sergeant hollered, 'Stailey, Gene Herbert, front and center,'" Stailey recalled. "I was sent to Barrack 16 to report to a lieutenant. Because I had typing in high school, I was assigned to the office. I had a 'real hard job.' I took care of the lost and found."

Next, he was told, "Grab your gear. You're heading out."

Several troops took a train to Oakland, California.

"They put us in a boat that was like a long canoe, with benches on the side," Stailey said. "Still not knowing where we were going, I thought it an odd way to go to sea. You could reach over the edge and feel the water. We docked at Treasure Island and were told, 'This is where you'll be stationed.'"

The island was the former site of the 1939 World's Fair, so the barracks and offices were in some of the buildings constructed for the event.

"My job consisted of processing records and giving leaves and furloughs to those eligible," Stailey said. "I'd have guys—chief petty officers with stripes from elbow to wrist—trying to get leave. It was 'Yes, sir' and 'No, sir.' Some guys with rolls of bills that would choke a mule also tried to get leave, but I didn't go that far.

"I was like a civilian," he said. "I had a special liberty pass and could go to shore anytime. I also had a special chow pass and could go to the head of the line. I had no musters, no guard duty. I'd roll out of my bunk and leave it like it was."

Stailey requested sea duty twice, because he had buddies going through a lot in the Pacific.

"I felt guilty," Stailey said.

The machine he used for his work had old IBM punchcards, and he could get it to "kick out names of New

Mexico guys serving in the war—Milton Hooker, Louis Johns, Ernest Rodriguez, Johnny Thompson and Pete Maldonado to name a few." Treasure Island was close to Alcatraz, and, during the riot at the Alcatraz prison in the summer of 1945, the troops stationed on nearby Treasure Island could see gunfire and hear shots.

"I did a few illegal things, but not much," Stailey admitted. "Milton Hooker was due to be shipped out the next day. We were trying to figure out how to get him out to see his wife."

Stailey went out the gate with his special pass, then went down the fence line and handed it through to Hooker, who went ashore with the pass. Hooker returned to base the same way by going through using Stailey's pass.

Another time, when Stailey has just come out of the barracks, the pay line was stretched out a long way.

"I bumped into a guy," he said. "It was Jimmy Barka from Gila [New Mexico]. I took him in the back door and told them to pay him off and let him go. When he got back to Gila, he went down to see my mom and told her what a big shot I was."

Stailey is the oldest of seven children and helped raise his siblings.

"After I paid for everything, I had nine dollars left on one payday and ten dollars the next," he said. "I couldn't do much with that, so I gambled. It wasn't always on the up and up. I had an older friend, who could palm dice. Naturally they were crooked dice. One time, he shook the dice—we played with two—and three fell out. Those guys went to work on us. Fortunately, the watch guard came through and with a bully stick, broke it up."

Sailors who were restricted to base wanted whiskey, which was not available.

"I took a big, thick Shakespeare book, cut out the middle, and brought whiskey back to the base," Stailey said. "They paid me well."

His cousin Robert "Coop" Stailey was restricted to his ship.

"I thought I'd go down to the pier and get permission to go see him," Stailey said. "I did, and he got permission to go with me for the weekend. We did that several times."

On V-J (Victory over Japan) Day, he said, there was no way that "swabbies" (sailors) were going to be kept on station.

"Hundreds of thousands of people were lining Market Street [in San Francisco]," Stailey said. "Cars couldn't move. The next day they found cars that had been pushed into liquor stores and servicemen asleep on the shelves.

"At the Pepsi-Cola Center, a woman had climbed onto a statue and started to do a striptease," Stailey said. "There was a lot of pushing and shoving. I stood on the curb and watched. All of a sudden, I hear a guy screaming and hollering above me. I recognized the voice. It was Owen Hubbard, who had shimmied up a pole. He was waving a fur coat in his hand. He would trade the coat for kisses, then take the coat back and do it again."

Stailey was a seaman first class at the end of the war.

"They wanted to promote me to yeoman first class, but I smelled a rat," Stailey said. "I refused it. I thought the rates would be frozen as well as the time required to serve, and sure enough, they were. The guy who took it was still there when I left."

In May 1946, Stailey was discharged from the Navy at Camp Shoemaker, Calif., on the point system, because of his helping to take care of his siblings.

"The day before I was to be discharged, I fell on the stairs with my arm out in front and hurt my shoulder," Stailey said. "During my exit interview, I said nothing was wrong because I knew it would postpone my discharge. I should have [reported it] because it still bothers me sixty years later."

Stailey said he has a friend who went to town on a pass, entered a rodeo and broke his foot.

"He draws disability," Stailey laughed, "and I don't draw a dime."

# CLAWSON, MAYETTA CECILA QUINTANA
## DOB 01/05/1925

"On my twentieth birthday, January 5, 1945, I enlisted into the Women's Marine Corps," Mayetta Cecilia Quintana Clawson (her married name) said. "I was living in Chicago. I went down to the recruiting station. A sailor was operating the elevator and he tried to talk me into going into the Navy. I told him I was signing up for the Marine Corps. He let me off at the Marine Corps floor and I signed up. I served as Mayetta Quintana."

Clawson said she was a senior in high school when Pearl Harbor was bombed. "I was sixteen and I remember that day. It was a Sunday. We had the radio on and we heard that the Japanese had bombed Pearl Harbor. I took the news to my friend Myrna and her family. They hadn't heard the news. That evening, I was a member of a young people's church group. That was all we talked about. I remember who was there—Myrna, Bob Parker, Gus Jones, Willis Jorgensen, Chuck Bowles, and Mary Saviss. It is imprinted in my mind."

Parker became a fighter pilot. His plane went down in the Pacific and he was never found. Jorgensen guarded German POWs in Florida. Bowles was a gunner on a plane that took part in the European invasion. Jones was exempt from the draft because he had diabetes, but he was very athletic, and he trained soldiers at Fort Sheridan as a civilian.

Myrna went to school at Kalamazoo, Michigan, after they graduated. "I enrolled in teacher's college," Clawson said.

The day after Pearl Harbor, everyone at school was called into the auditorium to hear President Franklin Delano Roosevelt's speech. "We also heard a bit of the Congressional hearings before they turned the radio off. That was the beginning that changed our lives so drastically."

"My perspective as a teenager at Chicago Teacher's College was that the world was passing me by," Clawson said. "I quit. I was already working as a part-time secretary to La Salle Extension University. I learned stenotype and got a job with the Quartermaster Corps after school. They bought all the perishable supplies for the military. They would get bids in for railroad cars full of turkeys and such. I was the teletype operator. That's what I was doing when I decided to join the Marines."

She said it was a time when people were pulling together. "My mother was working for the War Manpower Commission. It later became the United States Employment Office."

"When I was supposed to report to the Marines, I got on the train in downtown Chicago [Illinois]," Clawson continued. "It went as far as Washington, DC, where I had to take the bus to Camp Lejeune in North Carolina. It was a revelation, because, when we got to the nation's capital, the restrooms were segregated, and the buses were segregated. We arrived at Camp Lejeune. It was the middle of winter, but it was beautiful. We went through boot camp.

"It was a new experience living with all those people," Clawson said. "I ended up staying at Camp Lejeune my whole military career. I was assigned to the Military Police [MP] investigative division. The stenotype machine came in handy. I also did some court reporting while I was there."

She said she didn't do anything dangerous during the war.

"The Women Marine Corps slogan was: 'Free a Marine to fight.'"

When she was headed to boot camp, Clawson was given instructions about shoes. She said, "Shoes are important in the military. I was supposed to bring some cordovan brown shoes—oxfords. I dyed my loafers brown. The sergeant told me to get rid of those shoes. We needed to have well-shined shoes. The women officers could wear pumps at events. Enlisted women weren't supposed to wear pumps, but when we were off duty, we did."

"I worked hard, sometimes at night, investigating fights and accidents," Clawson said. "I had led a somewhat sheltered life before that, so it was a revelation to me. Camp Lejeune was large. It was like a little city, but I often worked long hours. Fights and accidents didn't usually happen in daylight."

The women had separate barracks, but they looked like all the other barracks. Theirs had been redone for them. In the bathrooms, they had private showers and private toilet stalls.

She worked at different parts of the base quite often. "There were four women in the police department and a lot of men. Some of the men had FBI experience. We were responsible to a major."

When she first went in, she had to do KP (kitchen patrol) duty, but once she became a corporal, she didn't have to do KP any longer. "This was early on, when some generals were coming down from Washington, so we were scrubbing, trying to get everything ready for them. They arrived early. We had a dishwasher. We piled the dishes on big wooden trays and shoved them through the tunnel where the water came out. We used a pole. We had just turned it off, and it was still dripping. A general came in, looked around and said, 'Very good, very good.' Right then, I knew he didn't know what he was talking about. It was a mess. Maybe he had never done KP. It was an easy life, other than working the long hours."

One time when she was working on an investigation, a Marine had been involved in a fight. The investigator asked what caused it. The Marine told the investigator that the man had called him a name. "Well, what did he say?" the investigator asked. "I can't tell you with her here," the Marine replied. "So, I had to leave, and I never did find out. I learned a lot of new words when I joined the Marines," Clawson chuckled.

Another humorous happening occurred when a man couldn't tell the barracks apart and came into the women's barracks during the night and bedded down. He left quickly the next morning.

"My friend Jackie was secretary to a major," Clawson said. "Dogs were being trained for the military. The major had adopted one that had been detrained. It was a huge dog. The major's wife wouldn't allow the dog to stay in their house when he wasn't there. So, Jackie got to walk the dog.

"We had good food, especially good seafood," she said. "One time, I established my reputation as being fearless. I had never been on a motorcycle, but one of the men asked me if I wanted to go to Wilmington [North Carolina] for lunch. We went on his motorcycle. I guess he tried to scare me, but since it was my first ride on one, I thought that was the way they rode. He told the guys that he tried to scare me, but I didn't scare at all."

She said they could walk for miles on the beach and never see another person.

"One Marine used to polish my shoes for me," Clawson said. "But I didn't meet anyone seriously, although I met a lot of men. While the war was on, they used to get shipped out. Most of the ones that stayed there were older and most had wives.

"When I still there, a fellow I worked with asked me to a dance on the base," she said. "It was very platonic. His wife was pregnant in Detroit [Michigan]. We called for a ride. The MPs drove up in a station wagon. It was raining, and the driver drove into a lamppost. We flew into the back of the front seat. I was bleeding profusely. The medical corpsman dealt with us and took us to the hospital. I was in surgery, and all I remember was the doctor looked like Clark Gable. He said the shot to deaden my upper lip will hurt as much as the stitch, so I told him to 'just do the stitch.' I still have a small scar. Bob Milligan is who I went to the dance with. He, too, got stitched up, but, somehow, I wasn't feeling as much pain as he was. We went back to work the next day and everyone was telling me to 'keep a stiff upper lip.' That was my World War II injury."

Clawson said she had a chance to go to Pearl Harbor during her service, which was well after the bombing, but her mother got upset, so she backed out. "I missed that opportunity."

"The war changed our lives," she said. "Many men I had gone to school with didn't come home, and others came back totally changed. My husband had been in the Army for five years before I met him.

"My dad's two brothers were drafted in World War II," Clawson said. "My dad was the oldest in the family and wasn't drafted. My mother's younger brother had been in the Naval Reserve and got called right away. I had numerous cousins who served. One was a nurse. The war affected everyone. As a teenager, I thought I was doing a very patriotic thing canning tomatoes."

Clawson has roots in New Mexico. Her paternal grandparents were from the area around Santa Cruz, New Mexico, and later moved to Durango, Colorado. "My mother's family moved to Bailey, Colorado. She had a brother in a hospital in Denver [Colorado] as a result of

World War I. My dad moved to Denver and took a job in that hospital. That's how they met. They went back to Indiana where I was born. They later moved to Albuquerque [New Mexico]."

After the war was over, she said she had seen a movie filmed in New Orleans. She and her friend and co-worker Jackie decided to go there. "We both got jobs with the War Assets Administration, getting rid of things left over from the war. We found a place to rent in the French Quarter. She was in the legal division, and I was in real estate. In New Orleans, we used to take a streetcar that stopped across the street from where German POWs were being held. They would whistle at us. It was another revelation to me that they were just like the guys I grew up with."

Jackie went back to Detroit, and Clawson went back to stenotype school, where she met her husband, Corporal David Lloyd Clawson. He served in the Army in World War II, including time in Okinawa.

He wanted to continue his education and was accepted at New Mexico College of Agriculture and Mechanical Arts in Las Cruces. The population there at that time was about 10,000, about the same size as Silver City is now.

When they were looking for housing, they talked to Dean O'Donnell. It was in April, not a good time to be looking for housing. "We went back to the motel. The next day, a man knocked at our door. Mr. Knox was head of the animal husbandry department and needed a secretary. He asked me, 'Would you like to be my secretary?' So, I had a job."

The university moved some surplus single-wides and double-wides in for married student housing. "We lived in a single-wide for the three years we were there. After we graduated, we moved to Albuquerque. So that's how we came to New Mexico. My husband received a bachelor's at Texas A&M University, and a master's degree at the University of New Mexico. He worked for various government agencies as an environmental biologist in various parts of the country, including Albuquerque, where he retired."

"In 1990, my husband, daughter and I moved to Silver City after I retired from teaching in Albuquerque," Clawson said. "My husband died in 1999."

# CHAPTER 12

❧

## IN TRAINING DURING WORLD WAR II, BUT SERVED MOSTLY AFTER THE WAR

GOD'S UMBRELLA

# Ryan, William Murray

## DOB 07/22/1922, DOD 01/072017

Former New Mexico State Representative Murray Ryan was born in Central, New Mexico, "sometimes called Santa Clara," he said. "I grew up in a brick house on Seventh Street in Silver City."

He cited his education at St. Mary's Academy as benefiting him.

"Sister Florencia at St. Mary's Academy made a great impression on me," Ryan said. "I was in grade one in 1928. I clearly remember I had to kneel on the concrete steps until I was relieved [by Sister from having to continue to kneel]."

Ryan had Sister Florencia as his teacher for grades one through three.

"I spent the rest of grammar school there and received an outstanding education," Ryan said. "It paid off in the long run. It helped me in college, too, because eighty-five percent [of students] didn't have such training."

He was a politician even in 1928. Ryan said that was the year that Al Smith was nominated for the presidency of the United States. Sister Florencia asked the students for which candidate they would vote.

"Herbert Hoover was a Republican," Ryan said, "but Smith was a traditional and devout Catholic. I didn't raise my hand, because even then my family was Republican."

He said he had the opportunity to meet Smith in 1942, when Smith was governor of New York.

"Back to grammar school," Ryan said. "I liked math and English and had a little bit of art in seventh and eighth grades. One of my best teachers was Sister Marie Assumpta."

Ryan's sister, Martha, was two years ahead of him in school. When she was attending the high school at New Mexico State Teachers College (now Western New Mexico University), she drafted him to perform a male role in a play in which she starred because the school had no boys. The play was slated to be staged at a career conference competition, he said.

"The curriculum and discipline at St. Mary's stood me well in high school," Ryan said. "I got good grades, but only because of the discipline. The fourth year I goofed off."

He had two years before he was slated to attend the United States Military Academy at West Point, so he took calculus at the State Teachers' College.

That benefited Ryan when he arrived at West Point, because the same calculus textbook was used there. Three nights a week, he, Donald Johnson of Ruidoso and William Sheen, who has since died, studied together.

"Everything was controlled and watched at West Point," Ryan said. "Most of the students had been Army brats and their fathers had served together, but I knew no one there."

He said that, as the years went on, he made good friends.

"I took my years at West Point too seriously," Ryan said. "I was scared I would fail, and I didn't know how I could face my parents if I did. I stayed with it because of my own personality and seriousness. I didn't get as much out of it in the way of socialization. I sprinted away from the graduation ceremony and was the first one on the bus."

He said "kismet" played a hand in his service career, because during the first part of July 1945 he was training at Fort Bliss for the invasion of Japan.

"Shortly after that, Japan capitulated," Ryan said. "I had the choice of Europe or Japan after the war. Even though I was only in the middle of my class, I got my choice of Europe."

Ryan and his wife, Marian, were married in August 1945 and he was sent to Europe in October. His wife joined him in June 1946.

"She had a heyday in Europe with her strong background in the arts," Ryan said. "It was an extra bonus for me."

He said the destruction in Europe was massive.

"I had a ten-to-fifteen-mile commute to the base," Ryan said. "I drove through demolished buildings there in northern Germany. It was one of the coldest winters in years in Europe."

One of the nicest assignments he had was in Bad Nauheim, which had no bomb damage.

"It was a happy and exciting time for us," Ryan said. "We took one tour to Rome and Florence, Italy."

His next assignment was at Fort Lewis, Washington, in 1948.

"It was a beautiful post," Ryan said. "I was in the 2nd Infantry, assigned to the Combat Engineer Battalion.

"We had lost a child in Germany, but our oldest surviving child was born at Fort Lewis," he continued. "We came home to Silver City in October 1949, and I've been home ever since."

He built a business venture—a Studebaker automobile dealership—with financing from his father.

"Studebakers were ahead of their time and marvelous little cars," Ryan said. "But they couldn't keep up and the dealership was liquidated in 1953."

He went into business for several years with his father in wholesale liquor distribution.

"A-1 [beer] was brewed in Phoenix and we got the franchise," Ryan said.

Ryan then went to work at Kennecott Copper Corporation for several years. At first, he did maintenance at the smelter, where the metal was melted at 2,300 degrees, he said. Then he was in security and safety. He retired in July 1987.

"In 1968, I ran for the [New Mexico] Legislature," Ryan said. "I really worked at the election part. I squeaked by with about a hundred and some votes. I was incumbent for sixteen terms.

"I had marvelous experiences in Santa Fe, [New Mexico]," Ryan said. "I was there to look after my district in Grant County, and I think I did. I concentrated on bettering the education system. I looked up and thirty years had gone by."

He said the one controversy occurred in the 1970s.

"I had my name in the Wall Street Journal, when I took it personally that a law passed making it disadvantageous to use a twelve-ounce can for beer," Ryan said. "Anheuser-Busch didn't take a stand."

He said a law was on the books that "spirits had to set the price in certain ways that I thought was disadvantageous to consumers. It didn't apply to beer. Only one word had to be changed to apply it to beer. It was a financial bonanza for lobbyists. That one word made it better for consumers."

He said his years in the Legislature were full of exciting times. In 1973, he was the state chairman of the Republican Party and got to meet President Richard Nixon and Vice Presidents Spiro Agnew and Gerald Ford.

"Midway in the 1997 session, I decided not to run again," Ryan said. "My wife was ill. My experience as a representative ended on January 1, 1998. I don't miss it except for the dear, dear friends and staff."

He maintained many of his contacts and stayed in touch with them.

"The political and commercial leadership through World War II was outstanding," Ryan said. "There were not a lot of politics at that time."

He said the county and state officials during World War II were overwhelmingly Democrats, but he proved years later that a Republican could be elected.

Ryan cited Bill Emrick, Forrest Delk, and Vincent Vesely as county and state officials.

"Their motivation was service to community at great personal sacrifice, especially financially," Ryan said.

After leaving the Legislature in 1998, Ryan provided volunteer service to the community. He was appointed by New Mexico Governor Gary Johnson to serve on the local housing authority. He was also active at the Silver City-Grant County Chamber of Commerce, in Rotary International's Silver City chapter, and on the Western New Mexico University Foundation's board of directors.

"My life was permanently interrupted in 2001, when Marian died," Ryan said. "It gave me more time than I need or want."

Ryan and his wife had two daughters and twin sons, one of whom died in 1991.

# JOHNSTON, GENEVIEVE

## DOB 02/17/1922, DOD 10/22/2014

Genevieve Johnston, a native of Silver City, was in nurses' training in Salina, Kansas, during World War II.

"I went to St. John's Hospital from 1941 to 1943," Johnston said. "I attended Marymount College along with St. John's Hospital."

The United States Cadet Nurse Corps, founded through the Bolton Act in 1943, was the largest and youngest group of uniformed women to serve their country during the war. More than 1,000 nursing schools throughout the country participated in the program.

The nurses received tuition help and a small stipend.

"Since I was already in school, I joined," Johnston said. "We were issued a couple of summer uniforms and a couple of winter uniforms and hats. I received a little bit of pay, but I don't remember how much it was."

The nursing stipend typically varied from fifteen to thirty dollars a month.

The program was created because almost twenty percent of the practicing nurses in the country joined the Army and Navy, and the nation's hospitals were in dire need of nurses.

"I just did regular nurses' training at the hospital," Johnston said. "Several of us also went to Marymount, which was about a mile away from our housing. None of us had transportation, so we had to hike up there."

Johnston's sister Celia Padilla was in Women Accepted for Volunteer Emergency Service, better known as the WAVES, a branch of the Navy. She did her basic training on the East Coast, and then was stationed in Chicago, Illinois.

"Once when she had a leave, she came to visit me in Salina," Johnston said. "She suggested we get our picture made in our uniforms. We gave them all away to our family."

Their aunt in Phoenix, Arizona, got the photo enlarged and later gave it to the girls' parents, Juan and Gregoria Gomez, in Silver City. Johnston had the enlargement hanging on her wall.

She has a strong memory of a certain day during her training at St. John's.

"I was taking care of a patient—an older German lady," Johnston said. "The radio was on, and we heard that Japan had attacked Pearl Harbor. The lady got really upset and said, 'That means Germany will get involved in that, too.'

"I would have ended up as an Army nurse, but when the war was over, they disbanded the Cadet Nurse Corps."

A graduate of St. Mary's Academy in Silver City, Johnston attended New Mexico Western College (now Western New Mexico University) for a year, but then decided she wanted to become a nurse. The nuns at St. Mary's are of the Sisters of St. Joseph of Concordia, and they told her about St. John's Hospital, which was operated by the order, so she headed to Kansas.

When Johnston married in 1943, she quit school; but when her husband went overseas, she wrote to the supervisor at St. John's Hospital, and "she let me come back to finish my training. I completed it in 1945."

After her husband, Jesse, returned from overseas, they moved to Long Beach, California.

"Our son, John, was born in California," Johnston said. "When we returned to Silver City, one of many times we came back, I went to Western and got my teaching credentials."

She taught at Raton High School for seventeen years.

Johnston remained active as a volunteer with the Gila Regional Medical Center Auxiliary.

"I worked at the old Watts Clinic up by the county courthouse, at Hillcrest Hospital and at the new Watts Clinic," Johnston said. "Dr. Watts was a wonderful doctor."

# LAFFERTY, FREDERICK REID JR.

## DOB 03/31/1926

Frederick Reid Lafferty Jr. was attending the United States Naval Academy during World War II.

He started at the academy in Annapolis, Maryland, on June 30, 1944, and graduated with the class of 1948.

"I'm fifth generation with the military with my name," Lafferty said. "I always knew I wanted to go into the Naval Academy. It finally came to me why. My father used to post photos of admirals in my room. He wanted to go to the academy and never did. I was brainwashed to go into the Navy. I should have gone into the Army Air Force, but I didn't. My dad was in the Army and finally the Air Force. He became a pilot at Fort Bliss in 1916. That was his first station. Then he was stationed in various places. The most interesting to me was his station at Terlingua, Texas. Mom and he lived in an adobe with dirt floors. It was a three-day trip to Marfa for Mom to get her hair washed. She had hair down to about mid-thigh."

He said his grandfather was a mercenary in Mexico and the Philippines. He tried to get into World War II, but he was too old.

"My great-grandfather was wounded in Texas Canyon in the Chiricahuas [Arizona]," Lafferty said. "I've been to the very spot."

In his time in the academy, Lafferty said that at least a third of those there had been in service in the war. "There were a lot of good people there. It was not what I had expected, and I kind of lost interest. As plebes, we had to be in bed by 10 p.m. I started going over the wall."

One time a friend of his at the Spanish Embassy called him and asked him if he wanted to go to a Navy party. He lived in Washngton, DC, but he picked the plebe up and took him.

"It was Admiral Nimitz's welcome home party," Lafferty said. "I was in uniform, and I went through the reception line. I shook Admiral Nimitz's hand. He looked me up and down and said, 'Aren't you supposed to be somewhere else?' I said, 'Yes, sir.' And he said, 'Well, have a good time.'"

Lafferty remembered that he lost two classmates during training when they were doing a landing. "We were doing maneuvers on the beach and a plane misjudged and slammed into the forward turret of an LCI [Landing Craft Infantry] and wiped out the crew, including two classmates."

During Academy days, the students went to the "gedunk," where they had sodas and ice cream. "They always had war updates on a loop film from the previous day's activities. We were getting the information as fast as intelligence was. So, we always knew what was going on in World War II."

The rest of the time, he said, he enjoyed life and graduated.

Lafferty said he didn't meet his future wife, Betty, until after he graduated, "but we lived in houses about a block apart in 1939."

In 1947, he met her when he and his family were invited to dinner at Colonel Vissering's home. "My dad wanted me to meet Vissering's daughter . She was only fifteen. My dad told me I should date her. 'She's only fifteen,' I said. 'You ought to date her,' he said. So, I asked her out and we went out for George Washington's birthday. I borrowed Colonel Vissering's Jeep and we went to the Army-Navy Country Club. It was beautiful weather when we went in and when we came out there were three or four inches of snow on the ground. In taking Betty home and returning the Colonel's Jeep, I slipped along Connecticut Avenue on the only big hill they have, and I slid the Jeep into a big black limousine. We had Betty's good friend and eventual bridesmaid in the back seat with her date. She said, 'Oh, that's my mother's bookie.' The chauffeur came over and they got to talking and everything was fine. I hit him right in the middle, but now, I have to laugh. Everybody agreed it was the snow and no charges. So, after wrecking her father's Jeep, I felt I had to date her to be nice. That's what developed as a romance and eventual marriage."

After graduation, Laffery went to flight training in Pensacola, Florida. "We dated during that time. Betty would come down to Pensacola."

When he was transferred to Corpus Christi, Texas, he had a few days between assignments because there was a delay in flight assignments for advanced flight training. The military was short on fuel for training missions. So, he and Betty Vissering married in 1948 and had five days before the assignment began. They moved to Corpus Christi, where Lafferty trained on F4U Corsair fighter aircraft.

As an aside, Lafferty said that his father had been stationed at Fort Ringgold in Rio Grande City, Texas.

"After I completed training in Texas, we went back to Pensacola to get carrier qualifications," Lafferty said. "I got my wings and Betty pinned them on me in 1950."

He received orders to go to CINC PAC (Commander-in-Chief, Pacific) Fleet. "There was the end of my career," he said. "The assignment officer said, 'You're going to VS-21.' It was the aircraft composite squadron. Usually it was F6Fs. I ran into a buddy, and he asked what I got. He said, 'You don't want that. You're going to be flying TBMs, which are planes that detect submarines.' I went back in, but the officers would not change my assignment, so I became an ASW [anti-submarine warfare] pilot."


Lafferty came back from one of his first flights in a TBM and everybody was in the crew shack. "They said, 'Hey buddy. Know what's gonna happen? We're going to war.'"

Without completing much training on the TBM, Lafferty said, "I went off to war. We were the first squadron to deploy from the States on July 4. The only interesting flying I did from then on was ASW. When Chosin Reservoir came up [in Korea], the squadron was ashore in Japan. They needed TBM pilots to fly to the Chosin Reservoir area, so we rolled dice, and I won. We got to Hung Nam, probably an hour-and-a-half drive to Chosin. Marines had set up airfields. We got there the night the Chinese overran everything. The executive officer said, 'Fred, you've been flying Corsairs, haven't you?' I said, 'Yeah.' He said, 'We're gonna have to burn some of these Corsairs or fly them out.'"

Lafferty took his stuff and headed out to a Corsair and found it fully armed. He went back inside and said, "That's fully armed! Do you want me to fly that?" The executive officer said, "Yeah, drop some of it on the Chinese." Lafferty said, "When we took off, the Chinese were about 10 miles away in the flight path. They shot at us, so I shot back."

At the end of that cruise, the squadron was dismantled, and they were told to get home however they wanted. "All the enlisted were smart and took sea transport. A small group of us got to Honolulu after about four days. I was a measly ensign at that time. It was getting boring, so I called CINC PAC Fleet and got the duty officer. I explained our problem. He said to be down at anchor the next morning. We were and flew to San Francisco. I got a flight down to San Diego. That was my first cruise. I came home, and [my daughter] Nancy was two months old."

He went back into training again. "I went to LSO [Landing Signal Officers'] school in the fall of 1951 and got qualified as an LSO."

Back in the squadron, he got a deployment on a different aircraft, an AF Guardian, which was the biggest plane the Navy had that could land on a carrier. "We were landing on an escort carrier, so we stacked up a lot of aircraft, including me."

On the flight deck, he explained, you have the hooking gear, which slows and stops the plane, then there's a high barrier to keep from flying into the planes on the other side.

"We had been offloaded at Guam," Lafferty said. "We were doing our initial qualification training. We had a new LSO, who had trained under me. I didn't train him very well. When I came around on my third pass, he gave me a cut [the engine]. They either gave you a cut or a wave off to go around again. You had to follow what they said. I knew I wasn't going to make it to the ship. I had green water between me and the ship, so I slammed on the power. My main gear landed on the ship, but my tail hook hit the ramp and broke, so I didn't have a tail hook, so I went into the barrier."

When he came back from that cruise, he knew he was going to be ordered out, so he said, "I and another lieutenant grade were assigned to start a COD [Carrier Onboard Delivery]. In those days, helicopters didn't have any range. They turned the TBMs into transport planes. They could carry seven people. We set up the first school on the West Coast. Then I was ordered to Kingsville [Texas] where I stayed from 1954 to 1957 and where I instructed pilots for ASW flights."

He also served in Vietnam, but he was stationed in Guam. Lafferty retired from the United States Navy in 1969.

Lafferty and his wife Betty moved to Grant County, New Mexico, where they retired after a fourteen-year career in real estate in El Paso, Texas.

# BURK, JACK

## DOB 06/18/28

Jack Burk volunteered for World War II when he was seventeen years old in Silver City, New Mexico.

"We moved to Silver City when I was eight years old," Burk said. "My dad was a carpenter. During the war, everybody seemed to be wanting to go into the service. My dad wouldn't let me because he had to sign for me. He finally let me go in, along with my buddy Jim York, who lives in California now. We joined the Navy on April 22, 1946; I think that was the date. I was sent to San Diego, California, and had about two and a half months of training. The fighting had mostly ended but declaration had not yet been made."

He said he didn't know whether he would face combat or not. Burk went from San Diego to Norfolk, Virginia. He traveled by coal-burning train. "We were black when we got there."

Burk was assigned to the *USS Adirondack*, a communication ship. "They put me on as a signalman striker. I raised the flags and took care of the lights, but I didn't stay there very long."

His next assignment was on the *USS Stormes*, a destroyer. "We went on maneuvers at sea for about three months. I got sick and, when we returned, they put me in the hospital in Norfolk. My next ship was a patrol craft. We patrolled the Atlantic for a while, until we went to Charleston, South Carolina, where they decommissioned the ship."

"I was transferred to a YP [yard patrol boat], a refrigeration ship, which carried fresh vegetables, fruits and milk to different places," Burk said. "We would pick up the food in Miami and deliver it to Cuba and Puerto Rico. I really loved that weather. I did that for two months."

One of the places they went was Jamaica. "What a beautiful place. We went through the coral reefs. Guy had to know what he was doing, or you couldn't get in and out of there. Canons were sticking out on the walls above the harbor. The amazing thing was we were supposed to leave that afternoon, but the tide went out and left the ship sitting on the bottom in the harbor."

He said small boats came around with people wanting cigarettes. "One guy was going to sell them some, but they knocked the cigarettes out of his hand and they fell into the boat and they took off, so we got nothing. Kids went up on a boom and were asking for pennies. We would toss them into the water. They would get the dime or quarter or whatever in the water before it got to the bottom."

The sailors weren't allowed to go ashore in Puerto Rico, because they had elephantiasis there.

"Then I went to the base at Guantanamo Bay, where I was put in the master-at-arms course," Burk said. "All we did was clean barracks and break up fights in the colored barracks. "

He served next as a radio operator in the Harbor Patrol in Cuba. "I stayed there a little over a year."

When Burk was in Cuba, he said that Batista was in power. "I think he took all the money out of Cuba and left. We took some officers ashore into Caimanera. Soldiers came in where an officer was sitting at a table with some civilians. The soldiers, who worked for Batista, told him to leave and he said: 'There's no reason for me to leave. I'm not doing anything.' Because he wouldn't get up and leave they slapped him up the side of the head with a sword. That same night, an earthquake hit. I was aboard ship and could see the waves coming in and the lights in town shaking. I didn't know at the time what it was. But that's what it was, an earthquake."

While he was in Cuba, a petty officer first class had a big monkey. "He would keep him in a big cage, but, every once in a while, he would take him for a walk. The monkey was mean and would bite people. One night it got loose and ran to the colored barracks and went in. It was about reveille, so when the men walked in and saw the monkey, they all went out through the screen windows. The monkey didn't like redheaded people or colored people."

"Another thing we would do at night is go out lobster hunting," Burk said. "They were called rock lobsters. They were good eating.

"I went on a ship to New York City to get discharged," Burk said. "It was February 1948. The ship was covered with ice and there was snow in New York City. While we were on the ship, I was on guard duty. We would check all the compartments and make sure everyone was OK. One night, I had just done my rounds and got back just as an officer caught some guys gambling. They were put on report and so was I. I was put on report because I hadn't reported them. Well, I didn't know they were gambling. I was going on report and would have extra duty, but there was an officer from Guantanamo Bay on board, and he got us out of it. The guys knew they weren't supposed to be gambling. You could play cards and use chips, but you couldn't have money out."

From New York City, he rode the bus back to Silver City, "seeing ice and snow all the way. It took almost four days. I was tired of traveling, so I spent the night in El Paso before coming home the next day about noon."

# BRYCE, ANDREW WALLACE

## DOB 08/30/1930 DOD 09/08/2018

Andrew Wallace Bryce volunteered for the Navy on January 4, 1946, at age sixteen.

"My fellow student, Sandy Valentine, and I joined the Navy in New York City," Bryce said. "He convinced me we should join the Navy, because it was clean, and the Army was dirty. He built and rebuilt cars and was always covered in grease.

"We left thinking we were in the Navy," Bryce continued. "We went on holiday in upstate New York, taking a long weekend in the Catskills, where my parents had a small cabin. Snow was still on the ground, and we had an enormously good time skiing. We told everyone we were in the Navy."

But the Navy didn't take them right away. After two or three weeks, Bryce said he was becoming antsy, because he wanted to be in the service.

"I'm going to join the Army," he told his mother and persuaded her and her sister to drive him down to the city in his little car. "I went in and joined the Army. It took me into the service. When I left that room, I was in the Army, and I did what the Army told me to do. I slept that night in a barracks in New York City. At 5:00 a.m., they awakened us and told us in no uncertain terms to get out of bed. We marched to a bright-lighted room filled with desks. They told us to take the tests as quickly as we could. Then they told us we were done."

At that point, "I had a name, a number and everything." He got a three-day pass to go home. When he got home, his mother told him the Navy had come looking for him. She had told them, "He's in the Army. Don't you know what you're doing?" They nullified everything and said it was good he was in the service and left.

For basic training, he was sent to Fort Knox, Kentucky.

"I was in the Army for about eighteen months," Bryce said. "I encountered Valentine in Larchmont [New York] one day after I was out, and he was spending four years in the Navy. Mostly under a truck. He had a miserable time in a garage.

"I had a great time," Bryce said. "For almost a year, I was sent from one camp to another across the country in the best trains of the 1940s. Every time a new assignment showed up, I applied for it. I wanted to go overseas. I applied for all kinds of openings. My time in the Army was wonderful. I was living a dream life."

He described the dream life as doing things he probably shouldn't have been doing but managing to stay out of trouble. "Girls were smitten with the uniform, so I could always find a girl."

After almost twelve months in camps throughout the United States, including California and Alaska, he embarked to Japan from Seattle, Washington, on Thanksgiving, 1946.

"They officially didn't have to let me go, because I hadn't been in the full twelve months required before going overseas, but I went," Bryce said. "The last view I had of our homeland was Mount Olympus in the flat waters of Puget Sound."

It was a Liberty ship voyage, the *USAT General A.W. Greely*, which had survived the war in good enough shape to continue in service. The servicemen aboard soon faced the rough seas of wintertime.

"I never threw up," Bryce said. "I felt sick all the time, but I didn't get sick. I wasn't interested in food. I was small and agile, so I used to climb to the highest points on the ship, because I didn't want people throwing up on me."

Aboard ship, he met a fellow soldier, a non-commissioned officer. "He liked the way I talked, and I liked the way he talked. He took me to the brig, where with nobody there, we assigned ourselves a bunk each in a different cell. Nobody bothered us until it was time to put someone in who belonged there. Then we were thrown out."

The ship arrived in Yokohama Bay, and the soldiers were taken to Shinodyama, which was the Japanese equivalent of West Point.

During the occupation of Japan, Bryce served as a driver of Jeeps, tanks and trucks. He actually wrecked three vehicles and thought he would get heavy disciplinary action. However, one time, he was driving a general to where he shouldn't have been going and wrecked the Jeep. The general covered for him and Bryce didn't get into trouble.

[Author's Note: This writer was only able to speak to this veteran briefly while he was ill. He died about 10 days later. The rest of this chapter consists of summarized pieces from Bryce's somewhat fictionalized memoir, *GI Junior: Coming of Age in the Army, Part 1, The Road to Japan,* which his wife said he had written from his memories and simply changed his name in the book.]

Bryce's first assignment as a driver was to drive the staff sergeant, who headed the mailroom. They traveled on weekly trips to pick up the mail.

One night an earthquake rousted the soldiers out of their old Japanese officers' quarters. They moved into newly built quarters, "which had plumbing, to our delight."

Because the main roads were pocked with bomb craters, the military often used the packed tracks between rice paddies to travel from place to place. On one regular mail run, Bryce and the sergeant encountered a truck, which had slid off the track into a rice paddy. Men were trying to use a water buffalo and bamboo pry poles to move the truck back onto the hard-packed track.

"The sergeant got out of the Jeep and surveyed the situation," Bryce said. "He instructed the men working to pull out the truck to hitch the cable from the Jeep to the truck. I slowly let out the clutch and the truck, which was much larger than our Jeep, began to move back onto the path ."

He said the men and women broke into cheers and shouts of joy when the truck was safely on the path . Several men unhitched the cable and rewound it onto the winch.

"A peasant woman polished up the Jeep's windshield and headlamps. Then they all lined up opposite the sergeant and bowed deeply."

"I thought to myself, 'The Jeep, ain't it something?'" Bryce said.

He wrecked his first Jeep by running it up under a half-sized truck, a so-called weapons carrier that was being used by the PX (post exchange) sergeant who was picking up supplies for the recreation hall—mostly beer.

Another night, the soldiers had to abandon their barracks when it caught on fire and the fire raged up the stairwell. Several, including Bryce, saved themselves by throwing a mattress out a window and jumping onto it.

After Bryce had wrecked three vehicles, he and his bunkmate became telephone operators. But the Army continued to need drivers.

While he was still in Japan, Bryce was issued another brand-new Jeep to carry a lieutenant, a staff sergeant and another corporal, who was a Japanese American. The corporal was born in Hawaii of Japanese parents, a nisei (second generation from Japan, born in the United States), who would be their interpreter and liaison between them and the Japanese civilians they would be educating on democracy through an "election tour." It was part of the post-war constitutional government brought to Japan by the occupying forces.

On the tour, they traveled through villages, seemingly empty of residents, until they stopped and were treated to "vats of tea," often in rooms filled with terrified villagers, who had never seen the "barbarian Americans" before. At each stop, the lieutenant would use chalk to draw on the floors the instructions on how to vote. The residents would quickly mark the ballots and scurry away.

Wajima was the destination that would become their headquarters. The men were met by a major, who said he was their agent and would lead them to where they would stay. For security reasons, they would be the only guests in the lodging. The agent also assigned them a young Japanese woman, who would be the liaison between them.

They stayed in a ryokan (traditional Japanese inn) with sliding translucent paper walls, tatami sleeping mats and bathing tubs to be shared by all. Toilets were simply a hole in the floor that led into a trench with foot ramps on each side of the hole where they squatted. The "night-soil" from the trench was used to fertilize crops.

Each soldier was assigned a girl to bathe him and take care of his needs, including feeding him each tiny bite at a time.

Dinner and each evening  set the pattern for the Election Team for the rest of the tour, which, with one notable exception, was spent entirely within the confines of the ryokan, the "Grand Hotel of the 25th Infantry Division's Social and Political Reconstruction Plan, 1947 Spring Election Tour, 35th Battalion, B Company Team, Rural Section."

The sergeant of the team informed the driver, Bryce, that he was taking the Jeep. The sergeant commandeered it every day, and one day Bryce discovered that the Jeep was damaged. He had signed out for it and was worried that he would have to pay for it before he could be discharged.

The one trip away from the ryokan was to a large house with land. The old man who owned it wished to alert the soldiers that he wanted them to talk to General MacArthur about the taking of his home and land. Bryce was unaware of what had occurred, and the nisei explained some of it to him without getting into the politics. The men soon left and went back to their "fast life" in the ryokan.

The agent, the nisei, Bryce and their "dates" also attended a Kabuki theater, which Bryce admitted was not to his taste and he didn't understand it, but everyone else seemed to enjoy it.

Although Bryce was threatened with having to pay for the damage to the Jeep, it didn't happen, and he was released from the Army to return home on time.

The soldiers returned home on the *USS Admiral H. T. Mayo* on calm seas across the Pacific.

When Bryce was officially discharged on July 4, 1947, he was at home in upstate New York and received the honorable discharge by mail.

GOD'S UMBRELLA

# CHAPTER 13

⊗

## Too Young to Serve, but Found a Way to Serve in a Different Capacity

GOD'S UMBRELLA

# Cunningham, John

## DOB 04/18/1931

John "Jack" Cunningham of Silver City said that the New York State Guard had a company in his hometown of Malone, New York.

"The armory where they met and drilled and all was a half a block from my house," Cunningham said. "During [World War II], we kids, and I think everyone else, were wrapped up in things [about the war]."

The State Guard, which he described as composed of old men and young boys, started a band for Company G, 6th Regiment in 1945. When word got out they were going to take high school students, "I jumped at it, quit the Boy Scouts and went into the State Guard," he said. He played clarinet.

"A friend, who played trumpet, and I lied about our age and said we were sixteen," Cunningham said. "I was fourteen years old."

He spent two years in the company—1945 and 1946.

"The bandmaster, my commanding officer, Fred Bova, was one of the nicest men I have ever met," Cunningham said. "My experiences and the friends I made in those two years are still vivid today, and probably had the greatest single influence on my development. I went in a boy, and thought I came out a man, although today I qualify it as a 'very young' man."

The first big event for which the group played took place on May 8, 1945, when the members received a phone call to assemble at the armory for a parade to celebrate the end of the war in Europe.

"We marched from the armory the length of Main Street and back again," Cunningham recounted. "So, I had the good fortune to partake in the V-E Day celebration."

The band often traveled by bus to play for various events. Because they had no radios, everyone sang for entertainment, "so we sang all the way there and back, usually in harmony."

One time, the band traveled to Chateaugay, New York, to a dairy that was getting an Army-Navy "E" award for excellent production.

"They gave us all the ice cream we wanted after our performance," Cunningham said. "They also gave us cartons of Neopolitan [ice cream] to take on the bus. Someone ate the strawberry out of his and gave it to me. I ate all the chocolate and threw the rest out the window. When I got home, we had chocolate ice cream for dessert, and for the first time in my life, I didn't want any."

One summer, the company, including the band, went to guard camp, near Peekskill in the Catskill Mountains of southern New York.

"We marched up and down the company street [in the camp] to wake up everyone," Cunningham said. "Then we played as they marched out to the field and did whatever they were going to do for the day. Then we had a rehearsal or two and had the rest of the day free."

The band also played for special events, such as parades and ceremonies.

"A couple of times, I borrowed coveralls from a guy who was little, got a rifle and ammunition and went out with the company," Cunningham said.

The last event for which the band played in 1945 was the V-J Day parade on August 14 to celebrate victory over Japan.

He stayed in the band until after the war was over and the State Guard disbanded, when the National Guard, which had been federalized, returned from their duties during the war.

"I didn't mind lying about my age to the state, but I wasn't going to get in trouble with the federal government," Cunningham said.

After the war, the band was "even better than the first year," he said. "A number of local boys returned [from the war] and joined the band. The band morphed into the Malone Town Band. We rehearsed once a week."

After finishing high school and college, Cunningham volunteered for the draft and went into the Army at the end of the Korean War. He was stationed in Tokyo, Japan, but never saw combat.

"I got out of the Army in 1955," Cunningham. "I started in the New York State Guard and from 1990 to

2000, I served in the New Mexico State Defense Force. After 9/11, I went back in for a couple of years, but then resigned again."

# RUHNE, CARL

## DOB 03/18/1934

Carl Ruhne of Silver City, from eight to twelve years of age, served during World War II as a mascot at the United States Merchant Marine Academy at Coyote Point in San Mateo, California, on San Francisco Bay.

He said the United States was building Liberty and Victory ships at a great rate, sometimes as fast as a ship in four days, and needed officers and engineers to man them.

Cadets, who were generally in the seventeen- to nineteen-year-old range, attended the academies to be trained in ninety days.

A neighbor was an officer at the base.

"He told me if I could learn to tie a bowline knot, he would introduce me to the captain of the base," Ruhne said. "My sister learned faster than I did, and I didn't want her to be the mascot, so I learned it."

His job was to report to the base every Saturday at eight o'clock and then "I had the run of the whole place, kind of a little brother to the cadets, many of whom had never been away from their home or farm."

"My mother remade one of the uniforms to fit me," Ruhne said. A chief petty officer took Ruhne in his

Hupmobile to San Francisco to get a uniform and took him to a "gin mill—the Five-Mile House" on the way.

"They did have good clams," he said.

One time while Ruhne and others waited for the crew bus next to the Greyhound Lines bus station, "a lady saw me and walked over and said, 'Now I've heard of this draft thing getting bad, but this is ridiculous.'"

The other students at school kidded him "something fierce" about his uniform. If something special was going on, he would usually go home immediately after school, put on his uniform and walk fifteen minutes to the base.

"I spent more time growing up at Coyote Point than I did at my folks' house," Ruhne said, "because my folks had a boat there, too."

He took part in academy inspections on Saturdays when the battalions were spread out on the parade grounds. He would stand between the battalion commander and the assistant commander.

"My uniform was blue," Ruhne said. "One hot day I thought I was going to pass out. One of the officers observed that I was in bad shape, so after that I stood by the band."

He said it would "be an eternity while officers wove in and out inspecting." The inspection was followed by the presentation of arms.

Often Ruhne would sit up with the officers.

"There were always a bunch of people watching," Ruhne said. "Sometimes I would see a classmate and, boy, I'd feel pretty big."

Ruhne got to play with what was "probably one of the first video games. I had to determine whether the planes coming toward me on the giant movie screen were friend or foe. I could shoot and could tell by the flash on the screen whether I had hit the plane."

The training instrument was "a real gun with electric guts to make the screen spark."

He also had an opportunity to fire a submachine gun and said his ears rang for a week afterward.

"I was so little, and the Thompson submachine gun shook so hard, I held on to it, including the trigger," Ruhne said. "By the time the instructor pried my hands off, the barrel was melted.

"I could clean a .45 faster than some of the cadets. Of course, I was there for four years and they were only there for ninety days," Ruhne reported.

He said he spent a lot of time by the harbor where a big pier had four lifeboats hanging in davits and a thirty-foot jumping tower so the cadets could practice abandon-ship drills.

At low tide, not much water remained, so two men stood by to pull trainees out of the mud if they got stuck.

His favorite place was the boatswain locker where seamanship was taught.

"I had my chores," Ruhne said. "A lot of times, I would eat with the chief petty officers because they got bigger cuts of meat. I was there for the troops. Everyone was really nice to me and got a kick out of me wanting to learn how to run boats."

Ruhne would just pick somebody to sit by and said, "The language often cleaned up. It was always a kick."

The cadets would go up and down San Francisco Bay practicing steering and maneuvering.

Ruhne said the band members were partyers and one of the guys, Elmo Tanner, got arrested for being drunk.

"No one could get away to pay his bail," Ruhne said. "They gave me twenty-five dollars to ride the bus to town to get him out. He was sure glad to see me because he had to be back on duty. It was done on the hush-hush, so the officers didn't find out that I was the one who went and bailed him out.

"I wasn't getting paid as mascot," he continued, "except for prime-rib dinners on Saturdays. We got to listen to the Ted Weems Band play and Snookie Lanson singing."

Many of the cooks and servants at the academy were Filipinos.

"I would lower a net into the water," Ruhne said, "and I'd get one dollar for a five-gallon bucket of fish, shiners. I would take them to the back door of the galley. I wasn't supposed to be doing that. They would fry them with heads on and everything."

GOD'S UMBRELLA

His stint as a mascot finished at the end of the war.

His name and photo as the mascot of the base are in a book about the United States Maritime Administration, he said.

"My service taught me a bit of independence," Ruhne said. "It was good and bad. My teachers didn't appreciate it."

When the base closed, "I knew where to get into the swimming pool, so my friends and I swam the whole summer. The water got kind of murky."

Ruhne said the guard had a noisy vehicle, so it gave them time to get quiet and hide.

The former academy became a junior college and is now a museum and includes a kind of a zoo with native animals, he reported.

"The only thing left standing of the school is the captain's house, which is used for the recreation department offices," Ruhne said.

Ruhne served from 1954 to 1956 as an active member of the United States Coast Guard. After that, he spent ten years as the skipper of a private yacht.

He lives part of the year in Silver City, New Mexico, since marrying Sudie Kennedy of Silver City, and part in Santa Cruz, California.

# ABOUT THE AUTHOR

The author/compiler of this collection of interviews reports the local news in Silver City and Grant County, New Mexico, as the founder and editor of http://www.grantcountybeat.com.

A proud American, the daughter of a man who served in World War I and World War II, Mary Alice supports veterans and appreciates their service and hearing their stories.

She was raised in far south Texas and has lived with her husband and their two daughters in Indonesia and Turkey, as well as time spent in Laramie, Wyoming; Denver, Colorado; and near Houston, Texas.

As a child, when her parents and her uncle and aunt got together for dinner or a visit, the women usually headed to the kitchen. Not Mary Alice. She preferred sitting near where the men were talking about their war experiences. This was the late 1940s and early 1950s, so the men's memories remained fresh, perhaps too fresh.

Oh, if only she could have somehow recorded their conversations or even remembered more than just bits and pieces of them.

This book is an ode to their service, for my dad—Joseph Francis Baingo, to whom this book is dedicated—and my uncle—Thomas Gambrell Edwards, M.D. Thank you for your service. Rest in Peace.

www.ingramcontent.com/pod-product-compliance
Lightning Source LLC
Chambersburg PA
CBHW021350090426
42742CB00009B/799